JOHN MIHEVC

Y0-CPE-441

THE MARKET
TELLS THEM SO

The World Bank
and Economic
Fundamentalism
in Africa

ZED Books Ltd
London and New Jersey

Third World Network
Penang and Accra

The Market Tells Them So:
The World Bank and Economic Fundamentalism in Africa
is published by:
Zed Books Ltd., 7 Cynthia Street,
London N1 9JF, UK and 165 First Avenue,
Atlantic Highlands, New Jersey 07716, USA
and
Third World Network,
228 Macalister Road, 10400 Penang, Malaysia
and P O Box 8604, Accra-North, Ghana.

copyright © Third World Network 1995

Printed by Jutaprint, 54, Kajang Road,
10150 Penang, Malaysia.

List of Abbreviations

AACC	All Africa Conference of Churches
AAF-SAP	African Alternative Framework to Structural Adjustment Programmes
ACLCA	Association of Christian Lay Centres in Africa
CBS	Cocoa Butter Substitutes
ERP	Economic Recovery Programme
GATT	General Agreement on Tariffs and Trade
GCA	Global Coalition for Africa
GDP	Gross Domestic Product
GEF	Global Environmental Facility
GNP	Gross National Product
HYV	High Yielding Varieties
IBPGR	International Board of Plant Genetic Resources
IBRD	International Bank for Reconstruction and Development
ICCAF	Inter-Church Coalition on Africa
IDA	International Development Association
IMF	International Monetary Fund
IPR	Intellectual Property Rights
LDC	Less Developed Country
NCCK	National Council of Churches of Kenya
NGO	Non-Governmental Organization
NIEO	New International Economic Order
OECD	Organization for Economic Cooperation and Development
PAMSCAD	Programme of Action to Mitigate the Social Costs of Adjustment
R&D	Research and Development
rDNA	Recombinant DNA
SAL	Structural Adjustment Loan
SAPs	Structural Adjustment Programmes
TNC	Transnational Corporation
UN	United Nations
UNCED	United Nations Conference on Environment and Development
UNCTAD	United Nations Conference on Trade and Development
UNDP	United Nations Development Programme
UNECA	United Nations Economic Commission for Africa
UNICEF	United Nations Children's Fund
UNPAAERD	United Nations Programme of Action for African Economic Recovery and Development
US	United States of America
WDR	World Development Report
WID	Women in Development

ACKNOWLEDGEMENTS

MANY people have provided valuable ideas, editorial comments and moral support during the writing of this book. Thanks are due to Lee Cormie who guided me through the process of research and writing. Charles Abugre, Jonathan Barker, Stephen Dunn, Marsha Hewitt and Harold Wells provided valuable comments on earlier drafts. Gregory Baum, Will Braun, Jenny Cafiso, Hugh Cheetham, Hilary Cunningham, Patience Elabor-Idemudia, Susan George, Lisa McGowan, Erich Mathias, Joe Mihevc, Ruth Rempel, Stephen Scharper, Kole Shettima and Leif Vaage provided valuable comments, suggestions, editorial assistance, and encouragement.

The members of the Economic Justice Working Group, staff, and Administrative Board of the Inter-Church Coalition on Africa have been very supportive of this work throughout. The Social Sciences and Humanities Research Council of Canada and Partnership Africa Canada have provided financial support for the research and writing of the book. The insight and commitment of African church partners like Omega Bula, Jephthah Gathaka and Jonah Katoneene have enriched and challenged my thinking throughout.

I would like to thank the Third World Network in taking the initiative to get this book published and to acknowledge the coordination work carried out by Pratap Parameswaran, Lim Jee Yuan for the cover design and Linda Ooi who did the typesetting.

My parents and family have been patient and unwavering in their support. Finally, a very special thank you to Rebecca Cunningham who has been involved in every aspect of this project and to whom I lovingly dedicate this work.

TABLE OF CONTENTS

PART I

PART III

INTRODUCTION

During the 1980s the debates and struggles concerning development strategies for Africa[1] focused dramatically on the issue of structural adjustment. Structural adjustment does not merely denote a set of economic policies to assist countries in addressing structural problems related to trade, growth and balance of payments. Structural adjustment also, and most profoundly, embodies a social, cultural and religious vision, not only for Africa, but for the world. This claim runs counter to the conventional characterization of structural adjustment as primarily a technical and economic set of policies to rectify the structural problems endemic to African economies. Unfortunately, those who oppose this agenda generally fail to appreciate the importance of engaging in a theological analysis of the structural adjustment agenda. This book engages in a theological critique of structural adjustment. It also provides an account of the variety of responses to structural adjustment by organizations and individuals from economic, religious and social scientific perspectives.

Unlike their counterparts in the North, theologians and social scientists in Africa, and in the South in general, understand intimately the fundamentally religious character of the discourses and visions of development promoted by agencies like the World Bank. Their responses draw increasingly upon a more integrated and coherent analysis of the various facets of development. *The Road to Damascus: Kairos and Conversion,* written by theologians and social scientists from Asia, Latin America and Africa, captures succinctly the insight that the political and economic crisis is profoundly religious and that the church is unavoidably a site in the struggle:

> Christian faith has now been introduced into the political conflict. Both oppressor and oppressed seek religious legitimation. Both sides invoke the name of God and of Jesus Christ, and Christians are found on both sides of the political conflict.[2]

The concerns outlined above converge into two dominant themes which provide the focus for the chapters that follow. The first theme illustrates how the numerous movements which are opposed to the structural adjustment agenda cut across a variety of social, ethnic, religious and class groupings. Amongst these groupings, church-based movements constitute key social actors in the struggles against structural adjustment. The second theme involves an intellectual commitment to these emerging alliances. The structural adjustment agenda represents a fundamental challenge to the piecemeal manner in which theology and the social sciences have approached development issues. This lack of coherency and integration seems especially prevalent among scholars and activists in the North who are critical of structural adjustment. The issue of theological relevancy challenges theologians and social scientists in the North and South opposed to the dominant development agenda to discover their common assumptions and together develop critiques and alternatives. An inter-disciplinary approach also provides a more integral understanding of questions of faith and values in development struggles and helps to explain why churches are so intimately involved and at the forefront of these struggles.

This book reports on a number of these developments by focusing on three aspects of structural adjustment in Africa. The first considers the theological dimensions of the structural adjustment vision promoted by the World Bank for Africa. The second provides an account of some of the criticisms of structural adjustment from a variety of social scientific perspectives. The third considers the religious responses to this agenda that have emerged from churches and church-based movements in Africa. The responses to structural adjustment challenge its factual arguments as well as critiquing its basic theoretical and conceptual claims. The range of responses to structural adjustment constitutes a compelling refutation as well as pointing to emerging alternatives. It invokes churches and social movements committed to social and ecological justice to respond in dramatically new forms. In the task of analysing, critiquing and creating alternatives, it is not uncommon to see theologians and social scientists forging partnerships with social movements of the poor and marginalized.[3]

The Setting

If the 1980s have been described as the "lost decade" for Africa, then the 1990s may well become the decade when "Africa [is] rendered irrelevant to global development, so marginal[ized] that its peoples' only real resource is to call upon the pity of the world by threatening to die in mass starvation on television".[4]

As the global economy is reorganized into regional trading blocs dominated by transnational corporate interests, sub-Saharan Africa is no longer even considered as an important source of cheap raw materials and commodities. During the 1980s, the cumulative effect of international economic developments on Africa has been over-whelmingly negative. Two-thirds of the countries defined by the United Nations (UN) as "least developed" are in Africa. Real wages have declined by 25 per cent and employment has fallen by 16 per cent. Over 30 million Africans are unemployed and an additional 95 million are underemployed. Per capita consumption in sub-Saharan Africa has fallen by one-fifth. Spending on health care has declined by 50 per cent and on education by 25 per cent over the last decade. As many as 10,000 African children are dying each day from the effects of malnutrition and rudimentary health care. According to the United Nations Children's Fund's (UNICEF) 1990 report, *The State of the World's Children*, children, the poorest and most vulnerable, have paid the Third World's debt with the sacrifice of their normal growth, health and opportunity for education. It is estimated that Africa's share of global infant death will rise to 40 per cent by the end of the decade.

In spite of efforts to meet their balance of payments, Africa's foreign debt grew faster than that of any other region in the Third World. In 1970 it was US$6 billion;[5] in 1993 it had grown to $300 billion. When measured in terms of export earnings and ability to pay, Africa's debt burden is twice as heavy as that of Latin America. Behind the pretence of Northern countries assisting in the "development" of the poorer nations lies a far more disturbing reality: over the past decade the South has transferred to the North approximately $418 billion – the equivalent of six Marshall Plans.[6] The ecological toll has also been dramatic: the intensification of rainforest depletion, soil erosion, famine and global warming.

During the 1980s a number of important agencies came to the forefront to provide their own analysis and solutions. In Africa, none has been more influential than the World Bank.

The World Bank

Over the 1980s profound changes occurred in Africa. Engineered by the World Bank and the International Monetary Fund (IMF), Structural Adjustment Programmes (SAPs) were put in place as a means of responding to the debt crisis and of putting African countries on a sound economic and development footing. This adjustment was deemed to be the necessary penance for past inefficiency and mismanagement.

Critics charge that the social costs of this adjustment have been staggering. They maintain that structural adjustment measures such as currency devaluation, the removal of food subsidies and cuts in spending on health care and education place a disproportionate burden on the poor – especially on women and children. In Africa, as in much of the South, women have been forced into additional forms of remunerative activities in order to survive as the farming of cash crops is consolidated into large, male-dominated and foreign-owned estates. Young girls are taken out of primary school not only because of the introduction of school fees but also because girls are needed to help their families grow and market food. The World Bank has countered that countries that postpone their day of reckoning and refuse to "adjust" are demonstrably worse off than those that courageously swallow the bitter medicine of adjustment.

World Bank Annual Reports are replete with examples espousing a theology of "faith" and "hope" to the poorer countries. Fantu Cheru remarks on the practices of World Bank economists in distinctly theological terms: "The old Christian missionaries have been replaced by an army of Western neo-classical economists who peddle their 'free market' ideology, which, it is hoped will take Africans to the 'Garden of Eden'."[7]

While many voices have supported the need for structural adjustment in Africa, it has been the World Bank that has assumed control of Africa's development agenda. Under the World Bank's tutelage, virtually every country in Africa has been forced to come to terms with the World Bank over the past decade. While other agencies like the IMF, multi-nationals, the governments of the G-7 countries, and commercial banks have also played a significant role, this book focuses largely on the World Bank as the key international development agency which has been at the forefront in advocating and implementing a structural adjustment development agenda for Africa during the 1980s.

The All Africa Conference of Churches (AACC) has called attention to the effects that SAPs are having on the poor and has called on churches, in Africa as well as in the North, to take a prophetic stand against what it describes as a "low intensity war" against Africa. According to the AACC, SAPs have led only to "the obscene widening of the gap between rich and poor and the increasing impoverishment and pauperization of the great majority of the African population."[8]

SAPs and the economic crisis have been identified in many churches as *the* most important theological issue confronting Africa, an issue about which the churches must speak out clearly and prophetically. Women's networks, lay centres and youth groups are beginning to implement programmes, workshops and seminars to study SAPs, and develop appropriate strategies. The theological responses and the movements to which they are giving voice, provide an important social space for organizing and implementing resistance strategies and alternatives.

Social scientists and theologians in the South have increasingly collaborated on development issues. This is especially evident in the area of economics and the study of the impact of SAPs. The growing interest in the theme of theology and economy has resulted in the characterization by a number of economists and theologians of the current global economic order as embodying a theology of death and cultural genocide. Collaborations of this nature are only slowly emerging in the North.

On the practical side, church development agencies are finding themselves overwhelmed in their attempt to address only the basic survival of the poor in their overseas programmes. In response to the calls of the church partners, they have become more involved in attempting to comprehend the global economic forces that have precipitated such a dramatic decline in basic living standards over the past decade. The churches are increasingly collaborating with other development and environmental NGOs in the North and South to form alliances and partnerships, to mobilize resistance against the imposition of harmful economic policies and to articulate alternatives.

A more comprehensive understanding of the forces that operate at the local level can be achieved by studying the dominant theories of development which attempt to explain the causes of poverty and their proposed solutions. A framework which considers the implications of development as a "global" phenomenon can illuminate the complex patterns and processes that contribute to the current crisis. Such a perspective considers the current crisis as multi-faceted, deeply rooted and global. In this respect, a global economy approach is a radical critique requiring a multi-disciplinary approach.[9]

In order to sustain this kind of critique, the traditional categories of development, i.e., growth, trade, debt, modernization and industrialization etc., have to be examined in light of their effect on local level impoverishment and land degradation. By remaining closely attentive to local level concerns, a global economy approach uncovers the connection between global development, impoverishment and environmental degradation at the local level.

The Theological Implications of a Global Economy Perspective on Ecology and Development

North American theologians generally struggle to articulate an analysis and vision which connects development and ecology. Much of this difficulty can be traced to the reluctance in appreciating the value-laden character of development discourse.

The theological task is even more daunting when the entire global political economy becomes the subject for enquiry. This has been an especially nettlesome problem in the field of social ethics. The reasons for this difficulty are many and complex. The most obvious, however, rests in the pervasive assumption that the market operates according to its own laws. For Franz Hinkelammert, the market can, "judge over life and death but cannot itself be judged in terms of the effect it has on the life and death of every individual".[10] The free market is claimed to be value-free, natural and most efficient at allocating resources. Another reason for the lack of theological critiques of development theory is to be found in the all too pervasive view that, while theologians and ethicists can inform economics by contributing general moral principles, they are "out of their depth" when they attempt to critique or propose specific economic policies.

The difficulty that has been encountered by social ethicists in naming the current crisis rests primarily in the complex task of penetrating the veneer of invincibility that neo-classical economics currently enjoys. What are often cited as the root causes of our current crisis are merely its symptoms. Moreover, the debates about alternatives often become mired in bitter disagreements between reformist approaches, which seek realistic opportunities for improving the conditions of the poor and marginalized within existing frameworks, and more radical approaches, which call for a complete transformation of the existing economic order.

Globalization as Social Control

When considered from the perspective of smallholder farmers, poverty and ecological degradation are elements of the same process of marginalization generated by the gradual loss of control over resources and land. The incorporation of the poorer countries into the global economic system (a process which began with their colonization) has radically transformed land use practices and has also firmly established unsustainable development practices on a global level. One of the most destructive features of this process has been the transfer of decision-making control over land from local economies into the global economy.

The value-laden aspects of development as a form of social control often elude most critiques. Grounded in what appear to be a set of self-evident natural law principles development theories often fall into the same conceptual traps as economics because they share many of the same presuppositions. Even alternative development theories do not result in a "rejection of the basic development paradigm but in merely broadening it beyond the parameters of pure economics."[11]

The Fundamentalist Theology of the World Bank

Structural adjustment needs to be understood as a clear agenda that has been undertaken by agencies like the World Bank to tie together a *set* of policies, the effects of which are known and understood. It is an agenda and a discourse which is, at its core, a fundamentalist one which not only denies the legitimacy of alternatives, but has actively sought, over the past decade, to ensure that all of the options available to developing countries have been narrowed down to one.

In the context of Africa this has meant the further marginalization of the region as a producer of commodities, an "open" trading system and the subjection of national priorities to a global corporate agenda. The World Bank has succeeded in narrowing the discourse around SAPs to one which is highly specialized and excludes alternative voices and perspectives.

The imposition of SAPs has had a dramatic impact on the churches in Africa. There are a number of movements within the African churches which are struggling to understand the implications of SAPs both locally as well as in terms of their relationships with their Northern counterparts. Many of these groups in the churches are in conversation with other groups, NGOs and movements which seek to put alternatives in place. Out of these dialogues emerges a challenge to the churches to rearticulate their mission within the context of these embryonic alternatives. These have not yet emerged as fully developed social or political movements. For the vast majority in Africa, the present struggle often involves mere survival. In these struggles there exist inchoate processes consisting of many faces and voices of transformative potential.

A Theology of Self-Reliance

The theological responses to the deepening development crisis have been varied. To the extent that theological responses engage in an analysis which regards economics, ecology and theology as discrete forms of discourse, the root causes of poverty and ecological degradation are partially understood. At the same time, there is a growing body of literature which bears witness to the voice and analysis of the impoverished and marginalized. This contextual approach recognizes that the poor do not speak of their faith, their poverty or the destruction of their land as distinct realms of discourse but in a language that illuminates their integrated or unitary character. The numerous women's networks, movements for popular participation, cooperatives and training for transformation programmes that are spreading across Africa are hopeful signs of change.

This raises a serious challenge to the traditional role which has been ascribed to theology and ethics as they relate to issues of development, economics and ecology. The traditional reluctance for theology and ethics to be directly involved in these conversations calls for a sober rethinking of the theological and ethical frameworks adopted for the study of these issues. This process is already seriously underway in Africa as well as in other countries of the South.

Part I of this book specifically considers the theological features of the World Bank's structural adjustment agenda for sub-Saharan Africa. Chapter one considers the World Bank's promotion of structural adjustment as a fundamentalist religious discourse. The manner in which the World Bank has presented, promoted and defended structural adjustment against its critics closely parallels fundamentalist interpretations of the Bible. The strategies employed the World Bank to guarantee the hegemony of its ideology and to deal with dissenters also correspond to those of fundamentalism. Our opening chapter sets the stage for a more detailed examination of the background and implementation of SAPs in sub-Saharan Africa by the World Bank which is taken up in chapters two, three and four.

Part II of the book draws on many of the insights provided by the critics of SAPs from a variety of disciplines. The terrain of analysis will be the responses to structural adjustment from the perspectives of trade, environment and biotechnology. These chapters consider a number of the counter-claims against SAPs in these areas through counter arguments and by exposing the assumptions and conceptual framework of structural adjustment.

Part III examines the churches and social movements in Africa as important voices resisting SAPs and providing alternative visions. The responses of churches to SAPs in Africa have taken many forms. The churches in Africa continue to be the dominant actors, especially in rural areas, in the provision of health care, education and extension services. In the wake of the removal of state support for these sectors it has been the churches who have been called upon to stretch their resources and serve as the "ambulances" for SAPs. As a result of this experience, religious responses to the economic policies of structural adjustment are emerging which focus on the idolatrous character of SAPs and their devastating impact.

Many of the insights and experiences related in this book have come about through my work at the Inter-Church Coalition on Africa (ICCAF) as a researcher on issues of debt and structural adjustment in Africa. This work has exposed me to the insights and analysis on questions of economic justice that have emerged from our church partners in Africa as well as from the countless solidarity movements, coalitions and non-governmental organizations. Many of the experiences and insights related in this book reflect my active involvement in these issues through my work at ICCAF.

Most significant, however, is my experience of the profound faith of the many African women and men I have come to know and work with over the years. The intimate connection to land, community and culture as integral aspects of their faith has had a lasting impact on my own faith and my understanding of theology, ethics and development. The chapters to follow are addressed to this network of communities and individuals around the world who struggle for social, economic and political justice.

Endnotes

1. This dissertation focuses primarily on the African countries south of the Sahara. I will distinguish between reference to the entire continent and the region of Africa south of the Sahara, especially when citing statistics and facts, by using the term Africa to denote the former and sub-Saharan Africa the latter.

2. *The Road to Damascus: Kairos and Conversion*, (London: Catholic Institute for International Relations, 1989), par. 26.

3. L. Cormie, "Christian Responsibility for the World of the Free Market? Catholicism and the Construction of the Post-World War II Global Order," (unpublished, 1991), p. 2.

4. Charles Bright and Michael Geyer, "For a Unified History of the World in the Twentieth Century," *Radical History Review* 39 (1987), p. 87.

5. Unless otherwise stated $ refers to US currency.

6. Susan George, *The Debt Boomerang: How Third World Debt Harms Us All*, (London: Pluto Press, 1992), pp. xv-xvi.

7. F. Cheru, *The Silent Revolution in Africa: Debt, Development and Democracy*, (London: Zed Books, 1989), Preface.

8. All Africa Conference of Churches, "Maseru Declaration on the Debt Crisis as it Affects Human Rights," (Maseru: AACC International Affairs, 1990), p. 20.

9. Gustavo Gutierrez writes in a similar vein about coming to grips with the complex reality of poverty and the need to adopt a variety of analytical tools to comprehend it: "The use of a variety of tools does not mean sacrificing depth of analysis; the point is only not to be simplistic but rather to insist on getting at the deepest causes of the situation, for this is what it means to be truly radical." "Introduction to the Revised Edition," *A Theology of Liberation*, (New York: Orbis Books, 1988), p. xxv.

10. F. Hinkelammert, cited in José Miguez Bonino, *Towards a Christian Political Ethic*, (New York: Orbis Books, 1983), p. 15.

11. Marc DuBois, "The Governance of the Third World: A Foucauldian Perspective on Power Relations in Development," *Alternatives* 16 (1991), p. 2.

— CHAPTER ONE —

The Fundamentalist Theology of the World Bank

At one extreme, the International Monetary Fund, the World Bank and the Paris Club for debt rescheduling are presented as a secular Trinity, converting African countries from their sinful ways and showing the route to salvation to an ignorant and ungrateful multitude. At the other, the Fund, the Bank, the Paris Club and the commercial banks are portrayed as a modern Four Horsemen of the Apocalypse complementing and completing the work of war, drought, epidemic and famine in a prostrate and defeated continent.[1]

The World Bank rarely finds itself the object of theological study. Its economic analysis and prescriptions for the development of the Third World are deemed to be value-free and, therefore, beyond the scope of theological enquiry. As the world's leading development agency, the World Bank's mandate encompasses a wide range of activities, from consolidating loans for large-scale development projects to imposing Structural Adjustment Programmes (SAPs) on countries experiencing balance of payments problems.

Recently however, the World Bank has come under consistent and heavy criticism from a wide range of groups in the North and South. These groups have called into question the kinds of projects that the World Bank approves for developing countries. Environmental groups argue that these projects have had a disastrous effect on the environment, have displaced people from their lands, and have led to massive deforestation and cultural disintegration. Other grassroots groups have targeted the World Bank's policies of structural adjustment designed to assist countries in correcting their balance of payments or debt problems. These groups argue that the austerity programmes imposed on poorer countries struggling to make their debt payments are exacting an unacceptable toll on the poor.

Churches in the North and South have been active both in opposing the environmental policies of agencies like the World Bank as well as speaking out against the intolerable effects of the debt crisis and the imposition of SAPs on the poor. Increasingly, churches and other groups in the North and South have directed their criticisms not only at the harmful effects of World Bank policies but also at the development agenda of the World Bank itself.

This chapter suggests a somewhat different approach to understanding the development policies of the World Bank. It argues for an explicitly theological critique of the World Bank and its development agenda specifically with respect to its policies of structural adjustment. Before engaging in this kind of enquiry, a number of methodological points need to be established specifically regarding the relationship between theology and development.

Development Discourse as Theology

Development thinking generally suffers from the delusion that its theories, pronouncements and analysis have little or nothing to do with religion or theology. However, a closer examination of the discourse of development reveals its fundamentally theological character.[2] Part of the reason for the lack of attention accorded by social scientists to the theological character of their discourse lies in the lack of appreciation of the role that theology plays in modern societies or in the shaping of the social sciences. The conceptual shift in thinking requires not only a consideration of the process of secularization in any given culture but also an appreciation of the religious re-orientation that accompanies it. This entails a recognition of the institutions which have assumed the mantle previously worn by churches as the authoritative theological voices in the process of secularization. It also requires a broadening of our conceptual framework to consider religion not only in terms of its institutional forms but as a genre of expression, communication and legitimation.[3] Development theory and Christianity share one fundamental assumption: the inherent right and duty to change the world. The view presented here claims that the World Bank has become the predominant theological institution devoted to changing the world in the area of development.

Religion posits a human relationship with the transcendent, a being and/or a reality that lies beyond our present experience. This transcendent reality is regarded as existing beyond this world or as part of a future possibility of this world. One of the basic features of religious discourse is its reference to a higher order towards which our present endeavours strive. Development discourse also exhibits this basic feature. It posits the existence of two worlds, the developing world and the developed world. It is the developed world which is held out as the "always not yet" to the developing world. By analysing the developed world and following its basic principles and precepts, the developing country can achieve the elusive status of becoming "developed". Philip Van Ufford and Matthew Schoffeleers note the salvific elements which characterize development discourse:

> These models are salvific in that they contain not only a promise but also a prescription to make that promise come true. The development experts are the "priests" who mediate between the two worlds. It is their task to keep alive the idea that to engage in development is a sacred duty: hence the continuous emphasis on mobilization of the public opinion. Their authority cannot be doubted, because they are themselves the products of the reality which has become normative for the underdeveloped world. At the same time this definition of development reflects... the inevitable hierarchy which evolves as cultures are integrated in the development effort. All this supports the idea that "development" may be viewed as a religious concept... even if the relationship with the transcendent is formulated in essentially secular terms.[4]

Not only does development discourse present essentially religious themes in secular terms, it also serves a crucial legitimizing role for the institutions that articulate these "secular salvation histories".[5] It provides these institutions, be they governments or development agencies, with the very basis of their authority. This claim to authority is based either on the institution's ability to demonstrate that its own vision of development is superior to any alternative one or that other alternatives simply do not exist. As Ufford and Schoffeleers argue: "in these attempts at legitimation the concept of development plays such an important role because it possesses the very combination of political meaning needed to mobilize a significant following."[6] As long as the dominant development agency can marginalize or eliminate alternative visions of a better world its own vision remains the dominant one.

The theological character of development discourse is clearly revealed in the recent ascendency of neo-liberal economic thinking. By subsuming all economic activity under the role and functioning of the free market, neo-liberal economics elevates the market to a divine status outside of human control. As Julio de Santa Ana declares:

> The laws of the market, which are not independent of the people involved in the market, come to be seen as transcendent. That is they undergo a process of sociological sacralization. Not only are they given a higher status, they actually become untouchable, like the laws of nature. They become a taboo which cannot be shaken... . In this way those who wield economic power shroud their privileges in mystery, and create a fantasy where only banal reality exists. But, as a result of this sociological sacralization, the fantasy becomes a vital principle.[7]

De Santa Ana goes on to demonstrate how, in neo-liberal economic thinking, the God of the Bible is replaced by the divinity described as the invisible hand of the market. This constitutes a new religion, "with a new Torah – the laws of the market – corresponding to the sociological sacralization of the latter".[8] To the economist, the suggestion that their discourse is fundamentally religious would be viewed as absurd. The disciples of economics are scrupulous in proclaiming economics as a science devoid of any analysis and reflection on issues of transcendence. Yet, in the very process of denying the human agency and reality of the market, economists imbue it with a metaphysical status: remote, untouchable, to which all economic activity submits.[9] Structural adjustment is, in effect, a more rigorous assertion of the divinity of the market, or what Franz Hinkelammert describes as the "total market economy".[10]

The consideration of development discourse as a form of theological discourse opens a wide variety of possibilities not only for research but also in the forging of alliances and the articulation of alternative development visions. It provides the opportunity for integrated approaches to the analysis of development issues from macroeconomic concerns like structural adjustment to grassroots concerns. Most importantly, however, using a theological light to explore the policies of development institutions exposes a number of issues and assumptions that typically elude social scientific analysis precisely because development policies are presented in the coded form of religious discourse.[11] This chapter provides an illustration of the usefulness of such an approach by subjecting the development discourse of the World Bank to theological analysis.

Sin, Redemption and Mission

The World Bank's major documents on sub-Saharan Africa over the 1980s encompass a variety of theological categories. One of the most prominent of these is the development of a theology of sin to describe Africa's failures. The sinfulness of Africa is characterized in all of these documents as economic inefficiency. The duality between the inefficient economies of Africa and the efficient economies of the industrialized countries is the central organizing feature of the World Bank's theology of sin. The redemptive call, issued by the World Bank, exhorts Africa to leave behind its sinful past to embrace the virtues of the market. This is most apparent in the World Bank's charter document for Africa in the 1980s, *Accelerated Development in Sub-Saharan Africa*, known as the Berg Report. Upon its release, the Berg Report was hailed by both its promoters and detractors as "the new testament for agricultural development".[12]

By 1989, in its second major document on sub-Saharan Africa entitled *From Crisis to Sustainable Growth*, the World Bank blames Africa for failing to reach the promised land of modernization. The moral failing identified by the World Bank, is clear: "Africa is simply not competitive in an increasingly competitive world."[13]

With this theology of failure, the ever-present prospect of salvation is offered. Those countries willing to turn away from their sinful past and swallow the bitter pill of adjustment will, with time and effort, reach the promised land of higher growth rates. This is accomplished through the use of projected growth rates models. These models usually illustrate three scenarios: high, medium and low. The

optimistic scenario depends upon a country's or region's willingness
to adopt "market-oriented reforms". To describe the difficult period
of transition, the World Bank borrows the biblical Exodus theme of
"crossing the desert".[14] The solution for Africa is as simple as it is
theological:

> The long-term strategy proposed here envisages a move away
> from earlier practices. It aims to release the energies of
> ordinary people by enabling them to take charge of their lives.
> Profits would be seen as the mark of an efficient business... .
> Foreign investors would be welcomed as partners, not dis-
> couraged.[15]

When it became increasingly apparent that the adoption of the
World Bank's policies was not bringing African countries into the
promised land, the theology of sin became even more prominent. The
sinfulness at the heart of Africa's failure to develop was further
elaborated. The state, and rampant corruption that pervaded African
culture, were identified as the real sources of Africa's failure to be
competitive.

The project of convincing reluctant countries to adopt SAP is
viewed in a similar light as the christianizing missions of the previous
century. Former World Bank official Robert Klitgaard reflects on the
missionary zeal with which World Bank officials sought to convert the
Third World to the virtues of structural adjustment:

> The term *mission* now seemed to me curiously appropriate.
> One of its definitions evokes pilots over enemy terrain, flying
> in close formation, dropping their loads, and returning home.
> Another meaning has to do with missionaries, aliens who
> promise salvation to the natives if only certain, shall we say,
> structural adjustments are made.[16]

Fundamentalist Discourse

In her illuminating study of Protestant fundamentalism, Kathleen
Boone builds on the ideas concerning the role and functions of
discourse elaborated by Michel Foucault. As Foucault argued:

> ...in every society the production of discourse is at once controlled, selected, organized and redistributed according to a certain number of procedures, whose role is to avert its powers and dangers, to cope with chance events, to evade its ponderous, awesome materiality.[17]

By uncovering the "rules" of a particular form of discourse, what is also made explicit is the governance over what is said and who enjoys the right to say it. Boone brings to light the relationships among the various elements of fundamentalist theology:

> The authority of fundamentalism arises in the "reciprocal relations" of text, preachers, commentators, and ordinary readers. And in studying these relations, one confronts the compelling power of the closed system, a power which cannot be localized but is of one cloth, a power woven in and through every thread.[18]

The rest of this chapter considers the fundamentalist threads woven into the World Bank's banner of structural adjustment.

The Theology of Structural Adjustment

> The proponents of the structural adjustment recipe, the neo-liberal recipe, have an enormous faith in their product, even in the face of "much previous experience, much professional doubt and obvious economic and political realities. In this it resembles more a brand of religious fundamentalism than a school of thought".[19]

The discourse of the World Bank's analysis and policy prescriptions for Africa closely resembles the discourse of fundamentalist theology. While it is not my intention to consider these parallels in detail, I will focus on a description of some of the key features of fundamentalist theology and compare them to the discourse of the World Bank. This kind of analysis offers a number of illuminating insights into the manner in which the World Bank succeeded in implementing its development agenda for Africa over the course of the

1980s.

In subjecting the World Bank to this kind of analysis, it should be understood that in an institution which employs over 6000 development experts, discourse is often varied and disagreements are common. The World Bank hires consultants around the world who generate studies and analyses on a wide variety of development concerns. Moreover, the World Bank represents a wide variety of political interests, including the US Treasury Department, the finance ministers and executive directors of its member countries, its shareholders, as well as the multitude of international finance interests, from banks to transnational corporations to elites in Third World countries. Yet, in spite of the various interests which comprise the workings of the world's largest development institution, it has maintained a remarkable degree of uniformity with regard to the fundamental principles of development and, during the 1980s, in its vision of the need for SAPs. It has succeeded in this agenda precisely by employing its army of technocrats, researchers and policy advisors as the new missionaries of development for Africa. The echoes of the colonial role of the missionaries is obvious to writers like Joel Samoff:

> ...it is important to recognize the power, influence, and academic and developmental consequences of this historically unique contribution of funding development projects and development research (note here the echoes of the early imperial era, when the metropolitan governments funded learned societies that in turn supported the field work of missionaries and adventurers who like Livingstone, also saw themselves as geographers, anthropologists, and historians).[20]

Appreciating the fundamentalist elements in the World Bank's SAP agenda is a helpful means of exposing the inner logic of its discourse. It challenges the bank's undisputed hegemony and self-confirming authority over the development of the continent. This self-confirming authority is achieved by employing the techniques and strategies of fundamentalist discourse. The fundamentalist strategies employed by the World Bank include the promotion of structural adjustment as the universal path of salvation not only for Africa but for all of the Third World, endowing SAPs with a moral authority and superiority over competing claims, condemning opponents of SAPs as irrational, inefficient or self-serving and, finally, fulfilling its anointed role of establishing, controlling and maintaining the SAP agenda.[21] Joel Samoff makes a strikingly similar observation about how the World Bank's financial/intellectual complex succeeds in giving privilege to a particular kind of development discourse:

> I want particularly to highlight the ways in which its assumptions, standard operating procedures, style and language structure the education and development discourse, specify the legitimate participants in discussions of education policy, entrench misunderstanding, accord official status to shaky proposition, and nurture a fascination with flashy but ephemeral understandings.[22]

Exposing the discourse of the World Bank as a fundamentalist one also serves an important strategic function for the many groups opposed to its development agenda. The strategy in dealing with an institution like the World Bank is refocused with the insight that its economic policies are really only a subordinate aspect of the much more important goal of controlling the agenda of development for the world's poorer countries. The challenge for groups opposed to the World Bank then becomes one of exposing and resisting this agenda and being less concerned with engaging in debates about the efficacy of specific policies.

Servants of the Text

Boone's assessment of the indisputable voice of fundamentalism is equally applicable to the World Bank's theology of SAPs. The production of incontrovertible arguments by the World Bank is achieved by the same methods employed in fundamentalist methods of interpreting the Bible. The first and most deceptive technique of fundamentalist interpretation is that of disavowing the interpretive role of preachers in reading the Bible:

> ...because fundamentalism so masterfully effaces the role of interpretation, fundamentalism has been successful in win-

ning and sustaining its converts. Preachers contend that they
do nothing more than expound the plain sense of the Word of
God, and so thoroughly do they lard their pronouncements
with Bible verses that it is indeed difficult for the ordinary
layperson to dispute a preacher's authority, derived as it
appears to be from the Word of God itself.[23]

This strategy is especially insidious and effective because it
disguises the interpretive role of the preacher as the actual Word of
God. It is a tactic, "drenched in humility, performed with righteous-
ness", assigning the preacher the role as the "servant of the text".[24]

This interpretive function is effectively carried out by the army
of technocrats who are employed by the World Bank, who, for the
most part, share the basic principles of economic rationality of SAPs,
or what R. L. Ayres describes as the "technocratic neoliberalism" of
the World Bank.[25] The World Bank disavows its own interpretative
role in what it passes off as the value-free scientific economic analysis
of Africa's economic crisis. The fundamentalist thrust of the World
Bank's arguments throughout the 1980s is revealed by the way it
defends its positions. Rather than employing a careful analysis of the
historical context or the lived experience of those affected by its
policies, the World Bank consistently refers to ideological constructs
to defend its positions. The World Bank's analysis remains unassail-
able in so far as it is able to fill the role of preacher or high priest whose
authority derives from the text of perfectly competitive markets.

The World Bank took advantage of a historical opportunity to
attain the undisputed hegemony of its agenda for Africa in spite of the
overwhelming evidence which should have occasioned a more critical
assessment of its policies. The consolidation of this agenda during the
1980s is framed around two key documents which serve as the
"ideological markers"[26]: the 1981 document *Accelerated Development in Sub-Saharan Africa* and the 1989 *From Crisis to Sustainable
Growth*. Although the World Bank has been intimately involved in
Africa's development since the 1950s, the (mis)conception conveyed
in these the documents is that it has only lately arrived on the scene,
called in to help rescue a continent on the brink of collapse. This
selective amnesia not only absolves the World Bank of any involvement or responsibility in contributing to the crisis or of re-assessing or

re-evaluating the assumptions and premises of its development policies of the 1960s and 1970s for Africa; it also provides a "fresh"
analysis and set of prescriptions for a newly-constructed problem. This
"new dispensation" is most apparent in the Berg Report, which
scarcely mentions the role of the World Bank in Africa in previous
decades.

Some of the other characteristics of the fundamentalist mindset
also resonate with the World Bank's theology of SAPs: the single-
minded commitment to a fixed concept (getting prices right or liberalized markets) and an attitude characterized as "authoritarian, intol-
erant, and compulsive about control".[27]

Throughout the 1980s the World Bank has succeeded in opposing and dismissing the legitimacy of alternatives. Over this period the
real economic options of most African countries have been narrowed
to one: the adoption of SAPs. The World Bank's response to the UN
Economic Commission for Africa's *African Alternative Framework*
provides a classic illustration of how the world's leading development
institution deals with dissent. As Julio de Santa Ana notes, the World
Bank's economic policies have attained undisputed hegemony by
means of tactics employed by fundamentalist religions:

> ...the most realistic proposals are set aside without being
> discussed. Everything has to be sacrificed for the sake of
> maintaining the prevailing ideas. Now this kind of resistance
> and rigidity and irrationality (which I would compare with the
> dogmas championed in authoritarian theologies) means that
> there is a sacred and therefore unassailable character from
> which taboos that cannot be infringed are promulgated. Those
> daring to suggest alternatives aimed at changes are regarded
> as dangerous or discounted as unrealistic... .[28]

Dispensationalism

One of the basic features of fundamentalist thinking is known as
dispensationalism, a method of biblical interpretation. The key feature
of this theological outlook is the division of biblical history into
distinct periods or dispensations, (e.g., Innocence – Pre-Fall, Law,
Promise, Reign of Christ). These dispensations are distinguished by a

change in God's method of dealing with humanity. "Each of the dispensations may be regarded as a new test of the natural man [sic], and each ends in judgement – marking his utter failure in every dispensation."[29]

Another characteristic related to dispensationalism is the adherence to premillennialist thinking. This refers to the belief in the utter futility of effecting social change because the end time is near. The role of the Christian is to evangelize individual souls and not engage in social or political activism.[30] While it is not possible to transform a lost society one can convert individuals in that society to the ethic of individual industriousness and personal virtue.

The World Bank's second major report on Africa in the 1980s, *From Crisis to Sustainable Growth*, is heavily laden with dispensationalist undertones. The World Bank's theology of crisis calls for more radical and comprehensive "solutions" than had been previously thought necessary. According to the report, the African state is beyond redemption. The task at hand is to focus on the few pockets of private industry in the continent and to bypass the state. This newly discovered problem provides a useful gloss for a sober assessment of the ability of SAPs to achieve their stated goals. Indeed, as SAPs continue not to work, the need to rediscover Africa's problems as rooted in the failure of its peoples and governments becomes increasingly necessary. By the end of the 1980s the World Bank had given up hope of converting African society and the state to the virtues of the free market and was content to save individual souls by encouraging investment in the private sector.

A Theology of Sacrifice

A theology of sacrifice is embedded in our Western Christian tradition. The crucifixion of Jesus stands as the central symbol for Christians of a self-sacrificing God offered up for the redemption of humanity. It has served as a powerful symbol for both the justification of as well as the resistance to oppression. This paradigm of self-sacrifice has been offered as solace for those who suffer injustice at the hands of the more powerful. In the fundamentalist order, the theology of sacrifice plays an important role in legitimizing suffering and oppression as part of God's inscrutable plan for the greater good of maintaining the divinely-willed existing social order. The poor are told that their poverty is their cross to bear and that their suffering will be redeemed in the world to come.

A liberative theology of sacrifice, in contrast, is rooted in the belief in a God who is on the side of the poor and oppressed in resisting the suffering imposed upon the victims of oppression. Sacrifice is liberative when it is directed toward resisting oppression and building a more just society. The Bible is filled with examples of a God who rejects an order where the strong are allowed to dominate the most vulnerable.

A fundamentalist theology of sacrifice plays an important role in the World Bank's theology of SAPs. SAPs are presented to African countries as a form of economic behaviour requiring sacrifice to the discipline of the market. This notion of sacrifice is also rooted in the assumption that sacrifices are required in order to pay off the debts incurred in the past. In the theology of sacrifice the morality of debt servicing is inverted. In a process that sacrifices the lives of millions in the Third World to pay the debt, the moral question that takes precedence is the one which asks whether it is lawful *not* to pay debts; what will happen to the international order if suddenly debts no longer needed to be paid?[31]

In spite of the many sacrifices that the African continent made in adhering to SAPs over the 1980s, the continent has become worse off. By the late 1980s, the theology of suffering becomes even more explicit in World Bank thinking. Those groups (women and children) who are suffering the worst effects of SAPs are comforted. They are targeted with special poverty alleviation programmes. However, the country's economy cannot escape the painful period of adjustment that is necessary before it can enter into the promised land of balanced budgets and high growth rates. This kind of expiatory theology, notes de Santa Ana, is indicative of a cultic piety based on tribute, expiation, guilt and conformity. Those who do not conform to the body of prevailing prescriptions are dangerous and unclean and must readjust to become acceptable.[32]

What is also implied in the World Bank's theology of sacrifice is what Franz Hinkelammert defines as "anti-sacrifice". The poorer countries are called upon to make sacrifices so that, in future, sacrifices will no longer be necessary. From the point of view of those who impose this logic, killing must occur, but there are no killers. This process turns into a cycle, which, once closed, submits all actions to its logic. As Hinkelammert notes:

> Once this sacrificial cycle has been closed, nothing is unlawful. Any human sacrifice, any violation of human rights is justified and no moral conscience in the world can legitimately interfere.[33]

It is the prevailing social economic order that must be preserved through the ritual of sacrifice, especially when the marginalized groupings threaten to disrupt this order. The entire SAP exercise of the 1980s can be regarded in theological terms as a ritual purification exercise to restore order to the international financial system. This exercise is described by economists as the need to restore stability to global financial markets which the debt crisis was threatening to disrupt. SAPs serve as a violent ritual without a perpetrator, a cultic sacrifice or an exorcism of violence that is transferred to the victim without guilt or confrontation:

> This idea is typically "religious"; it presupposes a society completely organized around these rites, depending on them to settle its problems, incapable on its own of handling confrontations in the social contract, or achieving reconciliation without making victims.[34]

For those who become the victims of the adjustment that is deemed necessary to safeguard the existing order, the role of high priests who determine the method, time and duration of the purification rite is all too clear:

> At present the prevailing "scheme" is administered by the IMF and the World Bank. The real power is in the hands of the international bourgeoisie, especially those working with finance capital. This is where the violence is really centred in our time. The appearances may not seem to justify that statement. Yet it is in the hush of elegant drawing rooms where plush carpets muffle the tread of footsteps that the most

violent actions affecting the life of peoples are devised. It is in places like this that the *economic readjustments* are imposed and they do not give life but take it away from the poorest sectors. This is where injustice is administered under the pretext that economic practice has nothing to do with social justice but is meant to generate wealth (as though the one were not closely linked to the other!).[35]

Filling in the Gaps

Another typical interpretive device employed in fundamentalist theology is the so-called gap theory, the practice of hypothesizing from what the Bible does not say in order to resolve textual difficulties. As Boone notes, "This technique can degenerate rather quickly into disregard for determining the actual facts of the case, effectively closing off discussion once the main objective – the protection of inerrancy – has been achieved."[36] The real agenda is not, as Boone notes, the logical coherency of the strained interpretations but first and foremost, the preservation of the *doctrine* of the text.[37] A closer examination of the African experience over the 1980s reveals that the World Bank consistently ignored or manipulated the evidence relating to Africa's economic crisis in order to preserve the inerrancy of the doctrine of structural adjustment. The clearest illustration of the World Bank's use of the gap theory can be found in a study the World Bank conducted with the UN Development Programme in 1988 entitled *Africa's Adjustment and Growth*. The study crudely attempted to prove that African countries which were adopting SAPs were performing better than those which did not by means of very questionable statistical manipulations. The document demonstrates the value attached by the World Bank to preserving the inerrancy of the doctrine of structural adjustment.

Justification by Correct Statement

Finally, in fundamentalist thinking a technique is required to distinguish true adherents from those who have interpreted the text incorrectly. This is achieved through what Boone describes as "justification by correct statement".[38] This involves employing the "correct" terminology, catch-phrases and principles in interpreting the text. Great care is taken to shield believers from the wrong words or combination of words for fear that exposure to them can destroy the faith.

The more recent writings of the World Bank demonstrate this kind of attitude towards any alternatives to structural adjustment that are put forward. These alternatives, to the extent they are even acknowledged, are subjected to the test of justification by correct statement. Because these alternatives do not employ the correct terminology and catch-phrases (such as adherence to the market, getting prices right) they fail to meet the standard of being considered as realistic or viable.

The correct statements, in the development theology of the World Bank, champion the virtues of an individualistic, free-enterprise "gospel of prosperity". This leads to a reductionist view of the human as *homo economicus*, the rational product of Western economic individualism. Many of the economic principles which form the basis of the World Bank's development theology are rooted in an ethical worldview predicated on extreme individualism.[39] This extreme individualistic worldview grounds many of the ideals championed by the religious right in the US.

For an international development agency like the World Bank, the appeal to a "gospel of prosperity" for a continent in "crisis" not only serves to provide a facile solution to the crisis, it also pre-empts any serious analysis of the virtues and effects of the policies proposed. As the SAP agenda became firmly embedded into the development agenda for Africa during the 1980s the "gospel of prosperity" attained a built-in invincibility. Failure to succeed could only be the result of individual or government shortcomings and not the fault of the policies themselves. In this respect the World Bank functions no differently than the countless right-wing evangelical movements spreading the gospel of prosperity throughout Africa. As Paul Gifford notes:

> This prosperity gospel has obvious socio-political effects. It tells the people of Africa, the world's poorest continent, that prosperity will be provided by a "miracle-working God", or (alternatively) that material prosperity will come as the inexorable result of the functioning of spiritual laws. It simply

ignores the political and economic reasons for so much poverty in Africa... .[40]

It is difficult to comprehend the World Bank's prescriptions for Africa during the 1980s without placing them in the context of the rise of what has come to be known as the "New Right" in the US. While not suggesting a direct correspondence between the theology of the New Right and the economic prescriptions of the World Bank for Africa, they share many assumptions and a remarkably similar political-economic agenda. This is not surprising given the convergence of political and economic interests that shape the ideologies of these seemingly disparate groupings. This is not to argue for a conspiracy theory of Third World Development during the 1980s, but for an analysis which demonstrates the common interests of particular elite groupings which succeeded in consolidating what has come to be termed the "New Right Agenda" during the 1980s. These interests cut across a number of institutions, think-tanks, TNCs, governments and elites. They also cut across agencies like the World Bank and many of the fundamentalist Christian churches.

As Gifford notes, one of fundamentalism's basic characteristics is its lack of historical or sociological awareness. This results in reading theological doctrines into the Bible which were developed centuries later.[41] Likewise, the World Bank engages in this kind of ahistorical analysis of the crisis in Africa as it offers up the free market as its uniform solution, while hardly bothering to consider the impact that these same prescriptions have already had. Responsibility for success is accorded to God and God's servants on earth, the preachers and high priests. Failure, however, is always the fault of the individual who did not believe correctly or fervently enough.

Many social scientists are beginning to characterize the policies and pronouncements of the World Bank in theological terms. Samir Amin has been one of the harshest and most consistent critics of the World Bank since the 1960s. His more recent writings expose the ideological underpinnings of the World Bank's development agenda. As he points out:

The [World Bank] "experts" love to brag of their political neutrality. They pride themselves on the hidden defect of many economists desirous of being technocrats, capable of shaping a "good development policy", "scientific", devoid of any ideological prejudice. But this kind of exercise has the supreme virtue of avoiding the real options facing currently existing societies. The truncated and superficial image of reality characteristic of the genre under discussion must of necessity lead to false conclusions.... . The critical analysis of the policies under way and consequently of the priorities proposed are governed by this disturbing vision of the global operation of the system and the fundamentalist prejudices of the Bank's Reaganite liberalism.[42]

A consideration of the World Bank's development agenda for Africa as theological opens up an area of analysis that connects what normally are considered disparate realms of discourse. It is also based on the conviction that any critique of the World Bank's SAP agenda must draw upon a wide range of analyses and disciplines. We must recognize that the World Bank's structural adjustment development agenda not only constitutes bad economics, it is also bad theology. Exposing the discourse of the World Bank as a fundamentalist one also serves an important strategic function for the many groups opposed to its development agenda. The strategy in dealing with an institution like the World Bank is refocused with the insight that its economic policies are really only a subordinate aspect of the much more important goal of controlling the agenda of development for the world's poorer countries. The issue for groups opposed to the World Bank then becomes one of exposing and resisting this agenda and being less concerned with engaging in debates about the efficacy of specific policies.

The struggle for a more just global order is greatly enhanced by the recognition of the fundamentally religious character of both the forces for change and those that uphold the status quo. The insights provided in the areas of development studies, economics, trade theory, anthropology, sociology, gender analysis, theology, ethics and ecology drawn upon in the subsequent chapters both serve to expose the World Bank's SAP agenda as a vacuous, dangerous and fundamentalist ideology as well as point in the direction of alternatives. As Walter Russell Mead suggests:

If we are going to have religions, then let us have real ones: religions based on things like love and human dignity, not on increasing the GDP. ...We may not ever be able to build a positive science of economics based on empirical knowledge, but that is no reason to wrap the little we know in a pseudoscientific fog of superstition.[43]

Endnotes

1. R. H. Green, "The Broken Pot: The Social Fabric, Economic Disaster and Adjustment in Africa," in B. Onimode ed., *The IMF, the World Bank and the African Debt*, vol. 2, (London: Zed Books, 1989), p. 31.
2. Phillip Van Ufford and Matthew Schoffeleers, *Religion and Development: Towards an Integrated Approach*, (Amsterdam: Free University Press, 1988), p. 6.
3. R. Robertson and W.R. Garrett, eds., *Religion and Global Order*, (New York: Paragon Publishers, 1991), p. xv.
4. Ufford and Schoffeleers, *Religion and Development*, p. 19.
5. L. Cormie, "The Sociology of National Development and Salvation History," in G. Baum ed., *Sociology and Human Destiny*, (New York: Seabury Press, 1980), p. 74.
6. Ufford and Schoffeleers, *Religion and Development*, p. 23.
7. J. de Santa Ana, "Sacralization and Sacrifice in Human Practice," in World Council of Churches' Commission on the Churches Participation in Development, *Sacrifice and Humane Economic Life*, (Geneva: World Council of Churches, 1992), p. 20.
8. J. de Santa Ana, "Sacralization and Sacrifice in Human Practice," p. 24
9. J. de Santa Ana, "Sacralization and Sacrifice in Human Practice," p. 25.
10. For Hinkelammert, "through this policy of total market economy which was promoted by the Reagan government, the eighties of this century became a decade of genocide in the Third World for the recovery of foreign debt, and made a holocaust of nature". F.J. Hinkelammert, "The Sacrificial Cycle as a Justification for Western Domination: The Western Iphigenia in Latin America," in World Council of Churches' Commission on the Churches Participation in Development, *Sacrifice and Humane Economic Life*, (Geneva: World Council of Churches, 1992), p. 72.
11. Ufford and Schoffeleers, *Religion and Development*, p. 26.
12. *Review of African Political Economy*, (editorial), 27-8, 1983, p. 186.
13. World Bank. *Sub-Saharan Africa: From Crisis to Sustainable Growth: A Long Term Perspective Study*, (Washington, D.C., 1989), p. 3.

14. See F. Stewart, "The Many Faces of Adjustment," *World Development* 19, 1991, pp. 1847-64.

15. *From Crisis*, p. 5.

16. R. Klitgaard, *Tropical Gangsters: One Man's Experience with Development and Decadence in Deepest Africa*, (New York: Basic Books, 1990), p. 207.

17. M. Foucault, *The Discourse on Language*, (Paris: Gallimard, 1971), p. 216, quoted in K. Boone, *The Bible Tells Them So: The Discourse of Protestant Fundamentalism*, (Albany: SUNY Press, 1989), p. 14.

18. Boone, *The Bible*, p. 3.

19. Hans Singer, cited in M. O'Neill, "Women and Children First: An Assessment of Structural Adjustment," CDAS Discussion Paper No. 59, Montreal: Centre for Developing Area Studies, (McGill University, 1989), (Unpublished) p. 16.

20. J. Samoff, "The Financial/Intellectual Complex of Foreign Aid," *Review of African Political Economy* 53 (1992), p. 70.

21. C.f., L. Cormie, "Christian Responsibility for the World of the Free Market?" p. 8.

22. J. Samoff, "The Intellectual/Financial Complex of Foreign Aid," p. 62.

23. Boone, *The Bible*, p. 2.

24. S. Fish, *Is There a Text in the Class*, p. 353, quoted in Boone, *The Bible*, p. 70.

25. R. L. Ayres, *Banking on the Poor*, (Cambridge, MIT Press, 1983), p. 75.

26. H. Bernstein, "Agricultural 'Modernization' and the Era of Structural Adjustment: Observations on Sub-Saharan Africa," *Journal of Peasant Studies* 18/1 (1990), p. 16.

27. Boone, *The Bible*, p. 4.

28. J. de Santa Ana, cited in A. Ndumbu ed., *Africa in the Debt Yoke: The Mission of the Church*, (Nairobi: National Council of Churches of Kenya, 1991), p. 138.

29. C. I. Scofield, *Rightly Dividing the Word of Truth*, quoted in Boone, *The Bible*, p. 50.

30. Boone, *The Bible*, p. 53.

31. In his characteristically blunt yet perspicacious style, Hinkelammert goes on to draw a number of important parallels between the logic of sacrifice imposed by the debt crisis and the Iphigenia sacrificial ritual which pervades Western thinking. As he declares about the consequences of the debt crisis: "Those who impose this Western morality see themselves as veritable Agamemnons, tragic heroes predetermined by fate to impose the law without regard for the consequences. They can admire the morality of those capable of carrying out the genocide with untrembling hands." Further on he notes: "And are not our banks making this tragic sacrifice when they collect the Third World's foreign debt and submit to being accused and find no one understands at all the moral necessity that obliges them to commit genocide? They are the ones with the tragic drama in their hearts – not those who have to die as a result! The slaughterers who carry out sacrifices really are

sacrificing themselves by sacrificing others." F. Hinkelammert, "The Sacrificial Cycle," p. 68.

32. J. de Santa Ana, "Sacralization and Sacrifice in Human Practice," p. 32.

33. F. Hinkelammert, "The Sacrificial Cycle," p. 67.

34. René Girard, *La Violence et le Sacré*, (Paris: Grasset, 1978), cited in J. de Santa Ana, "Sacralization and Sacrifice in Human Practice, p. 32.

35. J. de Santa Ana, "Sacralization and Sacrifice in Human Practice," p. 34.

36. Boone, *The Bible*, p. 63.

37. Boone, *The Bible*, p. 64.

38. Boone, *The Bible*, p. 83.

39. H. Daly and John B. Cobb Jr., *For the Common Good: Redirecting the Economy Towards Community, the Environment and a Sustainable Future*, (Boston: Beacon Press, 1989), p. 87.

40. P. Gifford, "Christian Fundamentalism and Development," *Review of African Political Economy* 52 (1991), p. 14.

41. "Fundamentalists put great stress on the depravity of the world and humankind, fathering their understanding of original sin on the Bible without realizing that it comes from Augustine... ." P. Gifford, *The New Religious Right in Southern Africa*, (Harare: Baobab Books, 1998), p. 90.

42. Samir Amin, *Maldevelopment: Anatomy of a Global Failure*, (London: Zed Books, 1990), pp. 35, 37.

43. Walter Russel Mead, "Why the Deficit is a Godsend: And Five Other Economic Heresies", *Harper's* 286 (May, 1993), p. 63.

— CHAPTER TWO —

Prelude to "The Crisis" – The World Bank and the Modernization of Africa

Introduction

The following three chapters provide a descriptive analysis of the World Bank's development strategy for sub-Saharan Africa during the 1980s. Through an analysis of the major World Bank documents on sub-Saharan Africa in the 1980s what emerges is a clear and coherent analysis of the root causes of Africa's development crisis and the urgent need for radical reforms. The pronouncements of the World Bank for sub-Saharan Africa during this period give the appearance of a well-reasoned "theology of crisis". Africa's problems are so profound and structural that they call for a radical break from the past; a conversion, as it were, to a completely new way of organizing its political, economic and cultural institutions. In effect, the World Bank's theology of structural adjustment, its programme for the restoration of sub-Saharan Africa, constitutes a moral exhortation to abandon an improvident and unproductive past to embrace a new way of thinking and acting which promises a brighter future.

These three chapters will highlight the World Bank's policies and documents for sub-Saharan Africa over the past decade. This will be carried out in the context of considering the dominant issues preoccupying the major interests in the North, particularly banks, transnationals and governments. How, for example, did the World Bank's self-perceived role change in light of a rapidly changing global geo-political and economic climate? This chapter considers the World Bank's involvement in sub-Saharan Africa prior to the 1980s.

The Structure of the World Bank

The World Bank is currently the largest multi-national lending and technical agency dealing with Third World development. Its administrative budget alone is over $900 million per year and it employs over 6,000 technical advisors and staff. It has an annual lending authority of over $20 billion and has recorded a profit every year since 1947. In 1993 this profit amounted to $1.1 billion. In 1993, the World Bank's total income was $9.4 billion. From this amount $8.0 billion came from interest and fees paid out by developing countries of which it returned $6.8 billion in interest to its various bondholders. In 1993 the World Bank's outstanding loans totalled $105 billion, not including the $56 billion owed to the International Development Association (IDA, the arm of the World Bank that provides concessional grants and loans to poorer countries).[1]

Behind the World Bank lie the financial interests of its donor countries dominated by the finance ministers of the Group of Seven or G-7 countries.[2] Since the 1950s, the mandate of the World Bank was to finance medium- and long-term projects to developing countries. In the 1970s, under the presidency of Robert McNamara, the World Bank grew dramatically in size and scope. In the 1980s, in large part due to the debt crisis, the bank served increasingly as a debt-management institution, lending in some cases as much as 50 per cent of a developing country's portfolio towards structural and/or sectoral adjustment lending. The primary feature of this kind of lending was to restore a troubled economy's debt servicing capacity by urging indebted countries to adopt major economic reforms.

The World Bank has wielded enormous power and influence in Africa especially over the last decade. Because of its vast technical and financial resources, the World Bank's analysis of Africa's development crisis has achieved virtual dominance in all Western financial and development assistance institutions. Over this period World Bank personnel have succeeded in inserting themselves into the highest economic decision-making levels of many African and other Third World countries. The solutions proffered for Africa's ills resulted in the radical transformation of every single African country in the 1980s.

A brief glance to the 1970s will help establish the backdrop for the adjustment decade of the 1980s and clarify the World Bank's role in Africa's development process during this period. It will also reveal the continuities and discontinuities in the World Bank's development agenda in the 1980s.

The Modernization Paradigm

During the 1960s and 1970s the World Bank's philosophy for the developing world drew its inspiration from modernization theories associated with the Chicago-based Economic Development and Cultural Change group.

A fundamental assumption of the modernization paradigm is that the problems of development are to be found within the confines of each individual country. Another key assumption of the modernization model is that the advancement of a nation depends primarily, or even solely, on its own efforts to maximize its own potential for growth. The corollary of this assumption is that obstacles to development are strictly endogenous. In his influential work *The Strategy of Economic Development*, A. O. Hirschmann shows that the major role for developed countries is to provide what he called the "demonstration effect", i.e. providing the model for developing countries to emulate:

> Once economic progress in the pioneer countries is a visible reality, the strength of the desire to imitate, to follow suit, to catch up obviously becomes an important determinant of what will happen among non-pioneers.[3]

The modernization paradigm, grounded in neo-classical and global Keynesian economic theories, considers development to be synonymous with economic growth and capital formation: the engines that will drive the modernization effort of the entire society. As such, the problem of underdevelopment can be adduced to a shortage of capital. Walt Rostow's *The Stages of Economic Growth* provided the classic model for the development of all societies based on growth and capital formation. Underdeveloped societies, in order to achieve self-sustained economic growth, had to pass through five stages to attain the most developed stage of the mass consumption society. The key to attaining "take-off", in the transition from a traditional to a modern capitalist society, was for a country to encourage its entrepreneurial class to be the catalysts for achieving industrialization. The key for developing countries was to increase investment and savings.

The pre-eminence of the modernization paradigm was such that its assumptions became part of the analytical framework of other disciplines involved in related fields. The assumptions of this framework can be summarized as follows:

- Development is an evolutionary process in which various societies find themselves at different stages.
- The relative stage of a particular society can be determined and measured through observable differences between developed and less developed societies.
- Development implies an imitative process by which a less developed society advances by imitating developed societies.
- The role of the social sciences is to analyse the qualities that obtain in developed cultures, to quantify them, and to assess the process by which they were achieved in order to synthesize them into principles of policy which can be applied in less developed societies.

These investigations extend into every realm of a society from its economic structures, to human attitudes, political institutions and cultural practices.[4] During the post-World War II period, the social sciences were actively engaged in determining the objective factors that could accelerate the development process.[5] For instance, the task of sociologists and anthropologists was to attempt to understand peasant consciousness in traditional societies in order to comprehend the obstacles that prevented the communally-minded peasant from becoming a self-interested surplus producer.

Internal resistance to change became the characterizing feature of traditional societies which had to be overcome. Writers, like David Lerner, speak of the moral change of heart required: "Modernization operates... through a transformation of institutions that can only be accomplished by the transformation of individuals – the painfully complex process which W. H. Auden epitomized as a 'change of heart'."[6] Others, like Christopher Hallpike, spoke of the resistance in terms of the lack of opportunity for the "primitive" mind to engage in abstract thought.[7] The epitome of the internalized version of the obstacles to development found in traditional societies is what David

McClelland referred to as "n-Ach", which stood for the need for achievement or "the desire to do well... to attain an inner feeling of personal accomplishments".[8] If the elites in a developing country did not possess enough n-Ach, then they would retard the course of development. Common to each of these perspectives was the belief in development as a "single, unilinear evolutionary path from the primitive or underdeveloped state to the developed modern one".[9]

Underlying such studies is the assumption that subsistence agriculture, and the mentality thought to accompany it, represents a less efficient and developed mode of production which needs to be overcome if the society is to develop. Countless volumes of research have devotedly studied such obstacles to development and how they can be overcome through institutional transformation or by introducing various aspects of modern technology.[10]

The primary arena for this transformation was the backward sector of subsistence agriculture. A generally shared assumption both in the North and South was that a "revolution of subsistence agriculture into a fully commercialized system was in the short term the critical task facing the development community".[11] Development was to be financed largely by external donor countries who would provide the infrastructural requirements to less developed countries. Properly coordinated, they would provide the engine of development for the continent.

As a multilateral lending institution, the World Bank sought to put this modernization agenda into operation by assuming the role of an agency that would garner and inject the necessary capital required for developing countries to achieve modernization. During this period the World Bank tolerated, and in some cases even promoted, neo-Keynesian approaches to development, which included state support for integrated rural development, health and education, small-farm credit, as well as import-substitution and even protectionism. The issue of redistribution as the means of achieving poverty alleviation received serious attention in the World Bank under the presidency of McNamara (1968-1981). This growing attention to poverty concerns can be traced to the growing influence and unity of the newly independent Third World countries in their call for a New International Economic Order. It was also a response to the increasing voices of dependency theory among Third World scholars critical of the assumptions of modernization theory.

During the 1970s, there was a marked rise in both bilateral as well as commercial investment. The World Bank, far from opposing this tide of investment and lending to the developing world, responded by dramatically increasing its own investments in a virtually unregulated environment. Under the tenure of McNamara, the World Bank expanded rapidly to become a $10 billion-a-year lending institution. Developing countries were emerging as political and economic forces. McNamara sought to manage these forces by manoeuvring the World Bank to the forefront of a development agenda which would direct investment and assistance towards Third World governments.

The World Bank dramatically increased its role and investment in Africa and also complemented and supported the tide of investment and lending by commercial banks and transnational corporations (TNCs). As Toye *et al.* note:

> In fact [the World Bank] saw high growth as the guarantee of
> the continuing creditworthiness of developing countries, and
> it had repeatedly soothed fears about the sustainability of the
> recycling operation.[12]

The New Orthodoxy

With the dawn of the 1980s a series of events culminated in a dramatic shift in the operation and philosophy of development within the World Bank. This reorientation can be traced primarily to the changes in the political and economic climate of several industrialized countries. The onset of the Reagan-Thatcher era corresponded with a decidedly neo-liberal shift in bank policy, symbolically heralded by the replacement of McNamara with an ex-banker, A. W. Clausen, as president.

In the wake of this dramatically altered political climate, the development philosophy and operational assumptions of the World Bank were reassessed. In the changing political economic climate this re-orientation became a matter of survival. In 1980, with the ascendancy of Reagan to the US presidency, the usefulness of the World Bank was called into question by a number of influential neo-conservative writers and think-tanks. The Heritage Foundation was foremost amongst the World Bank's critics. Articles appeared in the magazines *Forbes* and *Barrons* in 1980 which launched what amounted to a full-scale assault from the right on the policies and practices of the World Bank. The World Bank was criticized for encouraging the public rather than the private sector, for emphasizing redistribution over economic growth, for lending without sufficient conditionality or profit, and generally for its inadequate promotion of market-oriented policies in developing countries. Indeed, the usefulness of the World Bank as a tool for the projection of US political and economic interests was seriously questioned. [13]

In response, President Reagan ordered a full Treasury Department review of US participation in the World Bank. The review, released in 1982, vindicated the World Bank on many of the charges made by its right-wing critics. Other criticisms were supported, the most important being the charge that World Bank lending lacked sufficient conditionality. In order to correct this perceived shortcoming the Treasury Department recommended that the World Bank "exercise its leverage more effectively" by acting in concert with the IMF to apply "complementary pressure".[14]

Under the new leadership of A. W. Clausen, the World Bank adjusted quickly to the new climate in Washington. In short order, poverty alleviation and redistribution were banished from the lexicon. Structural adjustment, which in the late 1970s was used to refer to the need for *developed* countries to restructure their industries by dismantling such protectionist instruments as the Multi-Fibre Agreement,[15] was redefined to describe what was required of the indebted countries of the South. Rather than comprising the articulation of a new development philosophy, the shift to the structural adjustment agenda represented the rejection of what were viewed by its proponents as anomalies of modernization and developmentalist thinking. It represented a repudiation of one of the operational assumptions of the Rostowian stages-of-development paradigm which implied that developing countries must temporarily operate under a different set of laws from developed countries until they catch up. In concrete terms it spelled the demise of the loose neo-Keynesian consensus in the post-World-War II development debate. As Toye *et al.* note, the consequences were not surprising:

...in the end, the effect of the discrediting of neo-Keynesian ideas in the development debate was to open the way for the neo-liberals to establish their agenda and their policy preferences. These were eagerly picked up when the political mood decisively shifted to the right at the end of the 1970s.[16]

The Development of Structural Adjustment

The shift in World Bank policy towards structural adjustment lending was the culmination of both external pressures and an internal reassessment of its lending policies. John Toye *et al.*, in their two-volume study of World Bank lending over the past decade entitled *Aid and Power*, document this shift in internal policy in the World Bank which occurred at the beginning of the 1980s. The external climate was ripe for a reassessment of project-based lending which was the hallmark of World Bank lending during the McNamara era. Many, both inside and outside the World Bank, questioned the validity of the project-lending approach in light of the many "white elephants" that were beginning to be associated with this kind of lending. Of greatest concern, however, was the fact that project lending did not avail itself to the kind of macro-policy conditionality desired by high-ranking World Bank officials. Structural adjustment lending, the quick disbursal of funds for balance of payments support to needy countries, became the solution to both problems. Structural adjustment loans (SALs) could be offered to recipient countries conditional upon their acceptance of certain macro-level policy reforms. While resisted at first by some within the World Bank, structural adjustment loans quickly became operational as the debt crisis in developing countries deepened, rendering indebted countries more amenable to the conditions that were attached to new lending.[17]

A number of other factors contributed to the shift toward structural adjustment lending. Structural adjustment lending appealed to many within the bank because it provided the World Bank with an opportunity to "gain a purchase on high policy, to do so through direct negotiations at the highest level and to be offering enough resources to justify the attention of the country's top policy-makers".[18] The fact that many developing countries were in desperate need of quickly disbursed funds in the wake of skyrocketing interest rates and oil price hikes meant that the World Bank was able to fulfil this new role with little resistance. Since continued project lending was becoming less attractive, the World Bank stepped into the breach to offer countries balance of payments support loans, a function traditionally carried out by the IMF.

The explanation for the shift to structural adjustment lending was articulated as the generalized failure of the modernization project itself. Throughout the post-war period the modernization model promoted by the World Bank was centred upon the contrast between peasant and modern forms of production. However, modernization projects were not achieving the sought after transformation. Rather than rethink its own policies and assumptions, the World Bank redefined the problem as that of lack of incentives in agriculture and targeted the state in less developed countries as the chief culprit.[19]

According to the new thinking, the global economy operated under only one set of laws for all: the maximization of human welfare through the operation of the market. Interventions by the state into the market, previously tolerated as a necessary requirement for developing countries to catch up, was now considered anathema. The "stages" model of development which predominated in the 1960s and 1970s was rewritten to reject state intervention in the market-place. Peter Gibbon describes the policy consequences of this shift in thinking:

> As a group, LDCs happened to share in common only the unfortunate condition of subjection to administrative regulation in particularly comprehensive and entrenched forms. The "development" of these countries therefore depended on the removal of the administratively-imposed distortions which had prevented them taking proper advantage of their natural endowments. In practice this meant correcting administratively "overvalued" prices (typically currency and agricultural prices) and severely reducing the size of their public sectors, especially the productive sectors of their public sectors.[20]

In fact, the same policies that were heavily promoted by the international development and financial institutions for the South in the 1970s – investment in mega-projects and massive infrastructural development, coordinated by the state which served as the useful guarantor for loans and investment – were now to blame for the crisis which emerged in the early 1980s.

Underlying this reorientation is a coherent political economy of development, particularly in its vision of the relationship between the individual, the state and the economy. At the turn of the decade, these ideas became operational in agencies like the World Bank.

The key planks of this revised political economy of development are summarized by Toye *et al.* in the following three theses:

1) *Methodological Individualism*: This theory is based on the assumptions of neo-classical micro-economic theory, particularly the idea that when given the choice all individuals will be profit-maximizers. An extreme form of this assumption was then applied to Third World governments to explain not only the failure of their policies, but also their failure to adopt neo-liberal prescriptions. The explanation was that those in political positions of power will *always* be motivated by individual self-interest and therefore, will always choose to benefit themselves when given the choice between a public good and a private interest. Thus, Third World leaders are seen to be misguided, myopic, greedy and corrupt, always putting their own gain above the common good.

2) *Pessimism*: Stemming from the first principle is an over-whelmingly pessimistic outlook regarding the ability of governments to adopt the "right" policies, since it is not in the interests of their leaders to do so. Only by rolling back the state can these interests be curtailed for the benefit of all individuals.

3) *Developing Economies as Closed Systems*: This view represents a rejection of the aspirations for a New International Economic Order. The domestic policies of a country were exclusively to blame for its underdevelopment. The New International Economic Order, which called for basic structural changes in the way the richer countries related to poorer countries, was replaced by the doctrine of structural adjustment, which called upon developing countries to re-orient their economic policies to the exigencies of the global economy by liberalizing their own economies and rolling back the state.

As Toye *et al.* note, these principles represent not a doctrine, but a method, "within which a great variety of different models of reality can be constructed, but not *any* model of reality".[21] In the case of structural adjustment the cornerstones of neo-liberal theory translate into a specific analysis of a) the destructive character of interest groups opposed to liberalization (urban classes opposed to SAPs) and b) the overextension of governments. The vision put forward is one which represents "a dramatic shift away from a pluralist, participatory ideal of politics and towards an authoritarian and technocratic ideal based not on big government but on small and highly efficient government".[22]

The major pillars of this re-orientation to structural adjustment remained unchanged throughout the 1980s. What did evolve was the way this agenda gradually became incorporated into the aid programmes and the conditionalities for debt relief that dominated the development agenda in the 1980s. The next chapter examines the crucial role which the debt crisis played in facilitating the imposition of structural adjustment in sub-Saharan Africa.

Endnotes

1. *World Bank Annual Report* 1993. See Appendix 1 for more background information on the World Bank.

2. The Group of Seven countries are: Great Britain, Canada, France, Germany, Italy, Japan and the United States.

3. A. O. Hirschmann, *The Strategy of Economic Development*, (New York: W.W. and Norton, 1978), p. 8.

4. M. Blomström and B. Hettne, *Development Theory in Transition: The Dependency Debate and Beyond*, (London: Zed Books, 1984), pp. 20-24.

5. Myron Weiner, ed. *Modernization: The Dynamics of Growth*, (New York: Basic Books, 1966), p. 2.

6. D. Lerner, *The Passing of Traditional Society*, (Glencoe, Ill.: The Free Press, 1958), p. 388.

7. Christopher Hallpike, *The Foundations of Primitive Thought*, (Oxford: Clarendon Press, 1979).

8. D. McClelland, "The Achievement Motive in Economic Growth," in Bert F. Hoselitz and Wilbert E. Moore, eds., *Industrialization and Society*, (Mouton: Unesco, 1966), pp. 74-6.

9. L. Cormie, "The Sociology of National Development," p. 69.

10. Blomström and Hettne, *Development Theory in Transition*, pp. 19-24.

11. Peter Gibbon, "A Political Economy of the World Bank 1970-1990," (paper delivered to the Council for the Development of Economic and Social Research in Africa, 9-12 September, 1991, Dakar, Senegal), p. 4.

12. J. Toye, J. Harrigan and P. Mosley, *Aid and Power*, vol. 1 (London: Routledge, 1991), p. 23. Unless otherwise stated, all subsequent citations refer to volume one.

13. "Blood and Treasure," *Barrons*, June 18, 1980, p. 7, and "Is the World Bank Biting Off More than It Can Chew?" *Forbes*, May 26, 1980, pp. 122-6.

14. US Treasury Department, *United States Participation in Multilateral Development Banks in the 1980s*, (Washington, 1982), p. 80. See also, R. C. Pratt, "The Global Impact of the World Bank," in J. Torrie ed., *Banking on Poverty*, (Toronto: Between the Lines, 1983), pp. 61-4.

15. *World Development Report* 1978, p. 17; Toye *et al.*, *Aid and Power*, p. 22.

16. Toye *et al.*, *Aid and Power*, p. 11.

17. Toye *et al.*, *Aid and Power*, pp. 27-38.

18. Toye *et al.*, *Aid and Power*, pp. 43.

19. Bernstein, "Agricultural 'Modernization'", p. 15.

20. Gibbon, "Political Economy", p. 7.

21. Toye *et al.*, *Aid and Power*, p. 15. Boone makes a similar observation regarding fundamentalist biblical interpretation. A number of controls are necessary, she notes, to prevent *any* interpretation of the inerrant Word of God to be validated. These include elaborate systems to control who has the right to preach the Bible and the "correct language" that marks authentic interpretation. Boone, *The Bible*, pp. 61-75.

22. Toye *et al.*, *Aid and Power*, p. 16. A similar reassessment was occurring in Canada spearheaded by such interest groups as the Business Council on National Issues. By the early 1980s they had drawn up an agenda for Canada rooted in the neo-liberal principles outlined above on the role of the state in the economy. The following analysis on the urban public sector alliance blocking reform is illustrative: "The real concern over senior public servants' influence on policy formation stems not only from their ability to *initiate* policies but also from their ability to *frustrate* 'official' policy... by raising administrative hurdles or instituting tardy implementation schedules." See T. D'Aquino *et al.*, *Party Democracy in Canada: Issues for Reform*, (Toronto: Methuen, 1983), p. 38.

CHAPTER THREE

Rescheduling our Debtors

Introduction

... there is no general problem of developing countries being able to service debt. (World Bank, *World Development Report*, 1978, p.24)

Debt-service obligations are likely to become a more important element in the balance of payments of many African countries and may compel more of them to use the Paris Club and other arrangements of debt relief. (World Bank, *Accelerated Development in Sub-Saharan Africa*, 1982, p. 129)

Large revenues received by governments in the past have too often disrupted rather than promoted real development. The income has been spent unwisely, compounded by heavy borrowing secured on future revenues, which led to an excessive debt burden. (World Bank, *From Crisis to Sustainable Growth*, 1989, p. 11)

The World Bank's shift from "modernization" in the 1960s and 1970s to structural adjustment in the 1980s can be understood, not primarily by reference to the internal problems of African countries, but to the crisis in the international financial system. The opening section of this chapter considers the debt crisis as arising from a set of irreconcilable policies which characterized the post-World War II development decades. This perspective challenges a number of the prevailing assumptions about the origins and nature of the debt crisis, particularly the belief that it originated in the oil price increases and lending boom of the 1970s.

The second section looks closely at the World Bank's management of Africa's debt. By tracking the financial flows of the African region over the 1980s, a number of important trends are established that reveal those who benefited and those who lost as a result of Africa's debt crisis.

Financing Exports

The debt crisis originated in the pattern of global trade established in the post-World War II period. This is the position put forward by economist Cheryl Payer, whose analysis forms the basis for this section. In *Lent and Lost*, Payer details the extraordinary series of events, dating back to the late 1940s, which culminated in the debt crisis of the 1980s. The tracing of these events also identifies some of the forces determining the World Bank's structural adjustment agenda for sub-Saharan Africa.

The US emerged from the post-World War II period with an enormous, intact manufacturing capacity. The problem for US economists was how to maintain the wartime levels of high output and full employment. This, they argued, could be achieved only by establishing and maintaining large export surpluses with the trading partners of the US. However, the economists were well aware that repayment would be a problem. Eventually, countries would have to repay the US for these goods and this could be achieved only by increasing their exports to the US.

US elites side-stepped the "repayment problem" during the reconstruction of Europe. Rather than lend money for the Marshall Plan to rebuild Europe, the US government essentially provided it free as a way of avoiding the problem of having to "receive the massive flow of goods from European factories which [the US] would have been required to accept in repayment for the loans".[1]

By the 1950s, as markets were expanding, the US looked for ways to justify *lending* money to countries to enable them to purchase American goods, and thus allow continuing trade surpluses. Economists promoted the theory of ever-expanding markets and perpetual lending to explain away the problem of repayment. A general equilibrium could be reached, argued these economists, without the US ever having to suffer from an import surplus:

Thus servicing of development loans will generally not cause trouble in the future if we achieve the goal of an expanding free world economy, and the reasonable flow of such investment that the expanding economy requires.[2]

These interests provided the foundation for the major tenets of development theory which emerged in the 1950s and 1960s. One of the basic tenets of the modernization theory of Third World development was that developing countries lacked capital. Developing countries could achieve the take-off to self-sustaining growth if provided with the necessary infusions of capital. The World Bank was well suited to act as the financiers of this modernization project. By-passing the ordinary citizens of Third World countries, the World Bank targeted elites as the vanguards of development. These, as Pat Adams notes, were the principles of the World Bank's founding president, Eugene Black:

> The World Bank consciously strove to remove borrowing agencies from the fray of local politics, out of a conviction [that] the "job of development" would otherwise be botched.... Touted as "apostles of a new life", and as "the politician and the bureaucrat... [who] are very literally leaders as well as rulers", the local elites would "usher their societies into an age of enlightenment". For Black and the bank, as for the bank's founders, there would be no place for wide popular participation in development decision-making.[3]

Modernization theory incorporated the imperative of Northern countries to run perpetual trade surpluses by setting forth a Third World counterpart thesis based on the need for capital flows to finance development. The principle established was that the logical flow of capital was from capital rich to capital poor countries, a process that could continue until the poorer countries caught up. While it was accepted that capital flows to poorer countries were a necessary requirement for development, the *manner* in which these flows were achieved and the inevitable problem of repayment were never seriously considered.

A simple model outlining the life cycle of one loan on highly concessional World Bank terms dramatically illustrates how intractable the problem of repayment becomes in time. As Graph 3.1 illustrates, net transfers will be positive in favour of the borrower for the first twenty years. However, by year thirty, net flows shift dramatically in favour of the creditor, rising steeply before the debt is finally paid off. According to Payer, we are now at about year thirty on the graph in terms of the relationship between debtor and creditor countries. Latin American countries reached the reversal of flows stage in 1982; African countries reached the same point around 1984.[4] No matter how "soft" the terms of the loan are, the inexorable compounding of interest means that capital flows will eventually reverse themselves. It is the unwillingness to recognize this logic that explains in large measure the onslaught of the debt crisis in the early 1980s:

> In short, the cause of the debt crisis was an in-built contradiction between a macro-economic theory that holds it natural for Third World countries to import capital for long periods of time, and the micro-economic marketplace (or quasi-marketplace) instruments (commercial and government-subsidised loans) through which this transfer was accomplished.[5]

When the post-World War II development period is examined from the perspective of the North's trade and investment imperatives, a system built on two irreconcilable principles, is revealed. These two principles are: 1) the desire by the Northern countries to run a perpetually unbalanced trade with the South, financed by an unbalanced capital flow to the South, and 2) that this financing could be carried out through a mix of direct investment, loans and aid through agencies such as the World Bank. The post-World War II boom period can be described as the effort to keep these two irreconcilable goals in reasonable balance.

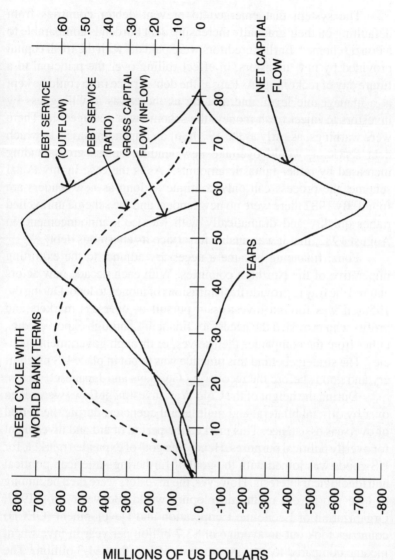

Graph 3.1: Capital inflows and outflows on a loan at near-market interest rates

DEBT SERVICE RATIO

.60 .50 .40 .30 .20 .10 0

NET CAPITAL FLOW

DEBT SERVICE (OUTFLOW)

DEBT SERVICE (RATIO)

GROSS CAPITAL FLOW (INFLOW)

YEARS

80 70 60 50 40 30 20 10

DEBT CYCLE WITH WORLD BANK TERMS

800 700 600 500 400 300 200 100 0 -100 -200 -300 -400 -500 -600 -700 -800

MILLIONS OF US DOLLARS

(Source: Payer, *Lent and Lost*, p. 6)

Ponzi Financing

The system that emerged to prevent debtor countries from defaulting on their gradually increasing debt burden is comparable to a Ponzi scheme.[6] Earlier creditors were paid off with the fresh capital provided by new investors, in effect rolling over the principal to a future day of reckoning. As long as the debt service ratio could be kept at a manageable level, and as long as there was a willingness by investors to inject fresh money, the scheme was manageable. There were warnings, as early as the 1970s, of an impending crisis in which debt servicing would overtake new lending unless gross lending increased by rather fantastic amounts.[7] As is the case in any Ponzi scheme, the process can only continue as long as new lenders are found. By 1982 there were no new lenders and the scheme unravelled rather quickly and dramatically with Mexico's announcement, in August 1982, that it was unable to service its enormous debt.

Ponzi financing became a necessary adjunct to the exporting imperative of the Northern countries. With each decade new actors entered the fray to provide fresh infusions of money to lend. During the 1950s it was foreign investors in pursuit of overseas markets and profits who provided the necessary financing, through export credits, either from the companies themselves, or through government agencies. The strategy behind this practice was to put in place US machinery and goods before the recovering Germans and Japanese.

During the height of the Cold War, investment flows were taken over by official bilateral and multilateral agencies, during the period of overseas assistance. This marked the period of aid and investment for overtly political purposes. Hence, the goal of expanded markets for US goods was joined with the goal of furthering American political and ideological interests. However, the investors were then beginning to take profits out of the developing world. Between 1964-1967, Organization of Economic Cooperation and Development (OECD) countries took out an average of $3.7 billion per year in investment income compared to new investments of less than $1.3 billion.[8] The difference was made up by new money from the bilateral donors.

During this period the question of repayment was hardly broached and was not considered problematic. The countries which were experiencing difficulties and threatening to slide below the crucial break-even point (the point at which the net flow is reversed in favour of the creditor) received fresh infusions of funds. The US, and, by now, the other industrialized countries, had no interest in seeing debtor countries make a serious attempt to repay their debt because this would mean that they would no longer be able to finance imports from the North.

The debtor countries noted this paradox and drew the conclusion they wished to draw (which was also, in a macroeconomic sense correct): the creditor governments did not expect them to repay debts with their own money, and in fact did not want them to.[9]

Debt negotiations were institutionalized in the Paris Club meetings, during which debtor countries would seek and invariably receive fresh loans to recycle old ones.[10] In most cases, however, this method of rolling over debts only meant that the countries found themselves even more deeply in debt. However, as Payer explains:

It was... a very effective means of allowing creditors to continue to sell goods to the debtor while exerting foreign control over the debtor's economy; and thus a telling indicator of the real agenda of the creditor governments.[11]

During the 1970s, it was the bankers who became the next set of investors in the Ponzi scheme. As early as 1970, however, it was clear to more thoughtful observers that a crisis was looming. The Pearson Commission, appointed by Robert McNamara, was established to address the concern generated by the growing debt burden of developing countries. The Commission forecast that, even with the increase of gross flows to the South of 8 per cent per year, debt service would consume anywhere between 60-89 per cent of gross lending by 1977. Unchanged levels would lead to an inevitable reversal of flows by that time.[12] Warnings such as these went largely unheeded in the orgy of lending by banks that was to follow in the 1970s.

Indeed, while concerns over developing countries' ability to sustain their ever-increasing debt load continued to be raised in World Bank circles throughout the 1970s, the World Bank's 1978 *World*

Development Report refers to the need for net annual lending to developing countries to continue to grow by 12 per cent per year until 1985. No concern was raised as to whether this debt load could be serviced. In fact, the report urges commercial banks to continue lending. It assures investors that its own studies clearly indicate the ability of developing countries to service their debts.[13] The World Bank's stamp of approval goes some way to explain why commercial banks behaved so irresponsibly and contrary to warnings of the impending collapse of the house of cards. In order to uncover a number of other factors, it is necessary to dispose of one of the most persistent myths offered by mainstream analysts as to the cause of the Third World debt crisis.

Almost all textbook analyses of the debt crisis cite the massive oil price hikes engineered by the major oil exporting countries during the 1970s as one, if not the major, factor contributing to the debt crisis of Third World countries. According to this explanation, the large commercial banks, flush with huge deposits from oil exporters like Saudi Arabia and Kuwait, were desperate to recycle these funds wherever they could find willing borrowers. This led to a universal lowering of banking standards, a disregard for normal lending criteria, and a concomitant frenzy of lending to any country willing to accept these loans.

According to Payer, this, at best, only partially explains the enthusiasm of the commercial banks for sovereign lending to Third World countries. The most telling argument against the oil price hike thesis is the timing of the banks' lending frenzy which began well before the onset of the oil price hikes. As an OECD study notes:

> In fact, it is absolutely clear... that the most decisive and dramatic increase in bank lending to developing countries was associated with the major commodity price boom of 1972-3 – before the oil shock in late 1973. From a 1971 figure of US$8 billion, bank lending expanded to more than US $18 billion in 1973.... Bank lending thereafter levelled off for the next two years, despite the enormous increase in oil bills.[14]

Payer offers a number of other answers to the "mystery" behind the banks' decision to embark on the largest lending spree in history.

First, commercial banks were simply following their corporate customers overseas who needed banks to finance their new operations. This was in response to the various nationalization trends occurring in developing countries. Investments were considered "safer", i.e., less susceptible to expropriation, if financed by Northern banks. Second, changes in international banking practice made sovereign lending easier and more attractive. The introduction of floating interest rates placed a greater share of the risk of lending money on borrowers. The contracting of large numbers of syndicated loans[15] also opened the way for smaller banks to get a "piece of the action". Third, banks were receiving very high interest rates on these kinds of sovereign loans, precisely because the borrowing countries were considered high risks. These extraordinary earnings were augmented by high front-end fees, the fees charged by banks for organizing the loans. Fourth, there were changes of governments and policies in a number of Third World countries which made them appear more friendly to foreign investors. Countries like Chile, Argentina, Indonesia and the Philippines are good cases in point. Fifth, the unprecedentedly high commodity prices coupled with a Club of Rome Report claiming the impending scarcity of these resources raised the confidence that Third World countries would be able to finance high levels of debt servicing.[16] Finally, the banks were confident that, in the case of defaults, either the debts would be rescheduled with an infusion of fresh money by creditor countries leading to even better rates of return for banks, or by Northern government bail-outs. The World Bank, IMF and the creditor countries would be there to ensure the continued stability of the international financial system.[17]

The World Bank was instrumental in convincing private bankers to enter into Third World sovereign lending. As the official collector of foreign debt statistics, the World Bank played a vital role in facilitating the commercial banks' entry into the fray. "Its pronouncements on the debt question carried particular weight, as it was assumed to be privy to the best information on debt and debt service burdens."[18] While the bank admitted that the debt-servicing burdens of Third World countries were already a serious concern in the 1960s, it nonetheless advocated increased levels of financing through a variety of channels. It also encouraged the commercial banks to enter the picture:

The World Bank group and other international organizations ... are making strenuous efforts to encourage and enlarge the flow of private capital into the less developed countries. There is no doubt that this flow can be expected to increase... thereby accelerating the pace of development and relieving the pressure on public funds.[19]

The World Bank urged both the wisdom and necessity of these loans and thus persuaded the banks to increase their lending. Through its efforts, the World Bank was able to attract $2-3 for every $1 it invested in Third World loans.[20] The implications of introducing into the Ponzi scheme new investors who offered their money on hard, non-concessional terms were not seriously considered.

In 1975 US Secretary of State Henry Kissinger led the call for "new ways to enhance the opportunities of developing countries in the competition for capital".[21] One of the chief means to this goal was to enhance the lending capacity of the World Bank. The overriding concern was not over the sustainability of these loans but on expanding markets and political stability for the US and its allies.

The World Bank was so eager to lend during the 1970s that it found customers that even commercial banks deemed bad risks. Over the 1970s, the World Bank increased its lending five-fold.[22] With this the World Bank, supported by the IMF, postponed the impending crisis yet another decade. The appointed debt management experts were in fact inciting developing countries to borrow far beyond their capacity ever to service their debts. As Payer notes:

> [I]n the short run it served perfectly the desires of the creditor governments which control those institutions to maximize their access to markets in the target countries. The Fund and the Bank must be considered among the major perpetrators of the debt crisis.[23]

Right up until the brink of Mexico's default the World Bank and IMF continued in their role of impresario. In a joint publication issued just weeks before Mexico's default the World Bank and IMF noted with optimism that "there is still considerable scope for sustained additional borrowing to increase productive capacity".[24] Soon after,

Mexico blew the whistle on the Ponzi scheme and defaulted on its debt payments, precipitating the international debt crisis.

Rescuing the Banks

> The only discernible achievement of multilateral involvement has been the bailing out of commercial creditors.[25]

The World Bank's shift toward a lending regime predicated on the discipline of structural adjustment corresponded with the dramatic upheavals occurring in the international financial system during the early 1980s. The World Bank's role in rescuing the collapsing international financial system is often overlooked. Yet, the World Bank played a very crucial role: assisting creditors by ensuring that the debtor countries (over whom the bank wielded considerable power) fell into line and maintained their debt servicing obligations. In the process of playing the role of enforcer for other creditors, the World Bank became the single largest creditor for sub-Saharan Africa. It achieved this status by stepping in to provide loans so that these countries could service debts owed to other creditors, primarily the commercial banks.

The agenda of the World Bank rapidly adapted to these realities, ushering in the structural adjustment regime of the 1980s. The concern for the economic growth of developing countries gave way to the exigencies of cutting imports and increasing exports as the necessary preconditions for the South to service their debts. The World Bank played a key role in preventing defaults by providing fresh lending to countries who would otherwise have no real incentive to honour their debt obligations. A mutuality of interests between the banks and the World Bank was thus established:

> On the World Bank (and IMF's) part, the debt crisis offered a chance to widen conditionality by cutting off the possibility of LDCs borrowing from the private banks to avoid policy reform. For the commercial banks, the fact that lending by *somebody* could continue while at the same time "responsibility" was imposed meant that their ultimate nightmare of a debtor's cartel receded.[26]

The interests of the international banking community dramatically shifted with Mexico's default in 1982. A 40-year low in the terms of trade for developing countries and a 50-year high in variable interest rates quickly also served to reverse the posture of the banks from one of unloading money on the South to one of trying to recover as much of it as possible.

By the late 1980s commercial banks were also benefiting from loan-loss provisions.[27] Citibank, one of the largest US creditors, took the dramatic step of adding $3 billion to its loan-loss reserves in 1987 with other banks quickly following suit. Banks not only enjoyed a tax break from these generous provisions, they were also free to collect whatever funds they could extract from debtor countries. As a result of the debt crisis, commercial banks have also enjoyed a huge windfall at the expense of Northern taxpayers through tax write-offs. The total amount that banks received in tax credits through loan-loss provisions between 1987-90 is estimated to be from $44-50 billion. As Susan George notes: "...the banks have transformed their 'historic mistake' into a near-bonanza and have managed to make the public pay for their ill-conceived Third World adventures."[28]

Table 3.1: Total Probable Tax Credits against Loan-Loss Provisions obtained by Banks in Major OECD Creditor Countries, 1987-90
(US$ billions)

Country	Probable Tax Credit
United States	8.8
Canada	2.7
Japan	0.17
Germany	10-16.7
United Kingdom	8.5
France	10.9
Switzerland	2.5
Italy	0.5
Total	US$44.1-50.8 billion

(Source, S. George, *Debt Boomerang*, p. 82)

One of the most prevalent myths surrounding the debt crisis in the 1980s holds that the commercial banks suffered huge losses from which they are still recovering. In fact, the debt crisis has turned into a significant boon for them. During the 1970s commercial banks recorded some of the largest profits on record, largely as a result of Third World loans. The 13 largest US banks recorded earnings quintupled from $177 million to $836 million during the first half of the 1970s.[29] Since Mexico's default in the early 1980s, banks have continued to have their debts serviced even though no new money has been lent out.

Throughout the 1980s debt service payments steadily increased. Between 1982-89 the total amount paid to banks was $615 billion in interest and amortization. At the same time, the amount owed to commercial banks soared from $493 billion in 1982 to $629 billion in 1989. As Susan George points out:

> It is, in fact astonishing that Third World countries could pay
> their commercial creditors an average of nearly $77 billion a
> year; more than $6.4 billion a month – yet find themselves as
> a group fully 28 per cent more in debt to these creditors than
> they were in 1982, in spite of a dearth of new lending.[30]

The World Bank has played a significant role in assisting developing countries to service their debts to the banks. The World Bank "came to the rescue" at a critical moment. It has provided fresh loans to debtor countries to the extent that multilateral debt now accounts for a larger proportion of the Third World debt than bilateral debt. Yet, in effect this new lending from the World Bank and IMF has been used to pay debt servicing to banks under the guise of structural adjustment lending. From 1983 to 1989, $32.7 billion in loans from multilateral sources went to service commercial bank debt, representing 17 per cent of total debt service over the period.[31]

The Debt Boomerang

Susan George's thesis about a "debt boomerang" assists in identifying the winners and losers in the debt crisis. The debt boomerang refers to the variety of adverse impacts that the debt crisis is having in the North. Among these is the upheaval in the manufacturing sectors of industrialized countries which has resulted from the loss of markets in developing countries.

As we have seen, since the 1950s, the driving force behind the lending flows to the South was the need for markets and trade surpluses. However, trends toward the globalization of production processes during the 1980s have led to a shift in the "national" character of industries. Instead of providing local jobs to produce goods for exports, many Northern-based industries have moved manufacturing operations to low-cost sites in Latin America or Asia. As a result of this transformation in production processes, the interests of capital and labour in running trade surpluses in the North no longer coincide. For instance, the US has become a net importer vis-à-vis many Third World countries while demonstrating little desire to resolve the debt problems of countries like Argentina and Brazil. Both these nations began to run large trade surpluses with the US from the early 1980s onward. The turnaround in the US trade balance has contributed to the severe domestic setbacks suffered by labour, through layoffs, wage rollbacks and plant closures. Other industrialized countries are suffering a similar fate as the gains made in the previous decades have been systematically rolled back by corporate interests no longer constrained by national boundaries.[32] This rapid trend towards denationalization is rapidly occurring in banks and corporations in the era of free trade.

The North has been affected by the debt crisis through the loss of jobs and markets in Third World countries. The fifteen most highly indebted countries export almost $20 billion more than they did in 1981 while importing $20 billion less. The $20 billion in extra earnings from exports has gone directly into servicing their debts, while the $20 billion drop in imports translates into lost jobs in Northern export manufacturing sectors in the North. Susan George concludes: "A genuine, if muted, conflict now exists between the banks on one side and the productive sectors of the economy on the other. So far, the banks have won hands down."[33]

In the 1990s the banks have consolidated their positions with respect to Third World debt. By successfully adapting to the new international financial environment and by taking advantage of loan loss reserves afforded to them by their governments, commercial banks continue to extract windfall profits from Southern nations. Economist Kari Levitt captures the current implications of debt servicing:

> The system today is more civilized and also more effective because the banks have been able to operate as a creditor cartel, under the skirt of the International Monetary Fund. It is not colonialism in the old sense, but it is an effective mechanism for transferring real resources from poor debtor countries to the creditor banks of the industrialized world.[34]

The World Bank and African Debt Management

The World Bank has taken over from the IMF as the lead agency in managing Africa's debt. The World Bank's financial flows to Africa increased substantially in the 1980s, quickly dwarfing those of the IMF. Another significant factor which has helped establish the World Bank as the premier debt-management institution in Africa is the credibility loss suffered by the IMF as a result of its failure to recognize the extent and depth of Africa's debt problems in the early 1980s. Treating Africa's balance of payments crisis like those of its other clients, the IMF lent funds to indebted African countries on the assumption that their problems were short-term ones.[35] The money was lent on very hard terms[36] and, as a result, when the crisis deepened the IMF found itself in the embarrassing position of being a net extractor of funds from Africa (Graph 3.2). In the mid-1980s the World Bank stepped in to provide what was regarded as a more appropriate long-term debt-management strategy. However, in recent years the World Bank also finds itself in the position of extracting net transfers from many African countries.

Although the appropriateness of the World Bank's debt strategy was being hotly debated, the bank did appear to be successful in generating badly needed funds for low-income African countries. The bank has also channelled highly concessional or soft loans to the most severely indebted African countries through its International Development Association (IDA).

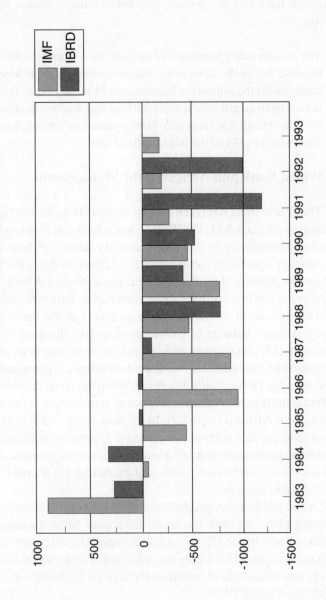

Graph 3.2: Net Transfers to IMF and IBRD Sub-Saharan Africa (US$ millions)

(Source: *World Bank Debt Tables*)

Myths about Sub-Saharan Africa's Debt

An examination of the overall debt picture of Africa over the 1980s, as well as a closer look at the financial flows to Africa's various creditors, reveals a number of striking features. As of 1993 the total debt of sub-Saharan Africa stood at $199 billion. For all of Africa it was $302 billion. Despite the various strategies to provide relief to highly indebted African countries, the overall debt has climbed inexorably. The countless reschedulings and debt cancellations for African countries, announced with great fanfare during recent G-7 meetings, have given the overall impression that African countries are the "basket cases" among debtors, always in need of more financial handouts.

That African countries have piled up huge arrears in their payments is not in dispute. However, until recently, the bulk of analysis on the debt has perpetuated a series of myths about why and how these countries have found themselves teetering on the edge of the debt precipice.

The first myth claims that African countries have been able to extract huge concessions from creditors and that they have not made significant efforts to keep up their payments. The second prominent myth about Africa's debt has been generated by its commercial bank creditors. The commercial banks have succeeded in convincing the general public that, having learned a painful lesson about lending to that region, they are "out of Africa". These creditors declare that they have resigned themselves to the fact that they will never recoup their losses. The third myth contends that many creditor countries have reduced the amount of money owed to them by African countries through debt cancellations and write-downs. The fourth myth involves the commonly held perception that the World Bank is providing positive flows to highly indebted African countries.

As Percy Mistry notes, contrary to the popular belief that Africa does not service its debts, the continent on the whole paid a total of $180 billion from 1982-1990. The total for sub-Saharan Africa was $81 billion. The composition of the flows is summarized by Mistry in the following manner:

To a large degree, the relief offered by bilateral debt reschedulings and by new money flows from multilateral institutions to North African debtors was absorbed by maintaining flows to private creditors.[37]

Table 3.2 shows the total debt of sub-Saharan Africa over the 1980s with its composite profile of major creditors. The most startling statistic is the rise in debt to private sources, from $27.5 billion in 1983 to over $40 billion for 1993. Of that amount it is estimated that the share of commercial bank debt is roughly $25 billion for sub-Saharan Africa. The rest of this debt is comprised of export credit debt and other unguaranteed debt. This increase is surprising in view of the fact that private investment to Africa virtually dried up in the 1980s.

Sub-Saharan Africa paid out close to $73 billion in debt servicing alone to private creditors between 1983-93. As of 1993, sub-Saharan Africa's debt to private creditors stands at approximately $41 billion.[38]

Sub-Saharan Africa's bilateral debt profile indicates that, in spite of efforts to find a coordinated debt-management strategy (the so-called Venice, Toronto or Trinidad Terms), the overall debt of sub-Saharan Africa to its bilateral creditors has continued to mount. It has also become increasingly non-concessional in nature; that is, loans and repayment schedules are being negotiated on much harder terms.[39] In other words, most of the debt relief that has occurred over the past few years has involved loans with concessional terms, often through rolling over this debt into longer term loans on non-concessional terms. Between 45-50 per cent of all non-concessional debt to the OECD countries was rescheduled concessional debt. In fact, by 1990, bilateral net resource transfers were in favour of creditor countries for the first time.[40]

It is after examining the composition of Africa's debt to its private and bilateral creditors that the World Bank's role can be clarified. What emerges is the central role that the so-called "soft" IDA loans play in the complex debt-management scheme. The IDA loans come primarily from the contributions of its richer member countries, who in turn generate their contributions from their development-assistance or aid budgets. Canada, for instance, channels one quarter of its aid budget to the African Development Bank and to the World Bank, of which a substantial amount is channelled to the IDA.

Table 3.2: Debt Profile – Sub-Saharan Africa (US$ billions)

	1983	1984	1985	1986	1987	1988	1989	1990	1991	1992	1993	TOTAL
TOTAL DEBT	79.8	83.3	96.5	138.5	165.2	166.3	173.9	191.0	195.5	194.2	199.0	
Bilateral	22.9	24.6	29.1	41.6	52.4	52.8	59.3	68.4	71.7	71.2	71.2	
Multilateral	18.1	19.1	23.4	28.4	35.6	36.0	37.9	43.6	47.1	48.5	50.9	
Private	27.5	26.7	30.3	40.9	51.8	53.2	52.2	50.5	47.7	42.1	40.7	
Short-term	11.3	12.9	13.7	27.6	25.4	24.3	24.5	28.5	29.0	32.4	36.2	
DEBT SERVICE												**TOTAL**
Bilateral	0.86	1.07	1.63	1.38	1.48	1.93	1.57	2.47	2.31	1.16	1.04	16.90
Multilateral	1.45	1.84	2.15	3.53	3.82	3.66	3.67	3.62	3.80	3.34	3.18	34.06
Private	4.91	6.00	6.54	7.68	5.94	7.08	6.26	7.52	6.64	8.21	5.93	72.71
Short-term	0.90	1.18	0.87	1.90	1.55	1.62	1.52	1.54	1.35	1.27	1.20	14.90
TOTAL	8.12	10.09	11.19	14.49	12.79	14.29	13.02	15.15	14.10	13.98	11.35	138.57
NET TRANSFERS												**TOTAL**
Bilateral	2.30	-6.00	1.00	1.57	1.53	0.86	1.59	0.17	0.39	0.75	0.52	4.68
Multilateral	2.41	-1.43	0.89	0.62	0.81	1.07	1.13	1.57	1.38	1.81	1.77	14.89
Private	0.27	-1.67	-2.65	-3.62	-1.88	-3.08	-3.29	-4.27	-4.61	-6.28	-4.53	-35.61
TOTAL	4.98	-6.24	-0.76	-1.43	0.46	-1.15	-0.57	-2.53	-2.84	-3.72	-2.24	-16.04
WORLD BANK/IMF DEBT SERVICE												**TOTAL**
IBRD	0.44	0.54	0.62	0.86	1.07	1.30	1.23	1.37	1.89	1.54	–	10.86
IMF	0.74	0.99	1.17	2.09	2.06	1.50	1.60	1.19	0.84	0.71	0.36	13.25
TOTAL	1.18	1.53	1.79	2.95	3.13	2.80	2.83	2.56	2.73	2.25	0.36	24.11
NET TRANSFERS												**TOTAL**
IBRD	0.27	0.31	0.03	0.03	-0.08	-0.73	-0.39	-0.56	-1.21	-1.00	–	-3.94
IMF	0.87	-0.04	-0.43	-1.36	-1.42	-0.47	-0.74	-0.46	-0.26	-0.19	-0.19	-5.09
TOTAL	1.14	0.27	-0.40	-1.33	-1.50	-1.20	-1.13	-1.02	-1.47	-1.19	-0.19	-9.03

(Source: *World Bank Debt Tables*)

Table 3.3: New Lending and Debt Servicing for Sub-Saharan Africa, 1992 (US$ billion)

Creditor	New Lending	Repayments	Net Flow
World Bank - IDA	2.09	0.21	1.88
World Bank - IBRD	0.54	1.54	-1.00
IMF	0.53	0.72	-0.19
Private	1.39	7.49	-6.10
Bilateral	1.92	1.16	0.76
Total	6.47	11.12	-4.65

(Source: *World Bank Debt Tables*, 1993-4)

The total amount of IDA money that has been lent to Africa has increased substantially. However, in light of the various other flows it becomes clear that a substantial portion of IDA money is simply "round-tripping", that is, it is being used to pay off other creditors. First in line to benefit from these new funds is the World Bank's non-concessional lending arm, the International Bank for Reconstruction and Development (IBRD). Next on the list of preferred creditors is the IMF, which has succeeded in siphoning off for itself a significant portion of any new financial flows. The commercial banks and other private creditors follow. In spite of the fact that they have substantially reduced their exposure in the continent, they still benefit significantly from the flows provided through the IDA. In effect, "what has evolved is a situation in which multilateral lenders, including the IMF, World Bank, the development banks, the OPEC [Organization of Petroleum Exporting Countries] special fund, etc. have acquired 'preferred status', gaining preferential claim on the foreign exchange resources of an indebted country".[41]

As Table 3.3 demonstrates, what begins as a $2.09 billion flow of new lending from the World Bank's IDA is scaled down to $0.88 billion after new lending and repayments from the World Bank's IBRD is taken into account. From there it is further reduced to become a net *outflow* of funds from sub-Saharan Africa to the creditors listed below. This means, in effect, that flows from other sources such as bilateral aid are being used to pay off these creditors. One must also keep in mind that the inflows from the sources named here are *loans*, and that a significant portion, from sources like the IMF, private creditors, and the IBRD, is on hard non-concessional terms. Nor does the World Bank use IDA funds to clear IBRD debts but merely to service them so that, in effect, they remain on the books.[42]

As of 1992 the World Bank accounted for about $28 billion of sub-Saharan Africa's overall debt, or about 15 per cent, more than triple its exposure in 1983 (see Table 3.4). In effect, the aid budgets of Northern countries are currently being used to maintain the fiction of the viability of the $28 billion debt that the World Bank has accumulated in bailing out the commercial banks, the IMF, export credit facilities, and other private creditors. It is taxpayers in the North who are, along with debtor countries, financing this subsidization, a fact that is being recognized increasingly, even by mainstream economists.[43]

The World Bank and IMF have attempted to deal with the so-called "repayment problem". The IDA, which is the arm of the bank set up to provide concessional loans and grants to the poorest countries, now provides a significant amount of these funds for "structural adjustment support" programmes. Secondly, the IMF created an Enhanced Structural Adjustment Facility (ESAF) which channels aid dollars from donor country donations to the poorest countries on more concessional terms. These measures have only added to the reality that "most foreign aid to indebted low-income countries is now going straight into the coffers of the World Bank and IMF".[44]

One economist proposes the application of US Chapter 9 bankruptcy laws to international debt, claiming that the principle should apply equally to the multilaterals:

> It is also patently uneconomic, rewarding those who, after disregarding the most elementary rules when showering money on the South, did not even care to build up reserves, in the hope that the government would not let them feel the consequences of the market.[45]

Highly publicized debt reduction schemes such as the Trinidad Terms call for deep cuts in the bilateral debts of low-income countries, most of which are in Africa. The Trinidad Terms would eliminate two thirds of the bilateral debt stock of these countries and refinance the remainder over a longer term. The most serious shortcoming of any of

Table 3.4: Debt and Debt Service Owed to the World Bank 1983-92

	1983	1984	1985	1986	1987	1988	1989	1990	1991	1992
IBRD Total Debt	3.86	3.96	5.28	7.04	9.28	8.42	8.43	9.18	9.03	8.43
IDA Total Debt	4.36	5.06	6.10	7.75	10.11	11.46	12.98	15.79	17.86	19.29
Total W B Debt	8.22	9.02	11.38	14.79	19.39	19.88	21.40	24.97	26.89	27.72
IBRD Debt Service	0.44	0.53	0.62	0.87	1.07	1.31	1.23	1.37	1.90	1.54
IDA Debt Service	0.04	0.06	0.08	0.09	0.11	0.13	0.13	0.15	0.19	0.21
Total WB Debt Service	0.48	0.59	0.70	0.96	1.18	1.44	1.36	1.52	2.09	1.75
IBRD Net Transfers	0.27	0.30	0.03	-0.07	-0.73	-0.39	-0.41	-0.56	-1.22	-1.00
IDA Net Transfers	0.60	0.72	0.80	1.31	1.57	1.57	1.57	1.89	1.80	1.88
Total WB Net Transfers	0.87	1.02	0.83	1.34	1.50	0.84	1.18	1.55	0.58	0.88

(Source: *World Bank Debt Tables*)

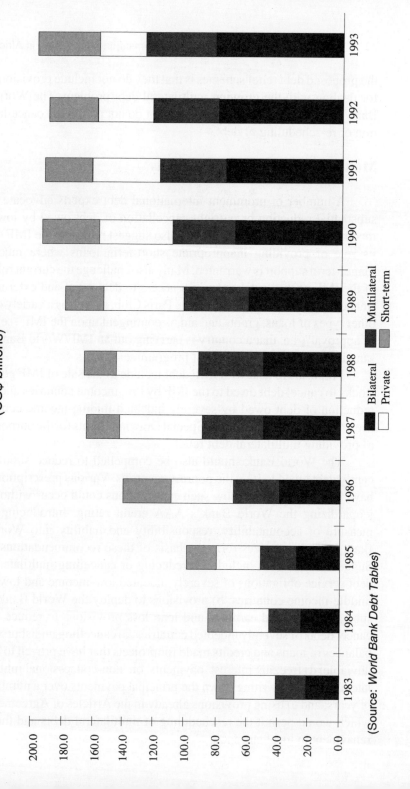

Graph 3.3: Debt Profile of Sub-Saharan Africa
(US$ billions)

Bilateral Private

Multilateral Short-term

(Source: *World Bank Debt Tables*)

the proposed debt relief schemes is that they do not include provisions for dealing with the growing multilateral debt problem. The World Bank's and IMF's Articles of Agreement do not permit the cancellation or re-scheduling of debt.

Multilateral Debt Relief Proposals

A number of prominent international debt experts advocate a substantial reduction or outright cancellation of debt owed by low-income countries to the IMF. They also suggest relieving the IMF of its role of providing inappropriate short-term loans where much longer-term support is warranted. Many also challenge the current role of the IMF as the "gatekeeper" for access to debt relief and external finance. Currently debt relief via the Paris Club, as well as a variety of other types of loans, grants and aid, is contingent upon the IMF "seal of approval", i.e. that a country is carrying out an IMF/World Bank-sanctioned structural adjustment programme.

Proposals to deal with IMF debt include a) the sale of IMF gold stocks to cancel debt owed to the IMF by low-income countries and a reduction of debt owed by severely indebted middle-income countries;[46] and, b) a special issue of Special Drawing Rights for the purpose of providing multilateral debt relief.[47]

The World Bank should also be compelled to reduce significantly debt owed to it by the poorest countries. Various prescriptions have been offered as to how such cancellations could occur without jeopardizing the World Bank's AAA credit rating. Introducing a measure of accountability, responsibility and liability into World Bank lending practices form the basis of these recommendations.[48] Suggested measures include: a) reducing or cancelling multilateral debt service obligations of severely indebted low-income and lower middle-income countries; b) provisions to deploy the World Bank's substantial retained earnings and loan-loss provisions to reduce or cancel debts of severely indebted countries; c) cancelling undisbursed balances of loans and credits made for projects that have proven to be unviable; d) freezing interest payments on non-concessional multilateral loans and writing down the principal payments over a number of years; and e) using provisions already in the Articles of Agreement which would permit the rescheduling of multilateral debts and their repayment in local currency.

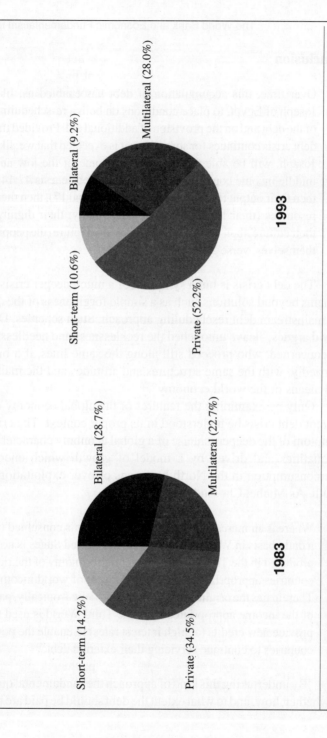

Graph 3.4: Sub-Saharan Africa Debt Service Burden

1993

Multilateral (28.0%)

Bilateral (9.2%)

Short-term (10.6%)

Private (52.2%)

1983

Bilateral (28.7%)

Short-term (14.2%)

Multilateral (22.7%)

Private (34.5%)

(Source: *World Bank Debt Tables*)

Conclusion

> Over time, this accumulation of debt has enabled us, like
> Joseph of Egypt, to place conditions on both a re-scheduling
> of the debt and on the provision of additional aid. Provided the
> debt crisis continues for some time, it is expected that we, like
> Joseph, will be able to demand from some of the low and
> middle income countries: first their money (Genesis 47:14),
> then their output (their livestock, verses 16 and 17), then their
> resources (their land, verse 20), and, finally, their dignity,
> their culture, their ability to define their own future (the people
> themselves, verse 21).[49]

The debt crisis is but a symptom of a much deeper crisis which
remains beyond solutions such as a simple forgiveness of the debt, or
the mainstream debt rescheduling approach. Such schemes, Douglas
Dowd argues, "leave untouched the recklessness and heedlessness of
all concerned, who proceed still along the same lines, if a bit more
worriedly, with the same structures and attitudes and the main ways
and means of the world economy".[50]

Only by examining the features of the global economy can the
current debt crisis be understood in its proper context. The crisis is a
symptom of the deeper malaise of a global economy characterized by
inequalities and driven by a model of growth which encourages
overconsumption in the North by means of over-exploitation of the
South. As Michel Chossudovsky suggests:

> Whereas an increasingly large share of what is consumed on
> a daily basis in Western Europe and the United States is now
> produced in the Third World, the rentier economy of the rich
> countries appropriates close to 80 per cent of world income.
> Therein lies the origin of the Third World debt. Ironically, part
> of the income appropriated from the Third World is used to
> provide new credits (at high interest rates) to enable the poor
> countries to continue servicing their external debt.[51]

By undertaking this kind of approach the fundamental questions
of whether, how, and to what extent the debt should be paid are brought

into clearer focus.

In her book *Odious Debts*, Pat Adams argues that many of the debts should not be paid as a matter of international law. She holds that the debts were contracted by corrupt regimes who did not represent the interests of their people along with lenders who were fully cognizant of how the money was being spent.[52] Citizens' groups and grassroots movements in the South are organizing around the principle that it is those that incurred the debts, and not the poor, that should be forced to repay.[53] The Freedom from Debt Coalition in the Philippines has succeeded in mobilizing grassroots organizations around this issue. Groups in Africa are seeking to draw attention to the debt that the North owes to Africa in terms of the gold that was stolen from the continent and the value of its people taken into slavery. They value this exploitation at over $2 trillion.

By all accounts, the 1990s is becoming another decade of reschedulings, coupled with meaningless debt reductions and cancellations as goodwill gestures to "reforming" African countries. Our next chapter considers how the debt crisis served as the backdrop for the ascendancy of structural adjustment as the new development model for Africa during the 1980s.

Endnotes

1. C. Payer, *Lent and Lost: Foreign Credit and Third World Development*, (London: Zed Books, 1991), p. 21.
2. Report to the President on Foreign Economic Policies, 1950, pp. 63-4, in Payer, *Lent and Lost*, p. 22.
3. P. Adams, *Odious Debts: Loose Lending, Corruption and the Third World's Environmental Legacy*, (London: Earthscan, 1991), p. 69.
4. Payer, *Lent and Lost*, p. 14.
5. Payer, *Lent and Lost*, p. 5.
6. Ponzi was a famous conman who in 1919 managed to persuade over 20,000 investors to put up $10 million with the promise of future profits. A Ponzi scheme is one where the original investors are paid off through money supplied by later investors. A "pyramid" scheme essentially operates on the same principles. See Payer, *Lent and Lost*, p. 16; also Adams, *Odious Debts*, pp. 104-9.
7. Payer, *Lent and Lost*, pp. 17-18.

8. Payer, *Lent and Lost*, p. 51.
9. Payer, *Lent and Lost*, p. 48. Cf. S. George, *A Fate Worse than Debt*, (London: Penguin Books, 1988), p.p. 233-4, who describes this state of affairs as Financial Low Intensity Conflict or FLIC.
10. The Paris Club is the name to describe the regular gathering of creditor-country governments who meet with debtor countries to discuss terms of rescheduling, refinancing or writing down of debts. Former World Bank Treasurer Eugene Rotberg describes the prevalent attitude that characterized Paris Club meetings during the 1970s: "If someone owes you money and you say 'You don't have to pay it for ten years,' then ten years go by, and you don't collect, and another ten years – well you may not wish to call that forgiveness for bookkeeping or political purposes, but you're not getting paid. 'Forgiveness is a legal term that says,' You owed me the money – you no longer owe it.' The Paris Club says 'You owe me the money, you haven't paid me and I agree that you don't have to pay me, but you still owe it.' Now I'm not going to talk about how many angels can dance on the head of a pin, but that is *de facto* forgiveness." Eugene Rotberg, former World Bank Treasurer, cited in Adams, Odious Debts, p. 90.
11. Payer, *Lent and Lost*, p. 55.
12. See Payer, *Lent and Lost*, p. 57.
13. *World Development Report* 1978, p. 24.
14. OECD, Twenty-Five Years of Development Cooperation, (Paris, 1985), p. 166, cited in Payer, *Lent and Lost*, p. 62.
15. Loans involving several creditors.
16. See also Adams, *Odious Debts*, p. 106.
17. Payer, *Lent and Lost*, pp. 70-2.
18. Payer, *Lent and Lost*, p. 65.
19. World Bank, *Annual Report* 1964-5, p. 62, cited in Payer, *Lent and Lost*, p. 66.
20. Adams, *Odious Debts*, p. 68.
21. H. Kissinger, Address to the Seventh Special Session of the UN General Assembly, Sept. 1, 1975, cited in Payer, *Lent and Lost,* p. 74.
22. Ayres, *Banking on the Poor*, p. 4.
23. Payer, *Lent and Lost*, p. 82.
24. Final Report of the Task Force on Non-Concessional Flows to the Joint. Ministerial Committee of the Boards of Governors of the Bank and the Fund on the Transfer of Resources to the Developing Countries, (5 April 1982), in Payer, *Lent and Lost*, p. 88. See also World Bank, *World Development Report* 1981, which assured commercial banks that there was no threat of an impending crisis: "Different countries are involved with different banks, and the degree of their involvement also varies. Loans rarely mature simultaneously. And no developing country accounts for more than 3 per cent of total international banking assets. *Developing-country risks are not synchronized* (my emphasis)." Further on the Report optimistically asserts that "banks that feel they are over-exposed internationally can generally be replaced by

others". World Bank, *World Development Report* 1978, p. 61.

25. P. Mistry, "The Problem of 'Official' Debt Owed by Developing Countries," (paper prepared for the Forum on Debt and Development Conference, Brussels, August, 1989), p. 17.

26. P. Gibbon, "The Political Economy of the World Bank 1970-90," p. 16.

27. Loan-loss provision involves bank putting aside money to prepare for the possibility of non-payment of all or part of an outstanding loan. Banks are not taxed on a percentage of these loan-loss provisions.

28. S. George, *The Debt Boomerang: How Third World Debt Harms Us All*, (London: Pluto Press, 1992), p. 93.

29. Salomon Brothers, *US Multinational Banking: Current and Perspective Strategies*, (New York, 1976), cited in Adams, *Odious Debts*, p. 96.

30. S. George, *Debt Boomerang*, p. 86.

31. S. George, *Debt Boomerang*, p. 87.

32. Payer, *Lent and Lost*, p. 108.

33. S. George, *Debt Boomerang*, p. 95.

34. Kari Polanyi Levitt, "Debt, Adjustment and Development: Looking to the 1990s," (paper delivered to the Association of Caribbean Economists, May, 1990), p. 3.

35. Percy Mistry, *African Debt Revisited: Procrastination or Progress?* (The Hague: Forum on Debt and Development, 1991), p. 44.

36. Money lent on "hard" terms refers to loans with little or no grace period, a short repayment schedule and market or near-market rates of interest. "Soft" loans, which are provided by the World Bank's International Development Association generally have a long grace period, long repayment schedules and low rates of interest.

37. Mistry, *African Debt*, p. 24.

38. Mistry, *African Debt*, p. 18, table 1.

39. Mistry, *African Debt*, p. 31.

40. *World Bank Debt Tables* 1991-2, pp. 124-6 and Mistry, *African Debt Revisited*, p. 30.

41. Richard Brown, "The IMF and Paris Club Rescheduling: A Conflicting Role?" (working paper – Sub-series on Money, Finance and Development – No. 30, May, 1990), p. 6.

42. Mistry, *African Debt*, p. 50.

43. J. Sachs, cited in K. Raffer, "Applying Chapter 9 Insolvency to International Debts: An Economically Efficient Solution with a Human Face," *World Development* 18/2 (February, 1992), p. 308.

44. Charles Abugre, "A Failed Recipe," *Economic Justice Update*, 8 November, 1993, p.4.

45. Raffer, "Applying Chapter 9," p. 309. The World Bank's Articles of Agreement do not permit the rescheduling, writing-down or cancellation of loans.

46. "IMF arrears, or at least the interest on these arrears, should be financed via the sale of IMF gold, so as not to 'waste' scarce donor resources on

maintaining the IMF's already 'super-safe' balance sheet." Helleiner, "External Resource Flows," p. 19.

47. IMF officials have argued that such a measure would be inflationary. Mistry counters this argument: "...such a danger is minimal and the prospects of a tailored SDR issue being inflationary are infinitesimally small. The current low-inflation environment reduces even more this insignificant risk of exacerbating inflation; in fact a case could be made in the present global climate for offsetting the negative consequences of deflationary forces." Mistry, "Multilateral Debt," p. 17.

48. Mistry, "Multilateral Debt," p. 9, "Aide-Memoire on Discussions of the Second Meeting of the Non-Aligned Movement Advisory Group of Experts on Debt," Feb., 1993, p. 7.

49. H. Rempel, "Exodus II: An End to the Debt Crisis," (background paper prepared by the International Debt Crisis Committee for the Mennonite Central Committee's Annual Meeting 1991), p. 2.

50. Douglas Dowd, *The Waste of Nations: Dysfunction in the World Economy*, (Boulder and London: Westview Press, 1989), p. 52.

51. M. Chossudovsky, "The Global Creation of Third World Poverty," *Third World Resurgence* 17 (1992), p. 20.

52. Adams bases her case on the principle of odious debts, developed by Alexander Sack, which absolve citizens of previous debts incurred by corrupt leaders: "The creditors have committed a hostile act with regard to the people; they can't therefore expect that a nation freed from a despotic power assume the 'odious' debts, which are personal debts of that power. ...One could include in this category of debts the loans incurred by members of the government or by persons or groups associated with the government to serve manifestly personal interests that are unrelated to the interests of the State." Alexander Sack, *Les Effets des Transformations des Etats sur leurs Dettes Publiques et Autres Obligations Financieres*, (Paris: Recueil Sirey, 1927), 157-8, cited in Adams, *Odious Debts*, p. 165.

53. "By the end of 1987 the foreign wealth held by the citizens of the 15 largest Third World debtors amounted to $300 billion – more than half of the foreign debts owed by their countries." From Adams, *Odious Debts*, p. 145.

—— CHAPTER FOUR ——

The World Bank and the Structural Adjustment of Africa

Around the beginning of the 1980s most of these [African] countries ran into very severe problems, these problems were not the kind that could be easily addressed through individual projects; they were starved for availability of liquidity in the countries, they had confronted a dramatic fall in their earnings from overseas, they were unable to maintain their imports and there were gross distortions in the economies. Now to help them overcome these problems of the structures of their economies, to help them turn their economies around and make them more competitive, to help create an environment where the investment projects would be more productive the idea of structural adjustment was brought about. Namely, that governments introduce a series of reforms to adjust the structures of their economies to make them more competitive, more responsive, more efficient, and that the bank and the donor community will provide some funds to ease the transition. That's where the name structural adjustment programmes has come from. It is very important to note that these are not things that are imposed by some bureaucrats in Washington, but they are the result of governments confronting rapidly changing realities in a very hostile environment and where, in fact, the past policies were simply unsustainable, and that some adjustment in the structures of the economies was absolutely inevitable and if the governments did not do it themselves it was going to result in a forced transition such as one sees in certain countries in Africa. (Ismail Serageldin, Vice-President Africa Region, World Bank, CBC Morningside, October, 1991)

The World Bank's promotion of its structural adjustment development philosophy for Africa in the 1980s has evolved over four stages. These stages overlap considerably with one another and the issues that dominated each particular stage continue to persist into the 1990s. The first, set out in the 1981 Berg Report, lays the foundation of the SAP agenda, addressing the central features of Africa's problems as well as establishing the required programme of reform. The second period, from 1984 onwards, is characterized by the politics of coercion, where the World Bank "convinced" reluctant African leaders to implement SAPs. After 1984 the third stage witnessed the emergence of a competing vision of development put forward by the UN Economic Commission for Africa (ECA). Finally, the period in which we now find ourselves can be characterized by the hegemony of the World Bank's SAP agenda with the added measures of poverty alleviation, democratization and good governance. These stages will be examined in turn, beginning with the Berg Report.

The Berg Report on Sub-Saharan Africa

The most influential document issued by the World Bank on sub-Saharan Africa over the 1980s was its 1981 publication *Accelerated Development in Sub-Saharan Africa* (hereafter referred to as the Berg Report after its lead author). Serving as the World Bank's manifesto for Africa in the 1980s, the Berg Report has garnered more attention, debate and criticism than any other recent economic study on sub-Saharan Africa. The document outlines the bank's wide-ranging and comprehensive analysis regarding the crisis in development that beset Africa in the 1970s and also includes the World Bank's recommended remedies. By the early 1990s virtually all of the policy prescriptions contained in this document had been implemented in one form or another in almost every country in Africa. The philosophy of development underlying this analysis is aptly summarized by the World Bank's president A.W. Clausen:

> ...the report suggests that African governments should not only examine ways in which the public sector organizations can be operated more efficiently, but should also examine the possibility of placing greater reliance on the private sector.

The report emphasizes that this is not a recommendation which derives from any preconceived philosophy of ownership. It derives from considerations of efficiency, which suggest that governments can more effectively achieve their social and development goals by reducing the widespread administrative overcommitment of the public sector and by developing and relying more on the managerial capacities of private individuals and firms, which can respond to local needs and conditions, particularly in small scale industry, marketing, and service activities.[1]

What Ails Africa

The Berg Report's analysis of Africa's economic and development crisis examines three areas: 1) Africa's export/import and exchange rate performance, 2) the prices which food and commodity producers received for their goods, and 3) the size, role and ownership of government. The report focuses on the alarming developments in each of these areas which characterized most African economies in the 1970s and which were the source of Africa's crisis at the turn of the decade. Each of these areas warrants a separate in-depth analysis since the response offered by the World Bank provided the basis for the bank's agenda to transform African economies in the 1980s.

Exports, Imports and Exchange Rates

The Berg Report begins by painting a gloomy picture of Africa's development performance, especially in agriculture, during the 1970s. According to World Bank statistics compiled over that decade, Africa experienced a marked decline in its exports, could not keep pace with population growth in terms of its food production, and imported ever-increasing amounts of grain. While agricultural export production was up by 20 per cent in the 1960s, it suffered a decline of 20 per cent in the 1970s. Food production only increased by 1.5 per cent per year compared to a growth in population of 2.7 per cent in the 1970s. Finally, imports of grain increased by 9 per cent per year in the 1960s and 1970s: "...the drop in production in this sector spelled a real income loss for many of the poorest."[2] The drop in exports and rise in food imports had also contributed to the balance of payments problem. From 1970 to 1979 the debt of sub-Saharan Africa had risen from $6 to $32 billion.[3]

The inefficient policies on trade and exchange rates are described as resulting from the "import-substitution" strategies which many African countries pursued in the years following their independence:

> Thus, an increasing number of African countries have been moving toward a trade and foreign exchange regime with the following characteristics: licensing of most imports; quotas or a complete ban on imports that compete with local production; automatic protection for any import-substitution industry; and priority allocation of essential imports to capital goods, raw materials for local industry, and food.[4]

Discounting External Factors

The Berg Report does mention some external factors which could be regarded as contributing factors leading to Africa's development crisis. These factors, however, are dismissed as peripheral to the real problems besetting Africa. The first is the negative terms of trade for Africa's primary products. While there was a significant price hike in oil and depreciation of mineral prices in the 1970s, there was also a boom in certain other commodities such as coffee. The Berg Report argues that terms of trade for non-oil exporting African countries were down only by 1.5 per cent per year in the 1970s. The report concludes that negative terms of trade do not explain Africa's slow economic growth in the 1970s, even though it boded ill for the 1980s:

> In brief, past trends in the terms of trade cannot explain the slow economic growth of Africa in the 1970s because for most countries – mineral exporters being the main exception – the terms of trade were favourable or neutral. All oil-importing countries suffered a strong and perhaps lasting downward shift in the terms of trade at the end of the 1970s. This compounded the balance-of-payments problems they all faced as they entered the 1980s.[5]

Another possible explanation, protectionism of the North towards Africa's exports, is also considered. According to the World Bank, removing restrictions on goods from the South would have benefited Africa only marginally. Moreover, the report argues, Africa enjoys preferential access to the EEC market for about 25 per cent of its exports and other goods are accorded Most Favoured Nation or Generalized System of Preferences provisions. The conclusion reached by the report: "...on balance, protectionism by developed countries had little effect on African growth in the last decade."[6]

Having dismissed external factors for the slow growth in exports, the Berg Report focuses on the internal causes for this stagnation:

Three factors explain the region's poor export performance: (1) a policy bias against both agriculture and exports which has led to slow overall growth in production; (2) rapid population growth, which, by increasing consumption, has reduced the exportable surplus of crops such as oilseeds and maize and raised the proportion of land used for domestic food production: and (3) the inflexibility of African economies, which has prevented their diversification into products with rapidly growing markets.[7]

Further, the report concludes that an over-valued exchange rate, which has discouraged production for export, has compounded the crisis in trade for Africa. Because food imports are cheaper, the report argues, an over-valued exchange rate has acted as a "tax" on exports, thereby serving as a further disincentive to producers to grow export crops.[8] Furthermore, these policies act, in general, as a bias against agriculture, subsidizing the urban sector through cheaper imported food at the expense of the agricultural sector.

Prices

It is now widely agreed that insufficient price incentives for agricultural producers are an important factor behind the disappointing growth of African agriculture.[9]

The Berg Report builds its case for a market-oriented strategy for African agriculture by citing poor producer prices as the key factor in Africa's agricultural crisis. The argument is premised on what is termed in the development literature as the "urban bias" thesis. The major proponent of this thesis is Michael Lipton whose influential book, *Why Poor People Stay Poor*, argues that the entire development enterprise undertaken in developing countries is structurally biased against the rural areas, especially small-scale producers.

Lipton's urban bias thesis rests on the claim that African governments subsidize the urban sector (their major constituency of support) by providing it with cheaper food, thus placing a burden on the backs of rural farmers who do not receive a fair price for their produce. This analysis extends into the import-substitution sector which is favoured through low exchange rates, subsidies, marketing boards and low producer prices.[10] These low producer prices are a result of government subsidies provided for imported food and an overvalued exchange rate which drives the price of locally grown produce down and which, in turn, makes imported food even cheaper relative to domestically produced food. Lipton argues that the interests of industrialists, urban workers and big farmers converge to steer the meagre resources allocated to agriculture to the big farmers to provide cheap food to the urban areas.

This process virtually ignores the plight of the small farmer who, while efficient, remains poor and powerless. Central to Lipton's argument, moreover, is his claim that international forces and donor practices contribute to this urban bias by restricting imports from developing countries and by ignoring the small farmer in their assistance programmes. Lipton points to the need for a shift in resource allocation towards the rural sector which would benefit small farmers.[11] This includes a fairer share of funds, assistance and fairer prices. The Berg Report relies heavily on a over-simplified version of Lipton's urban bias thesis.

The Berg Report also relies heavily on the ideas of Robert Bates, who extended Lipton's analysis to consider the African context. His book, *Markets and States in Tropical Africa*, argues that Africa's economic crisis is rooted in the diversion of rural resources to the urban sector through government intervention and inappropriate pricing policies. The real culprits, according to Bates, are the state marketing agencies who ensure that producer prices remain lower than the world market price.[12] Some of the other structural inefficiencies identified by Bates include overvalued exchange rates, the subsidization of inputs, and the protection of local industries.[13] Pitching its analysis in the context of the urban bias thesis provides the Berg Report with an appealing theoretical rationale for its solutions.[14]

The Berg Report reiterates Lipton's claim that the decline in exports is a direct result of the poor prices paid to farmers for their commodities. According to the report, the decline in Africa's exports is directly attributable to poor prices paid to farmers. Marketing boards and inefficient parastatals usurp a disproportionate share of the price of export crops. As a result, farmers end up subsidizing an overextended state bureaucracy through unfair prices for both export and food crops. In short, the state's attempts to ensure an adequate and affordable food supply through the setting of prices and control of supply, while laudable, has only exacerbated the food crisis in Africa in the 1970s.

> It is true, nonetheless, that the price policies described above have proved self-defeating. The policy of attempting to control prices and supplies of foodstuffs has, by and large, succeeded in securing only a limited supply of low priced (and often low quality) foodstuffs for a relatively small group of urban consumers. It has increased farmers' and traders' risks in producing and marketing food surpluses. It has failed to stabilize and indeed has actually destabilized supplies over the course of the year. Further, through its effects on farmers' supply response, it has probably resulted in higher overall level of food prices than would have pertained without government attempts to control supplies.[15]

The Size of Government

During the post-independence period the size and role of the state expanded rapidly. Because most industry was privately owned (in most cases by foreign colonial interests) the state moved in to take over key industries as a means of controlling essential resources and export income. This was necessary to help generate the income needed for health care and education, areas that were virtually ignored during the colonial period.

The Berg Report, while acknowledging the positive value of mobilizing economic surplus for public spending on health and education, is nonetheless alarmed at both the mounting cost and expanding bureaucracy associated with this process. Walking a fine line on the issue of national sovereignty, the report singles out three chronic problems with the state that were contributing to the continent's economic crisis. The first problem resulted from government spending on social programmes which was beginning to outstrip revenues. The second problem, the size of the bureaucracy, both with respect to government-owned industries and social programmes along with the cost of salaries and wages, was deemed unsustainable. The third area of concern lay in the free provision of basic services such as health care, education and water. As the report notes:

> While it is widely believed that goods of such fundamental importance should be supplied without payment, governments cannot afford to provide them; therefore, in the face of substantial demand, the services languish accordingly.[16]

The Berg Report's Solution

> The agriculture-based and export-oriented development strategy suggested for the 1980s is an essential beginning to a process of long-term transformation, a prelude to industrialization.[17]

The solutions proposed for Africa's economic recovery for the 1980s depended on using an agriculturally-based export-oriented growth strategy as the engine for recovery. In real terms it advocated abandoning the continent's fledgling attempts at developing its own industries and a re-emphasizing its traditional strength as a producer and exporter of primary commodities.[18] This model was accompanied by a related set of policy prescriptions. These policy prescriptions became tied into the export-growth strategy which was recommended for the continent in the 1980s. First to be examined, and the basis for the World Bank's optimism, is the idea that an export-oriented growth strategy based on commodities was the correct remedy for the continent.

Export Growth and Comparative Advantage

Assuming stability in the oil markets for the 1980s, the Berg Report went on to forecast a substantially improved trade picture for Africa's commodities:

> According to World Bank projections, world trade in the 22 non-fuel commodities of greatest importance to Africa is expected to increase by 2.9 per cent per annum during the 1980s, which is substantially higher than the average annual increase of 1.5 per cent for African non-fuel primary products in the 1970s. Moreover, the weighted price of Africa's non-fuel commodity exports is projected to rise slightly so that the average value of world trade in these commodities will increase by 3.4 per cent per year. Broadly speaking, projected trends for minerals and beverages will be the reverse of the 1970s; the value of world trade in minerals is projected to increase by 5.8 per cent per annum, with most of the increase coming in the latter half of the decade, while world trade in food and beverages will increase by only 1.6 per cent per annum.

The projected rate of growth of trade in Africa's main exports is lower than that of overall world trade. This dependence on exports of slowly growing primary products is a disadvantage, but exports can be diversified and Africa's share of world trade in most commodities could be increased with relatively small effects on prices.[19]

The report's recommendation to increase exports is built on the law of comparative advantage which holds that "a country [should] produce those things which it can best produce as compared with other countries and, second, [it must continue] producing them with the least use of limited resources".[20] As World Bank projections and statistics indicated, African countries should be able to double their earnings on most of their export crops. Essentially, the report holds that Africa's hopes for economic recovery lie in the fact that it can produce primary products most efficiently and cheaply and thereby finance its thrust towards industrialization and modernization. In the short run, however, this requires that the import-substitution strategy be abandoned and existing African industries opened up to foreign competition. When accompanied with a currency devaluation, an export-oriented growth strategy could be achieved without subsidies because of the higher prices that export producers would receive for their commodities.[21] The principle of correct prices forms the cornerstone of this strategy.

Getting Prices Right

With the assumption, borne out by macro-level studies, "which indicate substantial farmer responsiveness to price", the Berg Report continues to build upon the policy implications of its export-growth strategy for Africa. Higher producer prices for exports will not only induce the "market peasant"[22] to grow these crops, they will form the basis of improved and more efficient production of food crops as well. Dismissing the argument that a concentration on export crops occurs at the expense of food crops, the report argues that this is not necessarily demonstrable or a bad thing. The reason for this rests on the law of comparative advantage which holds that it is more efficient and profitable to import food if it costs less than producing it domestically:

> Even if it could be demonstrated that export crop increases have come at the expense of food production, the conclusion would not necessarily follow that a strategy of self-reliance requires a substitution of food production for exports. Most African countries have distinct comparative advantage in export crop production.[23]

The key assumption underlying this advice is that self-reliance in food can best be attained by exporting crops in which a country enjoys a comparative advantage and importing food that is cheaper than it would cost to produce locally. Also important to note is the assumption that the "fair" price for products is the world market price and, when the cost of inputs that are no longer subsidized is factored in, primary producers will be better off.

Privatization and Liberalization

The key requirement of a successful export-oriented growth strategy lies in allowing the market, and not the state, to allocate resources. This principle implies a number of policy prescriptions. These include removing subsidies on inputs and imports, allowing the private sector to buy and sell commodities, downsizing and cutting wages to the urban sector which will result in a healthy bias towards agriculture, and finally, instituting a user-pay system for basic services such as health and education to offset their growing cost and the increasing inability of governments to pay for them. Included in this recipe is the inducement not only to privatize large government-owned industries, but also to be open to foreign investment opportunities:

> Also, there is surely scope – at least in some countries – for larger-scale mixed public and private enterprises. Export crops are particularly suited to this option because the marketing skills and market connections that are often associated with foreign investment could be well utilized. Governments should also consider giving more room to agro-industrial enterprises (perhaps through concessions) whose external capital and technical know-how could be applied to plantations or irrigation crops as well as used in industrial processing.[24]

Finally, the report makes clear that the strategy outlined provides a comprehensive and long-term solution to Africa's economic problems:

> Devolution of marketing functions to private enterprise may be more difficult in some parts of Africa, where the tradition of indigenous entrepreneurship is weak, but this should affect only the pace of change, not the objective.[25]

Development Assistance and the Debt Problem

The final ingredient in the Berg Report's prescription for Africa is the need for the international community to increase its aid to the region in the 1980s. In fact, according to the report, without increased aid and significant policy reform, the continent will continue its economic slide. The section of the Berg Report on development assistance clearly suggests that the international community should begin to insist on policy reform as a condition of assistance in the 1980s:

> The level and pattern of donor assistance to a country must be determined in the framework of programmes of action prepared by individual governments, which address the critical policy issues outlined in the Report. In this way, donor financial assistance will effectively support the attainment of development objectives, and avoid financing projects that do not reflect a government's priorities or even run counter to these priorities.[26]

With a substantial aid increase to the region along with policy reform, projections called for an optimistic 5 per cent per annum increase in the region's GDP. The World Bank, in this report, was clearly signalling a new role for itself with respect to Africa in the 1980s. This was made clear in its intentions to form "consultative groups" to assist countries in planning and implementing policy reforms, and in its stated intent to begin providing Structural Adjustment Loans (SALs) to those countries willing to undertake serious policy reforms.

As of 1980 the World Bank had made SALs to four African countries: Kenya, Malawi, Mauritius and Senegal.

Debt, Aid and Policy Reform

While the rising debt of African countries was an issue of concern for the World Bank at the outset of the 1980s, it was nonetheless viewed as manageable if the needed policy reforms were implemented. The bank's projections indicated a modest rise in its debt-service ratio (the ratio of interest and amortization payments to export earnings). The report urges a closer monitoring of the debt picture by donor countries and increasing linkage between aid and debt. While the issue of aid conditionality in this context is not mentioned it is certainly strongly implied:

> It is in the interest of creditors and donors that economic and financial health be restored to the economies of borrowing countries, and that the separate treatment of aid and debt not jeopardize a promising attempt on the part of a debtor government to put through a viable policy-reform package.[27]

The World Bank urges a cooperative effort of increased international assistance and a commensurate "adjustment" in the economies of Africa in order to reverse the downward trend and put the continent on the road to growth and prosperity.

In the early 1980s the policy reforms outlined in the Berg Report were crystallized into the essential ingredients of SAPs which African governments were compelled to adopt as a condition for development assistance, a rescheduling of loans or further lending. The tone of cooperation increasingly took on the pallor of conditionality in the World Bank's, and the international lending and donor community's, relationship with African countries.

The Berg Report also called for a dramatic refocusing on the agricultural sector. The modernization literature of the 1960s and 1970s viewed so-called peasants as the primary obstacle to development because of their alleged resistance to change from subsistence agriculture. In the Berg Report, the characterization is one of peasants exploited by an urban alliance growing rich and inefficient through subsidized food. According to Berg, peasant producers are very responsive to price and will improve production considerably if given the right environment. Peter Gibbon sums up the World Bank's redesignation of the African farmer:

> Agriculture was no longer seen as a site of backwardness but of dynamism. This was because of its unique status as overwhelmingly the subject of private ownership. In the process the "subsistence" farmer was redesignated a "rural entrepre-

neur". By contrast, the industrial sector was viewed largely negatively and identified (often incorrectly) with state intervention, subsidization, inefficiency and general efforts at social engineering.... While LDCs still had to "pull themselves up by their bootstraps" it was neither feasible nor desirable for them to seek to emulate the specific sectoral mix of the developed countries.[28]

Before moving on to our next chapter it is useful to summarize the major arguments found within the Berg Report, since they become the key ideological refrains which are reiterated in the documents that were to follow throughout the 1980s.

SUMMARY OF BERG REPORT

I. **The Nature of Africa's Economic Crisis**
   A. Negative Growth Rates
      1. reduced exports
      2. higher imports, especially of food (grains)
      3. overvalued exchange rates

   B. The Urban Bias
      1. low prices to farmers
      2. bias vs. exports
      3. subsidizing imports

   C. Role and Size of Government
      1. inefficient parastatals
      2. ownership of major industries
      3. wages and salaries of the burgeoning civil service
      4. control of basic services
      5. free access to basic services

II. **Solutions to Africa's Crisis**
   A. Export-Oriented Growth
      1. comparative advantage
      2. lower exchange rates

   B. Getting Prices Right
      1. remove subsidies on imports for urban areas
      2. let market allocate resources
      3. market price = higher price for producers

   C. Reduce Role, Size and Cost of Government
      1. privatize parastatals, support private traders
      2. open up to foreign investment, agro-industries etc.
      3. cut wages and salaries to civil servants
      4. user pay for basic services
      5. privatize basic services

   D. Increased Development Assistance
      1. aid linked to debt management and policy reform
      2. increasing role of World Bank and donors in monitoring
         reform
      3. increased role to World Bank and donors in providing
         Structural Adjustment Lending

Endnotes

1. World Bank, *Accelerated Development in Sub-Saharan Africa: An Agenda for Action*, (Washington: The World Bank, 1981), p. 5.
2. *Accelerated Development*, p. 30.
3. The thesis of declining food production which forms the basis of the Berg Report has been seriously challenged by a number of sources. See, for instance Philip Raikes, *Modernizing Hunger*, (London: CIIR, 1988), pp. 17-32, where he convincingly disassembles the FAO production yearbooks upon which the World Bank data are based. Similarly, Jane Guyer, "Women's Work and Production Systems: A Review of Two Reports on the Agricultural Crisis," *Review of African Political Economy* 22-3 (1983), notes the systematic underestimation of food grown and marketed by women in the FAO estimates. Bill Rau argues that this assessment ignores the differential access to production resources, massive poverty and decisions regarding food security taken outside of officially marketed produce. As a result, the Berg Report does not bother to measure unofficial sales of goods as producers opt out of the market, an amount, he notes, significant enough to prove false the thesis of declining food availability. B. Rau, *Feast or Famine: Official Cures and Grassroots Remedies to Africa's Food Crisis*, (London: Zed Books, 1991), pp. 101-3.
4. *Accelerated Development*, p. 25. Samir Amin offers the following comment on the Berg Report's assessment on this issue: "The low productivity of agriculture in Africa is a platitude. What the Bank report neglects to point out is that this low productivity accompanying the extensive pattern of this agriculture has been and is profitable from the point of view of the world system's division of labour. In effect, it allows the West to acquire raw materials without having to invest. Transition to intensive agriculture, a necessity of today, entails a rise in the world prices of these raw materials if they are to be exported: land, along with oil or water, is no longer 'limitless' but becoming a scarce resource." Samir Amin, *Maldevelopment: Anatomy of a Global Failure, (London: Zed Books, 1990)*, p. 37.
5. *Accelerated Development*, p. 17.
6. *Accelerated Development*, p. 20.
7. *Accelerated Development*, p. 21.
8. *Accelerated Development*, p. 5.
9. *Accelerated Development*, p. 55.
10. M. Lipton, *Why Poor People Stay Poor: Urban Bias in World Development*, (Cambridge: Harvard University Press, 1977), p. 19.
11. Lipton, *Why Poor People Stay Poor*, p. 328.
12. R. Bates, *Markets and States in Tropical Africa: The Political Bias of Agricultural Policies*, (Berkeley: University of California Press, 1981), pp. 29, 136-45.

13. Bates, *Markets and States*, pp. 36-8, 49-54, 62-70.
14. John Toye *et al.* argue that Lipton's account was taken out of context to suggest that liberalization would "counteract the existing engineered economic biases in favour of a richer 'urban class'". Poor peasants in the rural areas would gain from liberalization, while parasitic urban rent-seekers would find their incomes being levelled down. *Aid and Power*, p. 15.
15. *Accelerated Development*, p. 58.
16. *Accelerated Development*, p. 43.
17. *Accelerated Development*, p. 6.
18. As Samir Amin remarks about the strategy outlined in the Berg Report: "If the words have any meaning this is an extroverted strategy of adjustment to the demands of transnationalization, a strategy of renouncing the construction of a diversified national and regional economy capable through its dynamism of becoming a genuine partner in the interdependent world system." Amin, *Maldevelopment*, p. 36.
19. *Accelerated Development*, p. 23.
20. *Accelerated Development*, p. 24.
21. *Accelerated Development*, p. 30.
22. J. Barker, *Rural Communities Under Stress: Peasant Farmers and the State in Africa*, (Cambridge: Cambridge University Press, 1991, 1989), p. 104.
23. *Accelerated Development*, pp. 63-4.
24. *Accelerated Development*, p. 52.
25. *Accelerated Development*, p. 65.
26. *Accelerated Development*, p. 125.
27. *Accelerated Development*, pp. 129-30. Foucault's understanding of the rigid government of the individual best approximates what is at the heart of this seemingly innocuous passage, for within it lies the blueprint for conditionality around the acceptance of structural adjustment packages for further aid or loans: "To govern, in this sense, is to structure the possible field of action of others." *The Subject and Power*, p. 221, quoted in Boone, *The Bible*, p. 84.
28. Gibbon, "Political Economy," p. 8.

—— CHAPTER FIVE ——

The Deepening Crisis

By 1983-84 it was becoming evident that SAPs would not be voluntarily adopted by African governments despite a variety of coercive and incentive measures. However, by the mid-1980s a number of factors converged to force the hand of many African governments to implement SAPs. The balance of payments problems of virtually all African countries had deteriorated dramatically and foreign exchange earnings had fallen precipitously. New investment and loans had virtually dried up as banks and other investors sought instead to recoup whatever they could from debtor nations and take advantage of deregulated domestic markets. Concessional flows and development assistance also dropped off in the wake of the recession in the North. Coupled with a severe drought in many parts of Africa, governments which had been able to resist the IMF and World Bank now saw their very survival tied to accepting the loans, and the conditions attached to them, in spite of the domestic unrest they were certain to cause.

In 1984 the World Bank issued another special report on sub-Saharan Africa aimed at reinvigorating the ideas raised in the Berg Report. *Toward Sustained Development in Sub-Saharan Africa* calls upon the donor community to focus its efforts around building an adjustment framework for African countries. Apparently, the message heralded in the Berg Report was not getting through. "Progress remains inadequate"[1] both in the rate and scale of adjustment and in the donor community's support for adjustment. *Toward Sustained Development* indirectly points to the need for more coercive measures to be introduced in the language of assistance. These calls for reform were issued in the language of incentive for countries to adjust while the donor community pledged to provide them the breathing space to do so. The opening lines of the document clearly set this out:

While the reform of the policy and institutional framework
within each African country is crucial, domestic reforms
cannot be fully effective unless supported by appropriate
levels and types of external assistance.[2]

The reason for the relative lack of enthusiasm for reform amongst
African countries is attributed, in more explicit terms, to the power of
the urban alliance. The report continues to argue for government to
disentangle itself from this alliance by adopting measures that will at
first require outside assistance but will quickly yield positive results in
the agricultural sector:

Cheap food, low import prices, and overstaffed state marketing
authorities all benefit some social groups and these groups can
be politically powerful. ...But if opposition to reform is to be
managed, governments need to show results quickly. This
implies a focus on policies that can yield results quickly from
existing capacity and will require an increased flow of imported
goods and services, which will initially have to be financed out
of increased external assistance to the country.[3]

The document goes on to target the donor consultative committees
as the arena for better coordinated donor policy for adjusting countries.
These donor consultative groups generally held annual meetings
during which the recipient country outlined its various needs and
requirements to the donor community who then divided up or coordinated the various projects. *Toward Sustained Development* suggests
that these meetings take on a "narrower and more operational focus".[4]

The theoretical justification for tightening donor conditionality
is also suggested in this report: "Agreement between governments and
donors might include, for instance, decisions to discontinue the
funding of certain types of projects; to provide more non-project
assistance or debt rescheduling... ."[5] The World Bank also sought to
use its International Development Association (IDA), which generally
provides low interest loans and grants to the poorest countries, to
provide highly concessional loans to low income sub-Saharan African
countries on the condition that they undertake programmes of economic reform.[6]

The report concludes with the suggestion that the World Bank serve as chairs to the reorganized consultative gatherings. Over the next few years the World Bank did assume control of the donor consultative groups. In the process it succeeded in bringing the donor community into line with regard to the kind of assistance, conditionality and development philosophy which should be provided to Africa in the era of adjustment. It was one of a number of measures taken throughout the 1980s to ensure that the adoption and adherence to SAPs became inescapable.

The World Bank also sought to steer any increased aid flows towards structural adjustment. An increase of aid flows of over $2 billion is requested from the bilaterals but with a clear condition attached to it: "...the additional funding should be placed in a special assistance facility to be used only when required to support reform programmes."[7]

The essential building blocks of the recovery programme laid out in the Berg Report are reiterated in *Toward Sustained Development*. The cornerstone of this growth model continues to be based on encouraging commodity exports. This advice persists in spite of the initial results of this strategy in the early 1980s. Between 1980-82 the terms of trade for non-oil commodities had plummeted by 27 per cent and Africa continued to lose the market share of its major commodities. In spite of these indicators the policy advice remained the same as that found in the Berg Report. African countries had to expand their exports and increase their market share.

The Debt Crisis

While the Berg Report all but ignores the precarious debt situation of African countries, *Toward Sustained Development* notes with alarm the implications of Africa's debt position for its development prospects. Africa's publicly guaranteed debt was rising rapidly. This debt, owed to multilaterals like the World Bank and IMF, could not be cancelled or rescheduled. Arrears were accumulating at an unprecedented rate: "Unless corrective measures are taken, the external resource position of sub-Saharan Africa is likely to become disastrous in the next few years."[8]

When this is juxtaposed with the dramatic decline in resource flows from private sources (by over 50 per cent between 1980-82), the 1984 report serves as an indicator of a crisis that was to worsen dramatically in the years to come.

Toward Sustained Development claims that the debt crisis was the result of extravagant spending and unsound fiscal management during the boom years of the 1970s. It signals the World Bank's attempt to disavow its own role and responsibility for its involvement in financing and encouraging these very same projects only a few years earlier. "...too much investment has gone into projects that have failed to generate significant increases in output. Genuine mistakes and misfortunes cannot explain the excessive number of 'white elephants'."[9]

In spite of this, and the fact that Africa was experiencing one of its worst droughts, the report adopts a theology of hope for the "basket case" that Africa had become:

> Such realities naturally cause pessimism. Yet analysis of
> development in sub-Saharan Africa and elsewhere suggests a
> basis for hope. A generation ago, it should be remembered, the
> prospects of Korea were regarded as dismal, 10 years ago
> Bangladesh was regarded as a basket case.[10]

The theoretical underpinning for the next stage of World Bank thinking was provided by Harvard economist Anne O. Krueger's elaboration of the concept of "rent-seeking behaviour". Krueger became vice-president of the World Bank's Economics and Research Department in 1982. According to Krueger, an added problem with regard to import-substitution strategies was the hidden and more debilitating costs of what she termed "rent-seeking" behaviour. A major source of economic inefficiency in developing countries was rooted in government itself and its "rent-seeking" behaviour. This behaviour denotes the appropriation of payments or taxes through government systems of regulation and the distribution of import licences. The elaborate system required to restrict imports and protect local industries was costly and inefficient, containing a number of added hidden costs such as the time spent by clerks filling out forms and standing in line. These costs were being borne by the rural producer. These rents could only be eliminated by replacing state regulation with that of the market.[11]

In this context the debate gradually shifted from one which saw the need for additional support for the state in its attempts to disengage itself from the interests of urban elites to one which advocated a weakening of the state. Support should be directed to non-state actors and groups that would foster 'reform' through parallel market activities and by-passing the state as much as possible. This theology of the corrupted state was promoted heavily by the World Bank from the mid-eighties onward. It involved a reassertion of the neo-classical laissez-faire role for the state and a repudiation of the post-war model of Third World Development which accepted the need for state intervention as a central element in the task nation-building.

Deepak Lal, who became Economic Advisor to the World Bank's Research Department in 1983, is one of the fiercest opponents of the development theories of the 1960s and 1970s or what he termed "development economics". His book *The Poverty of Development Economics*, constitutes a full-scale assault on the development practices in the post-World War II period, tainted as they were by misguided Keynesian ideals such as redistribution, import-substitution, and an interventionist state. According to Lal, the most telling error of development economics was its rejection of the neo-classical notion that individuals act economically, i.e., that when presented with an advantage they will take it. Development economics replaced this notion with that of the knowledgeable and compassionate government which redistributes wealth for the benefit of all. To this Lal replies:

> Numerous and empirical studies from different cultures and climates, however, show that uneducated private agents – be they peasants, rural-urban migrants, urban workers, private entrepreneurs, or housewives – act economically as producers and consumers. They respond to changes in relative prices much as neo-classical theory would predict. The "economic principle" is not unrealistic in the Third World; poor people may, in fact, be pushed harder to seek their advantage than rich people.[12]

The views of thinkers like Krueger and Lal soon prevailed in the operational strategies adopted by the World Bank in Africa. The model of the post-World War II development decades were abandoned, the overextended state was fingered as the cause of failure, and the conversion to the market through SAPs was held out as the only hope. With this analysis there also emerged the parallel consideration in the African context of the problems of cronyism and corruption that were rampant in the states of Africa fostering what was soon to become championed by the World Bank as the crisis of governance.

Dealing with the Critics

In the wake of its full-scale promotion of SAPs and the abandonment of poverty alleviation, the World Bank found itself the target of criticism within the UN family. During the mid-1980s a number of voices attacked the harmful impacts of SAPs on the poor. Most prominent among these were the United Nations Children's Fund (UNICEF) and the UN Economic Commission for Africa (ECA). While UNICEF focused on the issue of poverty alleviation (in effect resuscitating the World Bank's language abandoned in the 1980s), a formidable challenge to the World Bank's control over the development agenda for Africa was launched by the ECA and its Director Adebayo Adedeji. The ECA not only contested the economic underpinnings of adjustment and its suitability for Africa, it also charged that the World Bank was engaged in the distortion and manipulation of statistical data in its attempt to demonstrate the viability of SAPs.

The lightning rod for the ECA's major offensive against the World Bank and SAPs was the report prepared by the World Bank and the UN Development Programme (UNDP) to coincide with the Midterm Review in 1988 of the United Nation's Programme of Action for African Economic Recovery and Development (UNPAAERD). (UNPAAERD was the UN's five-year programme for Africa's economic recovery, launched in 1986.) The World Bank/UNDP report, entitled *Africa's Adjustment and Growth in the 1980s*, attempts to establish a statistical basis for the claim that countries adopting SAPs are achieving positive development outcomes. The essential thrust of *Africa's Adjustment* was that "... programmes of economic reform and adjustment have helped African countries begin to improve their economic performance".[13] In addition, the report argues that those countries adopting SAPs were clearly performing better than those that were not. "The evidence points to better overall economic performance in countries that pursue strong reform programmes than in those that do not."[14] The World Bank/UNDP report disagreed with the conclusions reached at the Mid-Term Review of UNPAAERD, in the UN Secretary General's Report as well as in the Final Resolution, both of which concluded that the situation in Africa had worsened since the onset of the UNPAAERD.

Playing the Statistical Game

By 1988 enough countries had undertaken SAPs to provide a statistical basis for assessing their performance. While Africa's overall development picture continued to look extremely bleak, the World Bank painted a rosy picture for those countries which had undertaken reforms. In order to demonstrate that Africa's development prospects were not as dismal as statistics suggested, *Africa's Adjustment and Growth* argued for the disaggregation of countries and the adoption of a longer perspective to assess the performance of SAPs.

Through a series of charts and the presentation of statistical data, the report attempts to demonstrate that Africa's terms of trade had actually improved since the early 1970s. The report claims that African countries were receiving a better price for their exports than the rest of the world, that development assistance to the region was up dramatically, agricultural production was ahead of population growth, and that GDP rates were rising. The report goes on to conclude that, "Africa's crisis cannot be satisfactorily explained as the result of an adverse international economic climate, low commodity prices, or dwindling foreign assistance."[15]

The problem of rising debt and the dramatic increase in the debt-service to export ratio is blamed on internal factors, namely the loss of market share for Africa's exports. If these countries had merely kept up with their 1970 levels, the report argues, their export earnings would have been up by $9-10 billion per year, equal to their annual debt-service payments. To emphasize the point further: "If Africa's export growth had matched that of other LDCs, its debt service ratio would be about half of what it is today." Africa was failing to keep its market share in spite of the fact that it enjoyed preferential access to European markets through the Lomé Convention as well as to the US relative to other developing countries.[16]

Africa's Adjustment and Growth attempts to break new ground in the chapters assessing the performance of countries that have adopted SAPs as against those that have not. The exercise is a complicated one as the analysis demonstrates, since the outward signs of improvement for adjustment are not immediately apparent using traditional indicators. For this reason, the World Bank/UNDP report resorts to a number of unconventional statistical methods to uncover what it regards as a SAPs success story.

Crop Prices

One of the cornerstones of structural adjustment is the liberalization of prices for farmers and the dismantling of government pricing and marketing boards. The preliminary assessment in this area provides mixed results. For export crops, the report boasts of a rise of 16 per cent in producer prices between 1983-86 reversing a decline of over 30 per cent over the previous seven years. For farmers in reforming countries, prices had improved by an average of 50 per cent between 1980-86. This success was "partly as a result of these reforms".[17] However, by 1987 this had again reversed itself "because of higher domestic inflation in some countries and a drop in international prices for several major commodities".[18]

As for food crops, there was a *decrease* in prices in spite of reforms, "because high production in 1985 and 1986 led to surpluses that depressed market prices and because official food crop pricing and marketing policies often were not enforced effectively before the reforms".[19] The report concludes its analysis of crop prices by noting that the relative price of export crops improved significantly over that of food crops between 1986-87, which led to shifts toward the production of non-food crops.

In assessing the overall performance of reforming vs. non-reforming countries the World Bank/UNDP report resorts to a curious mode of reasoning. It first attempts to demonstrate that reforming countries experienced a much harsher external climate than did non-reformers. Table 5.1 tries to indicate that reforming countries experienced a far worse climate for the prices of their exports and in their terms of trade. The current account deficit was rising in reforming countries and falling in non-reforming ones. Imports were on the rise

Table 5.1: Summary of Key External Economic Factors

| External factor | Period | Countries with strong reform programs | | Countries with weak or no reform programs |
		All	Excluding oil exporters[a]	
Change in export unit prices	1980-84	-3.5	-2.7	-4.4
	1985-87	-8.2	1.9	6.7
Change in export earnings[b]	1980-84	-14.1	-7.6	-5.2
	1985-87	-10.1	7.1	3.9
Change in terms of trade	1980-84	-1.3	-0.5	-2.1
	1985-87	-14.1	-4.7	1.4
Change in total net ODA[c]	1983-85	2.9	4.2	15.6
	1985-87	18.7	18.7	-4.7
Paris Club agreements (per year) Number	1980-85	4.3	4.3	1.8
	1986-87	8.0	7.0	1.5
Amount consolidated (US$ billions)[d]	1980-85	1.3	0.8	0.4
	1986-87	1.9	1.5	0.1

Note: Country coverage varies by indicator depending on available data over the entire period covered. Aggregate growth rates are weighted, based on total values summed across countries, computed using least squares. Periods are inclusive.
a. Trade data exclude only the oil exports of oil exporters.
b. Merchandise only.
c. Deflated by Sub-Saharan Africa's import prices.
d. Estimated annual reduction in debt service obligations through rescheduling.

(Source: World Bank, *Africa's Adjustment and Growth*, p. 27)

in reforming countries but continued to decline in non-reforming ones. The report does not measure the impact that this diversion of development assistance from "non-reformers" to "reformers" had in terms of basic economic indicators. It concludes that:

> Despite the difficult external environment, governments where economic reform programmes have been sufficiently strong and sustained to be supported by the World Bank and other international donors have clearly demonstrated better policy performance in numerous areas.[20]

These numerous areas are charted in the final table (Table 5.2) which is meant to indicate that reforming countries are outperforming non-reforming ones. These indicators provide the report with the basis for its spuriously optimistic assessment around the first two years of the UNPAAERD:

> Results from the region during 1986 and 1987 indicate that the compact of the UN Special Session on Africa is being widely followed. Where African governments implement reforms and donors provide additional resources, economic performance can, on average, be improved.[21]

Manipulating Statistics: The ECA Response

In the years following the 1986 UN Special Session on Africa which launched the UNPAAERD the differences between the World Bank and the ECA both in development philosophies and their assessment of SAPs became much sharper. The Mid-Term Review of the UNPAAERD and the widely divergent assessment of its success culminated in the ECA's comprehensive critique of the World Bank's promotion of SAPs. The focus for this attack on SAPs and the setting forth of an alternative was the response which the ECA mounted against the World Bank/UNDP's *Africa's Adjustment and Growth in the 1980s*. It is not possible here to analyse the ECA's response in detail, except to point out that it posed, for the first time anywhere in the decade, a credible and serious challenge to the World Bank and its development agenda for Africa.

Table 5.2: Summary of Economic Performance Indicators

Indicator	Period	All countries		Countries not affected by strong shocks	
		With strong reform programs	With weak or no reform programs	With strong reform programs	With weak or no reform programs
Growth of GDP (constant 1980 prices)	1980-84	1.4	1.5	1.2	0.7
	1985-87	2.8	2.7	3.8	1.5
Agricultural production	1980-84	1.1	1.3	1.4	1.8
	1985-87	2.6	1.5	3.4	2.6
Growth of export volume	1980-84	-1.3 (-11.0)	-3.1 (-0.9)	-0.7 (-4.7)	-5.7 (-2.1)
	1985-87	4.2 (-2.0)	0.2 (-2.5)	4.9 (3.5)	-3.3 (-6.0)
Growth of import volume excluding oil exporters	1985-87	1.7 (-7.7) 4.8 (6.8)	-2.7 (-3.0)	6.1 (7.4)	-4.0 (-2.2)
Growth of real domestic investment	1980-84	-8.1	-3.7	-3.5	-7.0
	1985-87	-0.9	-7.0	1.9	-4.8
Gross domestic savings (percentage of GDP)	1982-84	9.9	2.3	7.8	0.9
	1986-87	10.7	6.0	10.7	5.6
Growth of per capita consumption (real)	1980-84	-2.3	-1.1	-2.4	-1.5
	1985-87	-0.4	-0.5	0.7	-0.9

Note: Country coverage varies by indicator depending on available data over the entire period covered. Averages are unweighted except as noted. Growth rates are computed using least squares. Periods are inclusive. Figures in parentheses are weighted averages of country growth rates based on total values summed across countries.

(Source: World Bank, *Africa's Adjustment and Growth*, p. 30)

In early 1989 the Conference of Ministers of the ECA took the unprecedented step of issuing a separate report dealing with the specific conclusions reached in *Africa's Adjustment*, noting its "deep concern that in many respects the World Bank/UNDP report is at variance with the mid-term review of the implementation of the UNPAAERD".[22] In light of this it undertook its own analysis to set the record straight, especially given the fact that the World Bank/UNDP report was being widely publicized.

The ECA rebuttal refutes the basis for the World Bank's rosy assessment of SAPs. It questions both the assumptions and the methodological approach to the statistics and points out a number of serious flaws in the presentation of data to demonstrate the success of SAPs. The choice of reference years, base years and the inclusion and exclusion of data sets point to a high degree of selectivity geared to produce a pre-ordained conclusion. A major shortcoming of the World Bank/UNDP report is that its findings were impossible to replicate because of insufficient documentation and explanation of criteria.

One of the most glaring attempts to skew data to meet a pre-conceived conclusion is found in the World Bank/UNDP Report's use of base years to track various trends such as terms of trade, export prices, producer prices and GDP. To chart trends analysts traditionally use the first year of a decade (e.g. 1970, 1980). *Adjustment and Growth* departs from this standard practice. In its reference to terms of trade, the report uses 1970-73 as its base and concludes that Africa's terms of trade "are still 15 per cent higher than in the early 1970s". By charting trends in terms of trade according to accepted statistical methods, the ECA arrives at a different conclusion showing a steep decline in terms of trade, especially after 1985.

GDP: Weighing in Equally

The ECA uncovered a further statistical deception in examining the weighting of strong vs. weak adjusting countries in comparing their GDP growth rates in the 1980s. A number of anomalies is apparent. First, the World Bank uses 1985 as the first year when SAPs were adopted. In reality, however, many countries were adopting SAPs in 1980 and even earlier. Second, the World Bank curiously chooses to weight all countries equally in compiling its statistics for GDP and other indicators (Table 5.2). The ECA demonstrates how a proper weighting of countries provides a different outcome and indeed demonstrates that so-called strong adjusting countries were actually faring worse than the recalcitrant non-reformers (Table 5.3).

The African Alternative Framework

The open feuding between the ECA and the World Bank escalated with the release of the ECA's major document, *African Alternative Framework to Structural Adjustment Programmes* (AAF-SAP). The study is remarkable in that it is the *only* comprehensive sustained critique of the World Bank's SAP agenda for Africa from an institution of the ECA's stature. Most importantly, the AAF-SAP sets forth a holistic model of development based on the long-term transformation of Africa's economies.

The AAF-SAP challenges the World Bank's SAP agenda on two fronts. First, it calls into question the contribution that SAPs make to Africa's long-term development objectives. Second, it calls into question their social, economic and financial impact.

According to the ECA, SAPs have not achieved their macro-economic objectives:

> ...in many cases sustained economic growth has not material-
> ized, the rate of investment rather than improve has tended to
> decrease, budget and balance of payments deficits have tended
> to widen after some temporary relief and debt service obli-
> gations have become unbearable.[23]

The ECA regards the AAF-SAP as joining the growing chorus of international concern regarding the social costs of adjustment programmes, especially in the areas of primary health care and education. The AAF-SAP's rejection of SAPs as an appropriate macro-policy tool forms the basis of an alternative development path outlined in the second part of the document.

The AAF-SAP challenges what it considers to be questionable statistical reporting by the World Bank on the success of SAPs. According to the ECA, SAPs do not work because they address only the symptoms of fiscal imbalances in African economies and not their

Table 5.3: Growth of Gross Domestic Product in Africa 1980-87
(constant 1980 US$, market prices) (in per cent)

Country Groups	1980-81	1981-82	1982-83	1983-84	1984-85	1985-86	1986-87	1980-87 Aver.
Strong adjusting	-3.01	0.33	-3.85	-4.31	6.33	2.82	-1.97	-0.53
Weak adjusting	5.44	3.46	0.66	-1.29	0.13	4.01	1.88	2.00
Non-adjusting	3.92	3.35	3.53	3.68	6.40	3.62	-2.51	3.50
Sub-Saharan Africa	-1.05	1.01	-2.37	-2.94	5.44	3.09	-1.48	0.24
North Africa	-2.27	3.12	3.63	2.78	1.90	0.19	1.29	1.50
Africa Total	-1.52	1.81	-0.06	-0.66	3.98	1.92	-0.38	0.73

Note: Country coverage and classification of strong adjusting, weak adjusting and non-adjusting countries according to World Bank; average annual growth rates were calculated as arithmetic averages (preliminary).

(Source: UNECA, "Preliminary Observations," p. 25)

much deeper "structural deficiencies".[24] As a result, the AAF-SAP notes, the analysis of the World Bank regarding Africa's problems and its proposed solution with SAPs are incomplete, mechanistic and too short-term.

According to the AAF-SAP, the empirical evidence indicates that, contrary to the World Bank's analysis, countries adopting SAPs fared no better, and in most cases performed worse in areas such as GDP and debt servicing. The biggest oversight, according to the AAF-SAP, is the World Bank's obliviousness to the social costs of adjustment: increased poverty and unemployment and an exacerbation of structural weaknesses:

> That is why, in spite of the growth of GDP and exports, and in
> spite of improvements in external payments and budget bal-
> ances in some African countries, starvation and malnutrition,
> abject poverty, and external dependence have worsened,
> while the other structural weaknesses and deficiencies of the
> African economies have intensified.[25]

Coopting the Heretics: From Crisis to Sustainable Growth

The AAF-SAP has enjoyed very little success in influencing the mainstream policy debate on SAPs. Major donors have further entrenched a SAP-oriented approach to development. Although the AAF-SAP was endorsed in the UN (with the exception of the US which voted against it), its policy prescriptions have not been implemented or even seriously discussed. This failure can be largely attributed to the fact that the World Bank has seized control of the development agenda for Africa. Even the AAF-SAP's policy broadside against this agenda did very little to sidetrack it.

The internal dispute between the World Bank and the ECA had threatened to escalate into open confrontation. Hoping to mollify its critics and appear open to alternative perspectives, the World Bank modified and hastened the release of its second major comprehensive study on Africa for the decade.

World Bank President Barber Conable's opening statement in *From Crisis to Sustainable Growth* "strongly supports the call for a human-centred development strategy made by the ECA and UNICEF".[26]

A closer reading of the study confirms the World Bank's view that this human-centred development is only attainable through an even more comprehensive embracing of SAPs. The document is a further vivisection of African economies to uncover even deeper structural problems in need of remedy. In this instance the target has become the state itself.

This next stage of the World Bank's theology of crisis calls for more radical and comprehensive "solutions" than had been previously proposed. In some respects, the task at hand entails the radical overhaul of civil and political society as the only means of providing an adequate counterbalance to the control of the state. *From Crisis to Sustainable Growth* promotes NGOs "as an alternative conduit of development assistance as well as potential counterweights to government and basic constituents of an invigorated civil society".[27] This newly discovered problem provides a useful gloss for a sober assessment of the ability of SAPs to achieve their stated goals. Indeed, as SAPs continue not to work, the need to find ever deeper and more comprehensive problems with African countries intensifies.[28]

The scope of *From Crisis* is ambitious and comprehensive: "The time has come to take up this challenge and to put in place a development strategy for the next generation."[29] As in the preceding reports of the decade, *From Crisis* goes to great lengths to explain how Africa's problems cannot be traced to a hostile external environment, but are rooted in domestic failures. Terms of trade have actually improved since the 1960s. Africa is plagued by overpopulation, a steadily rising debt, and, as this report emphasizes, bad government. In short, "Africa is simply not competitive in an increasingly competitive world."[30]

From Crisis engages in an in-depth analysis of the political context of SAPs. While the message is often cloaked in language that appeals to grassroots participation and consensus-building the analysis constitutes a direct assault on the very legitimacy of the African state. At the same time the document engages in a sophisticated exercise of impugning the critics of SAPs either by delegitimizing or coopting them. Underlying this analysis is the attempt to deal with the populations, popular organizations etc. which were active in resisting the imposition of SAP policies.

The report also signals the next stage of the World Bank's

theology of SAPs in response to both its critics and lack of successes. Rather than question the basis for SAPs, the World Bank instead confesses that the problem lies in the fact that the World Bank did not realize that Africa's problems were so deeply rooted. SAPs, then, cannot succeed without the complete overhaul of the African economy and the African state itself. Africa must be transformed "from an expensive and difficult place to do business to an efficient one".[31] The analysis which claims that recalcitrant "vested interests" are blocking the path to true reform which would benefit the poor is restated in this document with renewed vigour. The root problem is a crisis of "governance", a failure in the "exercise of political power to manage the nation's affairs".[32] Corruption is rampant, officials remain unaccountable. The simple answer to this pervasive malaise is to roll back the state and to transform it into a promoter and not controller of private enterprise, including foreign private investors.[33]

The failure of the post-independence development experiment, according to the World Bank, lies squarely with the state's assuming the role of managing the economy and not allowing the private sector to take the initiative. This assessment echoes Deepak Lal's *Poverty of Development Economics* argument. *From Crisis* reiterates Lal's view that the post-independence development decades were a misguided neo-Keynesian quasi-socialist experiment where the state controlled every aspect of production to the point where it grew into an inefficient and corrupt behemoth that now needed to be dismantled in order for SAPs to work properly. SAPs have not failed, is the repeated message; they simply have not had a healthy environment in which to prosper:

> Alternative paths have been proposed. They give primacy to agricultural development and emphasize not only prices, markets, and private sector activities, but also capacity building, grassroots participation, decentralization, and sound environmental practices. So far such ideas have been accepted and tried only half-heartedly, if at all. The time has come to put them fully into practice.[34]

It is the state that has also largely been responsible for the suppression of local indigenous and popular initiatives, notes the report. *From Crisis* expresses support for grassroots initiatives:

The challenge is to build on this solid indigenous base, with a bottom-up approach that places a premium on listening to people and on genuinely empowering the intended benefici-aries of any development programme.[35]

In effect, what is sought is a "highly participatory approach... especially at the village level, in the decisions that directly affect [local peoples'] lives."[36] The report makes clear that this local empowerment is necessary to remove the barriers to the fuller implementation of SAPs. This curious assertion can only be understood in light of the neo-classical principle, elaborated by Lal above, that when provided with the opportunity all individuals are profit maximizers. Therefore, according to this logic, people at the grassroots must all want SAPs since they will provide them with the enabling environment to make a profit. Those who oppose SAPs must be profiting from the status quo, otherwise why would they be resisting? The problem, according to the World Bank, is that the enthusiasm and commitment for SAPs will be blocked at the local level unless the state is both rolled back and transforms itself to become the facilitator of private initiative at the local level.[37] Here reference is made again to the pervasive, "rent-seeking" behaviour of the state which hinders local initiatives.[38] It is important to understand this report's promotion of democratization and civil society, as well as more recent World Bank statements, as having little to do with political democratization and accountability. Its call for good governance is much more closely linked to its vision of unlocking the economic democracy of the market.[39]

In the area of rural development, the report argues for the complete removal of government involvement in the marketing and processing of agricultural products. The report claims that this would enable the potential for African entrepreneurship to be released.[40] This must be combined with greater security of land tenure, i.e., the privatization of land, which would encourage investment and land conservation.[41] The privatization of land, accompanied by the intro-duction of technological advances such as high yielding varieties (HYVs), fertilizers and pesticides, will enable Africa's farmers to increase production and improve their market share for the crops that it exports.

Donor Conditionality

In spite of the rhetoric around issues like popular participation and democracy, the report urges donors to take a hard line on conditionality:

> Those pursuing sound programmes should receive the external funding required; such external funding should fully reflect the adverse impact of world economic conditions and the debt burden on their import capacity. Countries with weak performance should receive much less assistance, limited where possible to programmes important to long-term development (such as research, health and education.)[42]

Such an assessment speaks more to the success of the World Bank from the mid-1980s onward in taking over the development agenda and tying development assistance to the acceptance of SAPs. The issue of donor conditionality from the mid-1980s onward is framed not in terms of punishing non-reformers but of not wasting valuable aid dollars.

The report concludes with the rather optimistic assessment that there is a universal consensus to this proposed agenda. Disagreements are few and the remaining problems are largely technical, in no way diminishing "the broad consensus on objectives, which is the starting point for working together".[43] This emerging consensus is considered to be occurring in three areas: 1) restructuring economies, 2) putting people first, and 3) fostering self-reliance. To convince donors that these principles do work the report holds up as a model the Nordic countries whose "success resulted from a social market economy with its combination of free-enterprise economic policies and active social policies".[44]

The report ignores the real opposition to SAPs both by groups in Africa and as expressed by a number of UN bodies. The World Bank claims to "reflect the evolution" of views embodied in the critical documents (no doubt a reference especially to the AAF-SAP). It claims to have achieved this by articulating the principles of "self-reliance" and respect for local African values. As far as opposition to SAPs in Africa is concerned, the report dismisses it as the work of "vested interests" clinging to rigid and outmoded "intellectual and ideological positions".[45]

Finally, the report calls for a new international compact for Africa for the 1990s. Claiming that this compact would take the UNPAAERD a step further, a global coalition for Africa would be established to create a forum for a wide range of interests to come together to agree on strategies for individual countries. This coalition is regarded as a new step forward for Africa and its partners.[46]

From Crisis does attempt to deal with the critics of SAPs. But in responding to these critics, the report invents a sector of African society to fit its theories. Contrary to the World Bank's view, it is not the so-called self-interested rent-seekers who have provided the most vocal opposition to SAPs. In fact, this group, often politicians or those tied to international capital, have managed to prosper in the era of SAPs, taking personal advantage of the privatization campaigns that have been associated with SAPs. *From Crisis* completely ignores the opposition to SAPs coming from the sectors that have been most affected: the poor, wage-earners, women, food producers, trade unions, nationalists, students, churches, NGOs and opposition parties. In some countries like Nigeria, opposition and protests to SAPs have been banned. Yet the World Bank argues that is the nationalists who are the torchbearers of a foreign ideology representative of foreign interests who are wrongly holding out a vision of modernization through state-controlled socialism. This vision, the Bank concludes, has demonstrably failed and SAPs provide the only alternative.[47]

According to *From Crisis*, SAPs incorporate programmes that will help the poor, through higher prices for their produce and through poverty alleviation programmes. The World Bank claims that those who will experience a drop in their standard of living are "the top 5 percent belonging to the formal modern sector and the recipients of 'rents'". The report confidently asserts that SAPs will benefit the poor by means of a redistribution of the unjustified subsidy which the rich now receive.[48]

The problems associated with SAPs, while recognized, never prompt World Bank analysts to question their basic assumptions. Past difficulties can be corrected by refining the process of design and implementation of SAPs. These refinements include taking into account proper sequencing, longer time horizons, and sector-by-sector approaches.

Consolidating the Agenda

The theme of poverty vanished almost entirely from the World Bank's pronouncements in the 1980s as the need for "adjustment" took centre stage. The growing criticism concerning the social and human costs of SAPs put forward by agencies like UNICEF were largely ignored by the World Bank when they first surfaced in the mid-1980s. One searches in vain for any considered analysis of the relationship between SAPs and poverty in World Bank documents throughout this period. In fact, little attention is accorded to the theme of poverty at all.

By the late 1980s, in part due to the success of UNICEF's *Adjustment with a Human Face* studies and campaign, and in light of the failure of adjustment in the area of poverty alleviation, the World Bank turned its attention again to the theme of poverty. In fact, many of the World Bank's proponents of development and poverty alleviation from the 1970s were called upon to renew the bank's focus in this area. However, while the World Bank's rediscovery of the language of poverty alleviation harkens back to the 1970s, the agenda behind this rhetoric had altered significantly.

Poverty Alleviation through Adjustment

It is false to suppose, as many critics of the institutions do, that adjustment is necessarily at the expense of the weakest.[49]

The World Bank's poverty agenda of the 1970s corresponded with the modernization development model. Poverty was defined especially with reference to the continuing preponderance of allegedly backward rural subsistence agriculture, and its alleviation required a crash programme of modernization through inputs such as larger farms, HYV seeds, fertilizers, increased production for exports and greater incomes which could finance investment and industry. The definition of poverty corresponded to income levels and its eradication with the raising of these income levels. In effect, "poverty alleviation and modernization represented simultaneous moments of a single movement".[50]

The message contained in recent World Bank pronouncements is that poverty alleviation is contingent upon adjustment and growth.

Economic growth can only come by way of furthering market reforms. In other words, the greater the extent of market liberalization and deregulation, the better the prospects are for the poor.[51] Hence, adjustment must be deepened to provide incentives for the poor to increase their production. These could be achieved through, for example, higher interest rates to attract investment, the privatization of land to act as collateral for borrowing, the elimination of marketing boards. On closer examination, this policy prescription merely echoes that of the Berg Report: a reaffirmation that adjustment helps the poor by providing them with better prices and allowing them to cast off the scourge of their exploitative "rent-seeking" urban counterparts.

Another important element in this approach to poverty is its advocacy of the need to re-allocate spending *within* the social sector. Contained in this policy advice is the recognition that SAPs do impose additional burdens on the poor which can be alleviated through Special Programmes of Assistance provided by the World Bank. These include programmes in retraining for laid-off workers, rural credit schemes, and a variety of other types of assistance.[52] Internally this involves transferring expenditures from universities to primary schools and from urban hospitals to rural health clinics to help cushion the blow of adjustment. Hence, user fees could be charged to those who could afford them while those truly in need would receive subsidies.

The final important piece of the World Bank's poverty alleviation re-orientation is its call for a systematic programme of social and economic research to be carried out to monitor the effects of adjustment on the poor (particularly those described as most vulnerable). Also suggested is the development of social-impact information systems to measure the impact of economic policies on the poorest sectors and technical models that would allow for the fine tuning of adjustment programmes to target these sectors. This approach to poverty alleviation is summarized by Elaine Zuckerman: "... there is considerable scope for policies and programmes which benefit the poor without undermining adjustment."[53]

The 1990 World Bank publication, *Making Adjustment Work for the Poor in Africa*, draws together a number of these conceptual threads to establish a comprehensive programme of research which examines the effects of adjustment programmes at the household level. In addition to this, the World Bank proposes a number of policy instruments within an adjustment regime for alleviating the burden on the poorest sectors:

> The *key policy problem* is how to assist target groups without at the same time causing distortions in economic mechanisms. If the latter are severe, neither economic recovery nor the poor will be helped.[54]

Yet, in the chapters that deal specifically with what are referred to as "poverty-sensitive adjustment programmes",[55] what is underlined are precisely the same macro-economic policy instruments (trade liberalization, removal of subsidies, instituting market-oriented reforms, demand constraint) which are the cornerstones of SAPs. A simple fine-tuning of these mechanisms to assist the poor is suggested. One of the recommendations is particularly striking in its simplistic understanding of poverty: "...the poor can sometimes reduce the value of their consumption without adverse nutritional effects by switching from superior foods to inferior foods that are less costly (but as nutritious)."[56] Other suggestions include ensuring that social sector spending which directly benefits the poor be exempted from cuts,[57] greater credit availability for the poor[58] and laid-off workers,[59] staging and better coordination of trade liberalization,[60] public works and re-training programmes.[61] All of these confirm a vision of poverty alleviation as a side effect or an externality that can be overcome either by fine-tuning SAPs or by providing special welfare-type programmes for the poor.[62]

The World Bank consolidated its renewed interest in poverty by focusing its 1990 *World Development Report* on that theme. In doing so it bestowed upon itself premier status as the leader in concern for poverty as well as in mobilizing support for its programme of poverty alleviation. It also served to "signal" to the donor community a change of heart and of policy around the harsh consequences of its adjustment agenda. In light of this, the adjustment paradigm remains inviolable; what has been added to this regime is a recognition that recovery through adjustment is a longer term process which in the short term requires special measures to assist the poor.

The 1990 *World Development Report*'s strategy to reduce poverty is premised on two principles. The first is "to promote the productive use of the poor's most abundant asset – labour". This can be achieved through policies that harness "market incentives" along with technological and infrastructural improvements.[63] The second is to focus on the provision of basic social services upon which the poor rely. These two elements, the report is quick to point out, are perfectly consistent with the longer term process of adjustment. These measures seek the protection of the poor in the short term.[64] While the developed world moves to more capital intensive production in the process of becoming more efficient and productive, the advice to the poorer countries is exactly the opposite:

> Switching to an efficient, labour intensive pattern of development and investing more in the human capital of the poor are not only consistent with faster long-term growth; they contribute to it.[65]

Poorer countries are urged to become more productive by lowering even further their cost of labour and to use this as a source of comparative advantage for competing with the developed world. In short, while there is a nod in the direction of considering ways to buffer the suffering of the poor while countries adjust, the report makes clear that the turnaround for the poor cannot be achieved through "narrowly focused anti-poverty projects, vital though these may be. It is a task for economic policy at large".[66]

According to the 1990 *World Development Report*, sub-Saharan Africa faces an especially long and difficult road to the promised land of recovery because of the combination of its reluctance to adopt reforms in the 1980s compounded by its internal problems of poor infrastructure, an over-reliance on primary commodities, and weak entrepreneurial and managerial capacity.[67]

In 1991 the World Bank released another policy paper on poverty alleviation during its annual meetings which heralded its new president, Lewis Preston. The document, *Assistance Strategies to Reduce Poverty*, essentially repeats the prescriptions contained in the 1990 *World Development Report*. It also reaffirms a new twist on donor conditionality: not only should donors tie their aid to the pursuit of sound economic policies (i.e. SAPs), they should also ensure that their aid and lending should be linked to a country's effort to reduce poverty.[68]

There are a number of reasons why the World Bank treats the issue of poverty differently than it did in the 1970s. Foremost among these is the declining interest and relative power of the Third World in geo-political as well as economic and resource terms. Studies which pointed to the negative impact of SAPs on the poor were being put forward by UNICEF as early as 1983. For several years in the mid-eighties these voices were virtually ignored.

Finally, of relevance is the fact that the entire issue of debt relief became rapidly framed within the context of the adjustment process with very little intellectual or other opposition to it, without questions of social reform or of the responsibility of the Northern banks coming under discussion or scrutiny. This major theoretical shortcoming has allowed the issue of poverty alleviation in the bank's recent pronouncements to be posed in isolation from the issue of structural adjustment. As Zuckerman admits,

> For the most part, little attempt has been made to identify the possible adverse effects on the poor of specific policy reforms supported by adjustment programmes and to redesign the adjustment programmes in order to lessen such impacts.[69]

At best, recent initiatives focusing on poverty, such as Ghana's Programme of Action to Alleviate the Social Costs of Adjustment (PAMSCAD), are geared only towards compensating those who might be severely affected by a SAP.[70]

The World Bank has recently moved to acknowledge the need to protect the poor against the adverse effects of adjustment. But as Frances Stewart notes, "it has not accepted that there is a need to redesign macro-policies in the light of the objective of reducing poverty".[71] The prevailing attitude in the World Bank's major documents continues to be that SAPs have helped farmers in Africa through improved prices. In its 1991 *World Development Report*, a special section promotes the idea that most farmers are better off under SAPs, not through hard data and statistical analysis but through "storytelling". The following passage provides an interesting illustration:

Regina Ofo is a farmer in Bendel State in Nigeria. For her, the structural adjustment programme of 1986, which included measures to increase farm prices, has meant something concrete: she is better off. Because she earns more from farming, she can afford to buy new clothes for herself and her two daughters, and she was even able to prepare a Christmas feast for the less fortunate in her village.[72]

These stories are followed by the admission that not all farmers are benefiting from SAPs. However, these are only short-run losers. In any event, "[a]djustment measures that favour agriculture will gradually pull up the whole rural economy".[73] As a solace to the worse off, the bank notes that "[e]ven the losers might soon have been worse off without the reforms...".[74]

At the level of policy, the response of the World Bank to the criticism of SAPs' immiserating effects is that the ultimate responsibility for the hardships experienced during adjustment does not lie with the SAPs; the critics are confusing cause and effect. In the words of Edward Jaycox, the World Bank's vice-president for Africa:

> The social dimensions are very difficult because clearly when the programmes – subsidies to food consumers or to university students – become unaffordable and governments have to print money or borrow money they can't afford to pay back in order to sustain them, then they are not sustainable. They are either going to go gradually or right away. Structural adjustment is really nothing but to try and make a soft landing when these conditions occur and to change the system fundamentally so it doesn't recur. That is very important to understand. The fact that food subsidies are no longer affordable in Zambia, for instance, is not the fault of structural adjustment, but of non-adjustment over a very long time and the fact that they ran out of money. We have confused the malady with the remedy and the causality of the pain.[75]

By maintaining its insistence on structural adjustment and increasing its profile on poverty alleviation, the World Bank succeeded in muting the mounting criticism that was being levelled against it. The resurgence of concern for poverty alleviation also served the interests of donor countries in maintaining their adjustment posture, due to their creditor status, within the context of their aid programmes. Understanding this connection more clearly would entail a closer examination of how national aid agencies are connected both departmentally as well as ideologically to their ministries of finance. The other reason for this neglect also lies in the lack of interest in the debtor countries in addressing poverty issues seriously. The inability to wrestle seriously with the issue of poverty can be attributed to the fact that in the 1990s "the laissez-faire market paradigm retains such intellectual dominance that no alternative views can gain real ground".[76]

The Global Coalition for Africa

In September of 1991, the United Nations convened another Special Session on Africa to assess the UNPAAERD. The programme had been launched with great optimism and the genuine hope that with donor support the crisis could be turned around. I was fortunate enough to be invited to attend the review session as an NGO delegate representing the Inter-Church Coalition on Africa under the sponsorship of the United Church of Canada and Partnership Africa Canada.

I will highlight the views presented at the session from a variety of perspectives and then conclude the chapter with my own observations. During the process, what began as a serious attempt to identify the various factors contributing to the crisis in Africa gradually deteriorated into an agreement full of meaningless platitudes.

A serious and comprehensive overview of the UNPAAERD was undertaken by the ECA. Its submission points to the various reasons for the failure of the programme. These include an unfavourable trade environment for Africa's commodities, the lack of serious reform on the debt issue and stagnating levels of development assistance.

In their review of UNPAAERD, African ministers expressed their sense of frustration and betrayal by the international community. In spite of the fact that most African countries adopted far-reaching economic reforms along the lines recommended by the World Bank and the IMF, the international community failed to respond in kind. Financial flows to Africa dropped dramatically in the 1986-90 period. Net financial transfers to Africa fell sharply from $13 billion in 1986 to $8.7 billion in 1989. Development assistance was stagnant, while investment in the region virtually disappeared. The debt of African countries had soared from $204 billion to $272 billion between 1986 and 1990. In 1990, African countries owed a staggering 46 per cent of their export earnings on debt servicing alone. Over $30 billion was whisked out of the continent as flight capital. Debt-relief measures only had a minuscule effect, making no dent whatsoever in the growing stock of debt and in many cases only delaying its payment for some future day of reckoning. As the final report of the African ministers notes: "These results can only lead us to conclude that our own efforts and sacrifices have not been matched by an equal effort on the part of our partners and that their response to UNPAAERD has disappointingly not been in line with their commitments in UNPAAERD."[77] In addition, the ECA acknowledged the contribution to the debt problem of domestic corruption and mismanagement.

The ECA unequivocally condemned SAPs as the major reason behind the failure of UNPAAERD: "...some of SAPs' instruments – such as repeated devaluation, across the board liberalization of the economy and high nominal interest rates – have actually undermined long-term growth prospects by fuelling inflation, discouraging domestic production and diverting savings to speculative activities."[78]

The first stage in the gradual watering down process of the UNPAAERD review came with the Report of the Secretary General. According to a number of sources, the World Bank had demanded a number of changes in the original draft. When it appeared, the report, while noting the severity of the crisis and the need for a massive outpouring of assistance, had practically expunged the vocabulary of structural adjustment from its assessment of the crisis. No mention is made about the impact of World Bank policies in the region.

The first week of the End-Term Review consisted of submissions from countries, UN agencies and NGOs. Three of these bear mentioning here: the IMF, the World Bank and the NGO submission.

The IMF submission by its director, Michael Camdessus, emphasized sound fiscal policy and the need to implement adjustment efforts. This came as no surprise. What was particularly striking, however, was Camdessus' tone of compassion and concern. He closed his remarks by assuring the international community that the IMF operates with the principle of "solidarity with the poorest".

The submission of the World Bank was delivered by Edward Jaycox, vice-president for the Africa region. Jaycox did not see any reason to co-opt the language of solidarity in his speech. The last five years were not a failure in Africa. Countries which had had the "courage" to adopt adjustment programmes and implement them fully were succeeding. SAPs were not the cause of Africa's downturn, they were the remedy. Plummeting commodity prices were not to blame – it was Africa's "lack of competitiveness" that was the problem.

Looking up from his text Jaycox stopped to address the African delegates like an admonishing parent addressing a group of disobedient children. "Africa needs to get competitive again." The speech of the World Bank was echoed by the submissions of the European Community, the US and Canada.

The delegation of NGOs brought together representatives from a variety of development agencies and church organizations from Africa, North America, Europe and Australia. As our own submission was discussed a consensus emerged: we should deliver our message clearly and prophetically, condemning SAPs and pointing to the intense suffering and death that these policies produce. We decided that at least one submission would challenge the IMF and World Bank and their SAP policies.

The NGO submission, delivered by Mr. Charles Karemano of Rwanda, referred to the "overwhelmingly negative role that World Bank and IMF policies have played during the UNPAAERD period". It went on to say: "The macroeconomic policies imposed upon the people of Africa have resulted in economic stagnation, increasing poverty and death. One cannot have 'solidarity with the poor' while denying them their livelihood."[79]

The NGO submission concluded by putting forward a set of concrete proposals which would provide the basis for recovery and development based on human-centred criteria and popular participation. These included the need for measures to cancel Africa's outstanding debt, the need to pursue economic diversification, and to find an end to war and conflict.

When Mr. Karemano completed his speech many of the African delegates rushed to congratulate him. Many of them thanked him for having the courage to say what they could not.

The third stage of the watering down process occurred with the proposed programme of action for the 1990s by the Organization for African Unity. Having heard the opening salvos of the IMF, World Bank and the other donor countries, the proposals were modest, calling for debt relief and increased levels of assistance.

During the negotiations around the final document it was the World Bank, along with the US and European Community, which ensured that no concrete commitments to assisting the region were made. Even in its severely watered down form, the US refused to sign the final document until even deeper concessions were made in the language of the document. The changes that were demanded by the donor countries, led by the US, on the issue of debt relief are most illustrative. The original proposal of the secretary general called for a cancellation of all official bilateral debt to the poorest and most heavily indebted African countries. It also proposed a reduction of private debt, as well as a reduction of World Bank and IMF debt. By the end of the Special Session's two week process this section of the New Agenda had been altered to suggest an option for the reduction of bilateral debt and only "serious consideration" for the reduction of multilateral debt. This wording was still unacceptable to the US. After three months of protracted wrangling, the final text eliminates any reference to the reduction of multilateral debt but instead refers to the need for a "growth-oriented solution of the problems of African developing countries with serious debt-servicing problems...." As Mr. Marks, the US representative noted, "it was important to avoid any action that might undermine the credit-ratings of the multilateral institutions".[80] This intransigence on the part of the donor community clearly reflects how anathema even a discussion of multilateral debt relief is to the World Bank and the G-7 countries.

The World Bank has succeeded in continuing to distance itself from serious accountability to the UN. The Global Coalition for Africa (GCA), a forum which the World Bank largely finances, is now the key forum for policy debates about Africa's development. Much like the Global Environmental Fund which the World Bank took control of after the 1992 UN Earth Summit, the GCA clearly demonstrates the extent to which the World Bank "owns" the agenda for Africa's development in the 1990s.

Proving Adjustment Works

In March, 1994 the World Bank released the latest of its reports on Africa, *Adjustment in Africa: Reforms, Results and the Road Ahead*, claiming still that African countries which were disciplined and adopted SAPs were faring far better than those which had strayed from the course.[81] There is nothing really new in this comprehensive review of how African countries have fared under structural adjustment. The World Bank has hauled out all of the same clichés about Africa that it has used for over the past decade in explaining Africa's economic crisis.

The tactic seems to have worked for now. After coming under increasing criticism both from within its own ranks on the failure of World Bank policies in Africa and from UN agencies like UNICEF, the UNDP and the United Nations Conference on Trade and Development (UNCTAD), *Adjustment in Africa* serves as a public relations ploy to justify the adjustment agenda. For the most part, the mainstream media accepted at face value the glossy prescriptions without wondering at all about the vested interests the World Bank might have in presenting the data to suit its own ends.

The message contained in the report was very straightforward, amounting to a re-assertion of the neo-liberal credo of structural adjustment: "In the African countries that have undertaken and sustained major policy reforms, adjustment is working."[82] Those African countries that vigorously adopted SAPs performed better than those that were less committed to undertaking the reforms. The bank warns, however, that while showing some promise, all African countries still have a long way to go.

By releasing the report at a critical juncture just before the celebration of its 50th anniversary, the bank effectively served notice of a public relations counter-offensive. *Adjustment in Africa* has come at a time when NGOs have succeeded in spotlighting the many shortcomings of World Bank policies. Africa represents the vulnerable underbelly of the bank's SAP agenda. Its own much less publicized studies have all but admitted to the failures of these policies. Yet, during the 50 years celebrations the World Bank was desperate to head off these criticisms.

In spite of what appears to be a very detailed and comprehensive analysis of SAP policies in Africa over the past decade, even a cursory read through reveals some of the report's more blatant manipulations which amount to statistical fraud. A thorough critique would require months of analysis and review of data from the countries case studies. There is no agency, within the UN or outside, with the capacity or courage to undertake such a comprehensive critique. For the time being, the World Bank has won the latest round in the public relations battle to maintain the credibility of its much-beleagured SAP agenda for Africa.

Conclusion

This chapter has provided an exposition of the World Bank's development vision for sub-Saharan Africa during the 1980s. For the bank, Africa's economic crisis could only be solved through the adoption of a comprehensive programme of economic reforms. We have noted the analytical framework adopted by the World Bank in assessing the nature of the continent's crisis and how that crisis can only be addressed through Africa's further integration into the global economy and on the basis of the trading advantages it enjoys. Finally, a number of developments in the late 1980s have induced the World Bank to adapt the SAP agenda to a number of concerns. The issue of poverty alleviation is examined in this chapter; chapters seven and ten consider the World Bank's latest attempts to integrate a concern for the environment and the role of women in development into the SAP agenda.

The chapters that follow provide an overview of the challenges to the World Bank's SAP agenda from a variety of perspectives. Our next chapter examines the trade orientation which forms the basis of the SAP thesis. We examine the key assumptions about trade that are implied in the SAP approach and the challenges that have been directed at the World Bank's export-oriented model for sub-Saharan Africa.

Endnotes

1. World Bank, *Toward Sustained Development in Sub-Saharan Africa*, (Washington D.C.: World Bank, 1984), p. 2.
2. *Toward Sustained Development*, p. 1.
3. *Toward Sustained Development*, p. 5.
4. *Toward Sustained Development*, p. 4.
5. *Toward Sustained Development*, p. 43.
6. See H. G. Petersmann, *Financial Assistance to Developing Countries: The Changing Role of the World Bank and International Monetary Fund*, (Bonn: Europa Union Verlag GmbH, 1988), p. 44.
7. *Toward Sustained Development*, p. 7.
8. *Toward Sustained Development*, p. 13.
9. *Toward Sustained Development*, p. 24.
10. *Toward Sustained Development*, p. 14.
11. A. O. Krueger, "The Political Economy of the Rent-Seeking Society," *American Economic Review* 64 (1974), pp. 291-301; also "Import Substitution Versus Export Promotion, *Finance and Development* 22 (June 1985), pp. 20-21. As Toye *et al.* note, the original statement of Krueger's rent-seeking thesis in the early 1970s was an attempt to demonstrate that there are added hidden costs to protectionist trading policies. These costs were identified as the added resources which were necessary for economic agents to compete for scarce resource licences. What is conveniently overlooked in this re-application of the thesis to African economies is the fact that in a context where import licences are awarded *without* competition to favourites, cronies etc., the consequences for the rent-seeking theory is precisely the opposite, i.e., there is less time wasted standing in line, filling out forms etc.. Toye *et al.*, *Aid and Power*, p. 18. Mark Gallagher, provides a more recent elaboration of the theory of rent-seeking wedded to neo-classical economic theories: "The neo-classical models assume that rational behaviour causes economic agents to choose between the most productive activities I posit that, instead, economic agents choose between those activities yielding the highest private returns and that these are not always productive activities." M. Gallagher, *Rent-Seeking and Economic Growth in Africa*, (Boulder: Westview Press, 1991), p. 53.
12. D. Lal, "The Misconceptions of Development Economics," *Finance and Review* (June 1985), pp. 10-13; also *The Poverty of Development Economics*, (Cambridge: Harvard University Press, 1985).
13. World Bank and United Nations Development Programme, *Africa's Adjustment and Growth in the 1980s*, (Washington: The World Bank and UNDP, 1989), p. iii.
14. *Africa's Adjustment*, p. iii.
15. *Africa's Adjustment*, p. 2.

16. *Africa's Adjustment*, pp. 2, 10.
17. *Africa's Adjustment*, p. 21.
18. *Africa's Adjustment*, p. 21.
19. *Africa's Adjustment*, p. 23. This suggests a rather curious application of the fallacy of composition argument, and does not take into account at all the effect that food aid and grain dumping by the North had on food prices over this period.
20. *Africa's Adjustment*, p. 28.
21. *Africa's Adjustment*, p. 31. The appropriateness of this kind of methodology has been challenged by a number of writers. As Frances Stewart notes: "From the point of view of the effects on human conditions, the counterfactual methodology is inappropriate, since it is not the performance compared with some postulated counterfactual, but actual developments which are significant. Macro-policies will only be satisfactory when they lead to sustained growth and rising levels of investment. This they have failed to do in many countries, especially in sub-Saharan Africa and Latin America." F. Stewart, "The Many Faces of Adjustment II", (unpublished, 1991), p. 6.
22. United Nations Economic Commission for Africa, "ECA Preliminary Observations on the World Bank Report: *Africa's Adjustment and Growth in the 1980s*," p. i.
23. United Nations Economic Commission for Africa, *African Alternative Framework to Structural Adjustment Programmes for Socio-Economic Recovery and Transformation*, (Addis Ababa: UNECA, 1989) p. i.
24. *African Alternative Framework*, p. 16.
25. *African Alternative Framework*, p. 25.
26. *From Crisis to Sustainable Growth*, p. xii.
27. P. Gibbon, "Political Economy," p. 25.
28. *From Crisis*, like the Berg Report, also seems to draw heavily on the ideas of Robert Bates. In a paper delivered to a conference co-sponsored by the World Bank and the University of California in Los Angeles (UCLA), Bates argues the importance of imposing stringent conditionality to persuade African leaders to adopt market-based policies. The task at hand is daunting, because it entails a radical conversion of African governments and of their constituencies of support: "Governments in Africa may have learned from their past mistakes. But the changes in their policy preferences may not result in changes in their policy choices. The situation within which they seek to retain power requires that to secure change they must alter basic beliefs and values, enlighten other major groups as to where their interests lie, and orchestrate reciprocal adjustments among them. Economic reconstruction poses daunting challenges to political leaders, and we can deservedly be sceptical of the prospects of success." This advice is followed up by Bates' suggestion that African policy makers are in need of basic training in economics: "Another appropriate investment would be in economic literacy. Many top policy makers in Africa fail to grasp even the rudiments of economic reasoning." R. Bates, "The Political Basis for Agricultural Policy

Reform," in S. K. Commins, ed., *Africa's Development Challenges and the World Bank*, pp. 125, 129.

29. *From Crisis*, p. 4.
30. *From Crisis*, p. 3.
31. *From Crisis*, p. 1.
32. *From Crisis*, p. 60
33. *From Crisis*, pp. 4-5, 55.
34. *From Crisis*, p. 37.
35. *From Crisis*, p. 191.
36. *From Crisis*, p. 60.
37. *From Crisis*, p. 62.
38. *From Crisis*, p. 61.
39. H. Bernstein, "Agricultural 'Modernization'," p. 21. Bjorn Beckmann argues that *From Crisis* and indeed the entire SAP agenda of the World Bank is profoundly undemocratic and a highly disruptive intervention into the politics of accommodation: "Foreign intervention tends to reinforce the impasse by propping up and shielding regimes from local political pressures. While succeeding temporarily in shifting the balance of forces in favour of ruling coalitions, such interventions simultaneously undermine the process of accommodation that may be required for more lasting solutions. The World Bank report is part of this intervention, obstructing a social contract. Its own contribution is the effort to de-recognize, de-legitimate the forces opposing SAP. It is unhelpful to the process of state formation as to that of democratization." B. Beckmann, "Empowerment or Repression? The World Bank and the Politics of African Adjustment," (paper to a Symposium on the Social and Political Context of Structural Adjustment in Sub-Saharan Africa, 17-19 October, 1990), p. 25.
40. *From Crisis*, p. 91.
41. *From Crisis*, p. 104.
42. *From Crisis*, p. 183.
43. *From Crisis*, p. 185.
44. *From Crisis*, p. 187.
45. *From Crisis*, pp. 192-3. Most reviews of *From Crisis* including those by traditional World bank critics subscribe to the World Bank's "consensus" building approach. One of the few who challenge the deception of this approach is Bjorn Beckmann who notes: "The picture of a consensus, where disagreements are minor and technical, and where the real challenges lie 'beyond', is a confidence trick. It conceals the ideological role of the report in enforcing SAP in the face of intellectual and popular resistance.

The political crisis of the African state is also the crisis of SAP. This explains why the World Bank sees itself obliged to enter the deep waters of political theory. The poor capacity of the African state to handle resistance to SAP casts serious doubts on the political feasibility of the reforms. The Bank seeks to boost this capacity, not by addressing the objections of the opposition, but by seeking to undercut its political and ideological legitimacy. Simultaneously, it seeks to construct new forms of popular legitimation under the banner of 'empowerment'." Beckmann, "Empowerment or Repression", p. 9.

46. *From Crisis*, p. 194.
47. *From Crisis*, p. 37.
48. *From Crisis*, p. 46.
49. Clive Crook, "The IMF and World Bank," *The Economist* (12 Oct. 1991), p. 38.
50. Gibbon, "Political Economy," p. 29.
51. Gibbon, "Political Economy," p. 29.
52. Stewart, "The Many Faces of Adjustment II."
53. E. Zuckerman, "Adjustment Programs and Social Welfare," (World Bank Discussion Paper No. 44, 1989), p. 14.
54. World Bank, *Making Adjustment Work for the Poor in Africa*, (Washington, World Bank, 1990), p. 3.
55. *Making Adjustment*, p. 93.
56. *Making Adjustment*, p. 96.
57. *Making Adjustment*, p. 99.
58. *Making Adjustment*, pp. 100-1.
59. *Making Adjustment*, p. 102.
60. *Making Adjustment*, pp. 106-7.
61. *Making Adjustment*, pp. 118-9.
62. Michel Chossudovsky provides an insightful critique of the World Bank's poverty alleviation programmes in the following: "The social consequences of structural adjustment are fully acknowledged by the international financial institutions. The ideology of the IMF and World Bank points, however, to the 'social sectors' and 'social cost' of SAP as something 'separate', i.e. according to the dominant economic dogma, these 'undesired side effects' particularly in the areas of health, child nutrition and education stem from the inner logic of the economic stabilization measures. The social consequences are an integral part of the economic policy model, of the IMF's hidden agenda." M. Chossudovsky, "The Global Creation of Third World Poverty," *Third World Resurgence*, 17, 1992, p. 18.
63. *World Development Report 1990*, p. 3.
64. *World Development Report 1990*, p. 3.
65. *World Development Report 1990*, p. 3.
66. *World Development Report 1990*, p. 4.
67. *World Development Report 1990*, p. 12.
68. World Bank, *Assistance Strategies to Reduce Poverty*, (Washington D.C.: World Bank, 1991), p. 20.
69. Zuckerman, "Adjustment Programs and Social Welfare", p. 5.
70. Fraces Stewart argues that, "these measures may be important for the political implementability of the programmes, but are trivial as a device to protect the poor during adjustment". F. Stewart, "The Many Faces of Adjustment II," p. 47.

71. Stewart, "Many Faces II," p. 59.
72. *World Development Report* 1990, p. 113.
73. *World Development Report* 1990, p. 113.
74. *World Development Report* 1990, p. 113.
75. Margaret A. Novicki, "Interview with Edward V.K.Jaycox: A New Scenario for Africa," *Africa Report* 34/6 (November-December 1989), p. 20.
76. Stewart, "Many Faces II," p. 61.
77. UN Secretary General, *Tackling Africa's Economic Crisis*, (New York: United Nations, 1991), p. 11.
78. UN Economic Commission for Africa, "Critical Economic Situation in Africa", (Addis Ababa: UNECA, 1991), p. 6.
79. "Beyond UNPAAERD: From Talk to Action," (NGO position paper for the final review of UNPAAERD, Sept. 1991).
80. *Africa Recovery*, Dec. 1991, p. 21.
81. World Bank, *Adjustment in Africa: Reforms, Results and the Road Ahead*, (Washington: World Bank, 1994).
82. *Adjustment in Africa*, p. 1.

—— CHAPTER SIX ——

Export-Oriented Growth, International Trade and Structural Adjustment

Introduction

> ...trade should be seen as a tool of sustainable development, not an end in itself. Trade **may** bring gains, but trade does **not necessarily** bring gains. Trade may bring an increase in growth and with it an increase in financial resources which may be used for environmental protection and the reduction of pollution. But neither of these effects follows automatically.... Trade can be environmentally benign, or it can be an engine of environmental destruction and resource depletion. Since it cannot be assumed that trade is automatically good, it follows that neither is more trade necessarily better. Nor does it follow that less trade is necessarily bad.[1]

Trade is one of the cornerstones of development. It is by trading with other nations that a country can develop its own enterprises and foster economic growth. For most countries, trade also brings in supplies of raw materials or manufactured goods necessary to carry out their production processes. Because these imported items must be paid for, whether in an internationally accepted currency, or through barter, a country which has imports must also have exports. A country seeks to export as much or more than it imports. If a country imports more than it exports than it must borrow in order to cover the difference. The only way a country can repay this debt is by running a trade surplus; that is, by exporting more than it imports.

In the simplest terms, the fundamental principles of trade amongst nations are captured in the above paragraph. In the real world however, the issues are complicated by the fact that trade occurs between countries with different resource endowments, levels of military and economic power, and control over mechanisms of international trade.

Increasingly, global trade occurs within a single transnational corporation across a number of countries. Also, countries needing to borrow to cover an excess of imports over exports do so not only from the country whose products they are purchasing, but from a variety of other sources, such as private banks, export-import banks and multilateral institutions like the World Bank. It is not the quantity of exports or imports that is important but the *value* that is assigned to these goods. This value is in theory determined by global market forces.

In spite of the variety of complicating factors such as the involvement of transnationals and commercial banks in the arena of trade, it nonetheless remains a development imperative for countries to register a surplus of exports over imports. However, a country can only maintain an export surplus over long periods of time by lending. Conversely, a country can only maintain a lengthy import surplus by borrowing. Implicit in this borrowing is the recognition that the debt incurred must be paid for at some point by means of an increase in exports.

This chapter is devoted to an examination of the export-oriented policies promoted by the World Bank for sub-Saharan Africa in the 1980s. Such an examination opens onto a set of related issues which will also be considered. These include an overview of the development literature on issues of trade and an assessment of the appropriateness of export-oriented strategies not only for sub-Saharan Africa but for developing countries in general.

The thesis of this chapter is that the World Bank's policy advice to sub-Saharan African countries to increase its commodity exports was geared to serving the interests of Northern creditors and TNCs. The cumulative effects of the promotion of this kind of trade strategy for the region are examined in terms of their impact on poverty, food security, women, land tenure, and the environment. The promotion of export-oriented policies across the board in all developing countries is considered in terms of the effect on supply and prices in the global market. Finally, the impact of export-oriented polices on the servicing of debt is examined. In this context we will consider the case of Ghana's experience with a structural adjustment programme based on export-oriented growth. Finally, we provide a brief overview of the prospects for sub-Saharan Africa under the recently concluded round of negotiations around the General Agreement on Tariffs and Trade

(GATT) and the role of the World Bank in the process.

Throughout the chapter, special attention is paid to the World Bank's analysis of the nature of sub-Saharan Africa's structural crisis and the trade strategy it offers to the region as the panacea for these ills. It is an analysis based on a series of hypothetical assumptions in a theoretical world of perfect competition and free trade. It is an ideology which has little historical or factual connection to the real sources of Africa's problems. As a result, the solutions offered have only served to exacerbate Africa's difficulties. This chapter accumulates some of the empirical evidence demonstrating the effect that these policies have had on sub-Saharan Africa over the past decade.

Comparative Advantage: The Organizing Principle of International Trade

Comparative advantage... has acquired a powerful ideological role and has been used to rationalise almost any type of international division of labour. Politicians, journalists and other professionals use the term with universal and accepted ease, without ever questioning what it really means. Theories of free trade based on comparative advantage have never evaluated the nature of specialization – who developed, who controlled and who used the productive knowhow.[2]

The key indicator of a country's economic strength is its ability to trade successfully within the global economy. According to neo-classical trade theory, the gains from trade will outweigh the losses if countries base their production and trade on the law of comparative advantage. The law of comparative advantage encourages countries to produce and trade those goods which they can produce most efficiently and cheaply. Canada, for instance, would be considered to enjoy a comparative advantage in areas such as wheat production, forestry products and mining. The comparative advantage of developing countries are considered to lie in the areas of commodities, chiefly metals and minerals, petroleum, and agricultural products, or in manufactured products which require a great deal of unskilled or semi-skilled labour.

Outward vs. Inward-Oriented Development

Since World War II the debate on the issues of trade and development has centred on two opposing strategies. The first is the outward-oriented strategy, where national production is largely geared toward export for the global economy, while the second is the inward-oriented or import-substitution strategy, where a country concentrates on producing goods primarily for the domestic market. For developing countries, the outward-oriented strategy is favoured by development agencies like the World Bank because this kind of export-oriented strategy will bring in valuable foreign exchange which, in turn, can be used to finance the development process. The prerequisite for the success of the outward-oriented strategy is an open international trading system with few tariff barriers. The inward-oriented strategy focuses on reducing foreign exchange spending by attempting to produce previously imported goods. One of the necessary policy prescriptions for the implementation of this strategy is the erection of tariffs and the provision of subsidies to fledgling industries.

The 1980s have witnessed the ascendancy of the export-driven model built on the assumptions of free trade and comparative advantage as the preferred path of development. It is a strategy that has been vigorously promoted and imposed throughout the Third World as one of the key elements of structural adjustment. Perhaps more significantly, Southern economies were also forced to open up their markets to foreign goods, investment and competition as part of their structural adjustment programmes. While liberalization did occur in certain sectors in Northern economies, these economies continued to discriminate against developing country exports by maintaining high tariffs and quotas on imports.

This chapter examines the performance of one African country: Ghana. Ghana's economic "recovery" in the mid-1980s has been hailed by the World Bank as the success story not only of outward-oriented growth but also of structural adjustment. Before looking at Ghana, some general observations about the World Bank's promotion of outward-oriented growth are in order.

The World Bank has devoted countless studies written by a number of the most influential trade experts to demonstrating the superiority of the outward-oriented trade and development model.

This was especially the case during the period when a number of Latin American countries' experimented with an inward-oriented approach to development. During the 1970s World Bank studies compared the progress of outward-oriented economies of countries like Korea, Singapore and Taiwan with that of inward-oriented economies of India, Chile and Uruguay. As one World Bank study by Bela Ballassa concluded, "... outward-oriented countries succeeded in rapidly expanding their exports and reaching higher growth rates than inward-orienting countries... ."[3]

By the 1980s, the inward-oriented, import-substitution strategy had largely been discredited by mainstream development economists.[4]

The implications of the outward-oriented growth strategy on development policies are far-reaching in both the North and South. The predominance of countries with outward-oriented strategies in the global economy is having a dramatic impact on the role that governments play in managing their economies. It also has obvious implications for the economies of the North which have to contend with the massive influx of inexpensive foreign goods which results in the large-scale displacement of workers in Northern manufacturing sectors. Northern economies continue to discriminate against certain imports from developing countries to protect what is left of certain manufacturing industries, or to give them time to adjust.

Critics point to a wide array of factors which suggest that export-led, free-trade strategies lead to greater dependency, continuing deterioration in terms of trade and greater impoverishment for the poor. The success stories of the South-East Asian economies do not provide hopeful models of development for several reasons. The most important of these is that there are fewer untapped markets in the Northern economies which would allow for a continuing expansion of developing country exports. The success of a number of Asian economies is also partly due to the relocation of production by TNCs. TNCs have escaped high labour costs in the North and moved to areas where cheap labour is made available to them through repressive working conditions and the agency of repressive governments.[5]

Export-Driven Growth and Commodities

The markets for the traditional primary commodities have been greatly altered by major changes in the structure and functioning of the global economy since World War II. Services, rather than manufacturing, have become the major source of GDP and value-added for more and more developed countries. Biotechnology research projects point to the possibility of reducing the demand for primary commodities even further or to replace them altogether.[6] Changing tastes and human priorities threaten the market for some traditional commodities, while imports are cut down in developed countries to take advantage of protected locally produced substitutes. For several commodities the net effect of these trends, both for the present and the future, is the threat of structural oversupply, especially for most primary commodities.

An important consequence of the commodities-led export promotion strategy, especially since the early 1980s, has been the suppression of the manufacturing/processing sectors of adjusting economies as a result of sweeping deregulation and privatisation. The dumping of goods as a result of trade liberalisation added to the anti-industrialisation bias of SAPs on the adjusting countries. Diversification is limited essentially to increasing the number of commodities for export rather than their value. The collapse of commodity agreements for coffee and cocoa have led to substantial losses for producers as a result of collapsing prices. Attempts to re-establish commodity agreements are hampered by regulations in the current North American Free Trade Agreeement (NAFTA) as well as the GATT.

Given the importance of commodity production and trade to the development prospects of the Third World and poor people in particular, the features of commodity markets have direct implications for sustainable development and environment management. Where there are few, or no alternative options to resource intensive methods of production, the exploitation of natural resources is bound to increase.

The majority of Third World producers of agricultural commodities are small rural farmers. In some cases, producing commodities for exports means forgoing food production. The behaviour of commodity prices – locally and internationally – impacts substantially on the abilities of millions of families to feed themselves, not to mention their ability to re-invest into improved resource management. Simply put, the decline in commodity prices, be it caused by the world market or government controls, leads to increased poverty for millions. The focus on increasing commodities for exports also tends to undermine the food security efforts of women farmers. Agricultural policies under structural adjustment favour cash-crop production which is dominantly male-oriented. Through this process, women are exploited and marginalized and encounter further barriers in terms of access to production resources. **Feeding people should be the objective of production. Resources must not be locked up for export purposes while people starve.**

(Source: Charles Abugre, "Understanding the Commodity Problem in the Context of the Changing Order: The Need for a Third World Strategy," Commodities: Third World Network Briefing Papers for UNCED, Paper No. 16, 1992).

The Assumptions of the World Bank's Export-Oriented Growth Model

The World Bank's policy of outward-oriented growth is embodied in the prescriptions of a typical structural adjustment programme. The major pillar of this approach rests on a set of assumptions relating to trade. While most of these assumptions are present in the Berg Report they bear mentioning here, since they all have a direct impact on the kinds of policies pursued by African economies in the 1980s, most particularly by Ghana.

The first and most crucial assumption relating to trade is the dictum that it is essential to "get the prices right". Essentially, any skewing of prices through subsidies, protection or overvalued currency leads to inefficiencies and ultimately lower growth rates. What is assumed in this policy prescription is that the "right" price which will allow a country to allocate its resources most efficiently is the current international market price. It is the strict adherence to this principle of trade that has compelled many commodity-producing countries in Africa to undergo massive currency devaluations and to eliminate subsidies on inputs and outputs. However, as economist Michel Chossudovsky argues, a more accurate picture is gained by considering the effect of what he describes as the "internationalization" of commodity prices on wages and labour:

> [The] global market system is characterised by a fundamental duality in the formation of wages and labour costs between rich and poor countries. Whereas prices are unified and brought up to world levels, wages (and labour costs) in the Third World and Eastern Europe are as much as 70 times lower than in the OECD countries.[7]

The second assumption is that international trade must be structured according to comparative advantage. Developing countries are pressured to export what they can produce more cheaply than other countries and import products which other countries can produce more cheaply. In the case of African economies this has led to the World Bank's policy advice to abandon import-substituting industries and concentrate instead on expanding production of the commodities in which they enjoy a comparative advantage.

Besides being pressured to implement comparative advantage strategies, African countries are also chastised for failing to retain their market share in commodity exports. This failure forms the basis of the World Bank's attack on the structural defects of African economies. In the World Bank's 1988 study, *Africa's Adjustment and Growth in the 1980s*, the argument is presented in terms of the continent's failure even to measure up to its developing country counterparts in Latin America and Asia: "If Africa's export growth had matched that of other LDCs [less-developed countries], its debt service ratio would be about half of what it is today."[8] What is implied in this rather specious argument is that throughout the 1980s African countries were engaged in misguided import-substitution development schemes.

However, this argument overlooks two considerations that are crucial in any analysis of trade issues and of the "successes" of the East Asian countries. The first consideration is the distinction between primary commodities and manufactured goods. The overwhelming evidence points to declining terms of trade in primary commodities. This has certainly been the case for Africa during the 1980s; over the course of the decade the continent's terms of trade dropped precipitously. In 1986 alone, terms of trade plummeted by 32 per cent translating into a loss of $19 billion for African countries.[9] Yet, in spite of the accumulating evidence of falling prices for commodities, the World Bank urged African countries to increase production with the assurance that these increases "would have little effect on prices".[10]

The second consideration relates to the difference between a country's *static* comparative advantage – what a country can produce more efficiently and export in the short run, and its *dynamic* comparative advantage – what a country can develop the potential to produce efficiently and export in the long run.[11] The World Bank has clearly promoted a policy of export growth for African economies based on their *static* comparative advantage in primary commodities. This is precisely the opposite of the development policies pursued by the East Asian countries which were clearly designed to develop a dynamic comparative advantage in manufactured exports.

It is not only the World Bank which has advocated an approach based on static comparative advantage for African economies. A study by the UN Secretary General's Expert Group on Africa's Commodity Problems provided similar advice:

> During the course of economic development, the relative importance of the commodities sector invariably declines over time. The speed with which it declines is a product of development itself. In the African context, the most obvious route to overall transformation is thus, paradoxically, to strengthen the commodities sector... the required changes will not take place without a macroeconomic policy and institutional framework that enable and encourages product expansion, productivity growth and increased competitiveness.[12]

One of the most articulate and consistent critics of the commodity export approach has been the development economist Hans Singer. In a joint article critiquing the UN Expert's Group Report, Singer and Hewitt point to the range of analytical flaws in the comparative advantage thesis for Africa's commodities. The trends, they note, point unmistakably to a decline in demand for commodities, declining terms of trade and an over-dependence by African countries on commodity exports. The most significant target of their criticism is the Expert Group's constant refrain that Africa must recover its "market share" in its commodities. Hewitt and Singer note:

...the achievement of greater market share can by definition only be at the expense of somebody else's market share – perhaps another developing country in the case of tropical commodities. Attempts to lower production costs in order to increase market share would provoke similar action by rival producers, often with stronger technical and financial backing, leading to further impoverishment of African producers and nations. To a great extent, and to the benefit of consumers and manufacturers, this phenomenon has occurred throughout the 1980s for a wide range of commodities, as debtor nations have been persuaded to keep up commodity-based foreign exchange revenues.[13]

As former World Bank official Percy Mistry has noted with respect to the continued reliance on primary commodities, it is a strategy by which Africa is "cutting its own throat".[14]

The third assumption relating to trade is that which postulates an irreconcilable opposition between import-substitution policies and export-led growth policies. The World Bank holds that the choice between these two options is the determining factor for development and trade policy. A quasi-theological dualism is established between the evil of import-substitution which is a violation of the natural law of comparative advantage and the inherent goodness of the export-led approach.

The World Bank's 1987 *World Development Report* is devoted to examining the relative merits of these opposed approaches. The report compares the performance of three countries (South Korea, Singapore and Hong Kong) labelled as strongly outward-oriented with the performance of a number of other countries, including some African ones like Zambia, defined as inward-oriented. The World Bank reaches the conclusion that outward-oriented countries performed better because of their open, non-discriminatory policies and because their resources were allocated more efficiently under an outward-oriented regime. Developing countries, then, are urged to adopt export strategies as the best means of financing development and encouraging economic growth.

Overlooked in this analysis is the fact that the World Bank's comparison pits a number of middle income countries against a group of low income countries experiencing a variety of other problems. Indeed, after studying the experience of a number of African countries, Gerald Helleiner concludes:

> As far as external influences are concerned, then, there is no evidence to support the proposition that the degree of export orientation is associated with growth performance either in Africa or in poor countries more generally; and there is support, especially powerful in Africa, for the view that greater import volume instability is associated with slower growth.[15]

In addition, a distinction must be made between the kinds of goods which are being produced for export.[16] Studies that have examined the performance of countries exporting agricultural goods have found a lack of correlation between export promotion and economic growth.[17] Moreover, the distinction between outward- and inward-oriented countries is a misleading one. Many of the East Asian countries were, and continue to be, highly protectionist and interventionist. Economist John Loxley questions the appropriateness of the export-oriented model when the clear trend was toward greater protectionism by industrialized countries: "How much less generalizable is the model when the capitalist countries themselves are in crisis?"[18]

In spite of these trends, the World Bank and other development institutions encouraged sub-Saharan African countries to increase their production in crops in which they enjoy a traditional comparative advantage, and to use the foreign exchange generated for sales of these crops to buy more imported food than could be grown locally with the same resources. On the surface, this seems to be a perfectly rational economic argument. However, the comparative advantage-based model of trade overlooks the way in which the benefits of trade are distributed. There is no guarantee that the income from the sale of export crops accrues to the producer. Nor does this approach consider which sectors, classes, gender and regions of a country adopting this model will benefit from this strategy.[19]

The fourth trade related assumption concerns the association of export promotion and trade liberalization. The World Bank has closely linked the promotion of primary commodity exports for Africa with non-interventionist trade policies. SAPs not only compelled African economies to increase their exports; they required them to remove protectionist barriers to imports and privatize government-run industries. Protectionism is inherently biased against exports and privatization favours exports through the increased prices exporters receive for their products. This advice is motivated by the World Bank's belief in a world of perfectly competitive markets. The World Bank assumes that the market will shift resources away from the protected import-substitution sector to the export sector. It also assumes that countries will automatically be able to export those goods which their resource endowments prompt them to produce. Again, this is in contrast to the experience of East Asian economies which actively discriminated in favour of certain exports through tariffs, subsidies and government interventions.[20]

The argument for trade liberalization is also based on the widely-held perception that the complex, and often corrupt systems of trade controls, marketing boards, export-import licenses and tariffs have been important contributors to the dramatic economic decline of developing economies. These kinds of state controls, it is argued, have resulted in smuggling, skewed prices and overvalued exchange rates.[21] When it is further claimed that it has been the better-off urban sector that has largely benefited from this regime of state intervention, liberalization can also be framed as a policy choice which will help the poor farmers.[22]

While there is some basis for these views, placing the major blame for Africa's woes on an urban-biased regime of state controls is an oversimplification of the cause of Africa's economic crisis. Manfred Bienefeld, in examining the case of Tanzania, challenges the so-called "urban-bias" thesis, demonstrating that the urban sector in that country did not reap the benefits of a system which exploited the rural sector.[23] The World Bank's characterization of the urban coalition is largely a fiction, according to Bienefeld. The World Bank presents "the urban coalitions as essentially domestic, political phenomena and largely ignor[es] their links with international economic interests".[24] The effect, as with the rest of the World Bank's analysis, is to analyse the structures of economic inefficiency as residing only *within* African countries and having little or nothing to do with external factors.

The fifth assumption related to trade concerns the fallacy of composition. This is not so much an assumption of World Bank trade policy as a glaring oversight. It is in this area that the World Bank's policy advice to African economies, and indeed to the entire Third World, can be exposed as a disastrous experiment. The fallacy of composition problem can be summarized as follows: by encouraging developing countries individually to increase production and export of its primary products, the World Bank set in motion a process leading to an oversupply of these commodities and an ensuing plunge in prices received for them. Stephen Smith describes this structural defect in the World Bank's trade strategy in the following manner:

> At the World Bank, project analysis and funding are quite decentralized. A myriad of small, regional departments are charged with promoting exports for their assigned countries. The staff of each department apparently assumes that, since most of these countries are small in the context of the world economy, their extra output will be too small to have an appreciable impact on world prices. World Bank analysts usually assume that prices will hold up, rather than fall as the supply of promoted exports (e.g., coffee, cocoa, tropical oils, sugar cane, rubber, or minerals) increases. This approach may simplify the task of the analyst, but it is likely to backfire for the countries receiving World Bank advice.[25]

Astonishingly, as Smith notes,[26] there is no mechanism to accumulate and analyse the effects of the "collective wisdom" given to individual countries. Loxley's warning to African countries in the early eighties has been realized with tragic results:

> African countries would do well to check out the kind of advice the bank is giving to primary producers elsewhere in

the world before blithely accepting its price projections or its exhortations to diversify production.[27]

An issue related to the fallacy of composition is that of price forecasting. The World Bank, in the Berg Report throughout the 1980s, encouraged countries to increase their commodity exports based on their own optimistic price projections. As became increasingly apparent throughout the 1980s, these forecasts were hardly ever realized as prices for commodities continued on a downward slide throughout the decade. The motive for these optimistic forecasts, as Robin Broad argues, was not any realistic assessment of the price prospects for commodities but was part of an incentive package to push developing countries towards outward-oriented policies:

> Bank growth projections for both output and trade have – year after year after year – turned out to be far higher than what was subsequently achieved. Rather than correcting this annual over-optimism, the Bank seems to have realized that few take the time to go back and check whether projections matched reality. To the contrary, the high projections have served admirably to justify Bank policy prescription that have continued to urge export-oriented development.[28]

In its 1989 report *From Crisis to Sustainable Growth*, the World Bank did recognize that the outlook for its commodities was not favourable. Yet, it continued to view the problem as an internal difficulty, one that can be solved if each country increased its output and expanded its markets. While acknowledging, in passing, the dim prospects for Africa's commodities, the World Bank continues to predicate structural adjustment on the assumption that the continent can increase its exports and that prices will improve. Jonathan Barker suggests the real motives which lie behind the World Bank's insistence on this strategy for sub-Saharan Africa:

> Ample production means low prices, and the industries which process these raw materials and market the products benefit from the low prices. International lenders are more likely to get their service and principal payments from economies that

are still earning foreign exchange. Peasant farmers will keep the goods and repayments flowing without changing the international pattern of manufacturing or challenging the position of international capital.[29]

Ghana's experience with cocoa, examined in the next section, illustrates the effects of the World Bank's trade policy advice on a country that faithfully adhered to it.

Case Study: Ghana

For the international financial institutions which have been the main financial backers of the Ghanaian programme... the stakes are particularly high. Ghana is their showpiece, the testing ground for their version of appropriate economic policy, and the success from which they draw the moral authority to apply structural adjustment programmes generally through the rest of Africa and in the developing world as a whole. The importance of the Ghana case study, therefore, extends well beyond the boundaries of this relatively small African country, and assumes truly global dimensions.[30]

This section evaluates Ghana's attempt to adopt an export-oriented solution to its economic crisis. It considers Ghana's decision to rehabilitate cocoa production along with its attempts to increase production of other exports such as gold and timber. Also included is an examination of the macro-economic effects of these policies on the country and a consideration of which sectors of the Ghanaian population benefited from this strategy. Particular attention will be paid to the impact of these policies on small-scale farmers.

A World Bank comprehensive report on Ghana served as the basis for the country's decision to adopt a SAP in 1983. The World Bank painted a ghastly portrait of the Ghanaian economy. Per capita national income was down by 30 per cent, while real income had fallen by 80 per cent, the volume of exports was down by 33 per cent, and income from exports dropped by 52 per cent between 1970 and 1982. Cocoa production had fallen precipitously from 418,000 tonnes in 1970 to 258,000 tonnes in 1980, and to 159,000 in 1983. By 1983 real producer prices for cocoa had fallen to one third of their 1970 level.[31] In 1983 there were also chronic food shortages and severe declines in food production. On the other hand, Ghana was coping with a severe drought; it also had to deal with the return of over a million Ghanaians from Nigeria. Ironically, Ghana's external debt was not large, totalling just over $1 billion in 1982. However, it rose rapidly from 1983 onward.

In 1983, Ghana sought assistance from the World Bank and the IMF. In return for fresh loans from these institutions, the government embarked on an Economic Recovery Programme (ERP). The ERP embraced the classic structural adjustment measures. A drastic reduction in the exchange rate coincided with a policy of improving incentives for the export sector. In Ghana, this meant focusing on cocoa, a crop which represented 98 per cent of its agricultural exports. This focus stemmed from the World Bank's position that declining cocoa export volumes were the major source of Ghana's problems. By improving the price paid to the producer, the volume of exports could be increased *without having any impact on the world price of cocoa*. Rehabilitating the cocoa sector thus became the centrepiece of Ghana's ERP.[32] Part of this rehabilitation involved laying off close to 30,000 Cocoa Board workers.[33] The revenue saved with this measure would give farmers a higher percentage of the export price of cocoa, thereby increasing production and eliminating smuggling.[34] The ERP also involved massive layoffs of government employees, the introduction of user fees in health and education, the privatization of government-owned industries, the liberalization of prices and the removal of subsidies, and a severe curtailment of the power of unions in order to improve the climate for investment. World Bank project lending was primarily used to assist the rehabilitation of the export sector through improvements in the transportation, communication and energy sectors.

By 1986 Ghana's ERP was being hailed as an unqualified success. The World Bank literature began to refer to Ghana as the model for all African countries to emulate. The figures used to demonstrate the remarkable recovery of the Ghanaian economy are indeed impressive. The economy experienced a growth rate of 9.7 per cent in the first year of the programme followed by rates of over 5 per cent per annum afterward. By 1990, however, the growth rate had dropped to just 2.7 per cent. The production of cocoa and other foodstuffs also rose dramatically, while the real volume of exports rose by almost 60 per cent between 1983 and 1985.[35] Most importantly, cocoa farmers received much better prices for their crops, one of the planks of the SAP. The manufacturing sector experienced a strong recovery with the mining and forestry sectors also growing rapidly. The inflation rate also fell by over 90 per cent between 1983 and 1985. Finally, Ghana's ERP was accompanied by a large inflow of new lending from the World Bank and IMF. Ghana received about $1 billion in additional funds between 1983-86, enabling it to service its debt and take care of its arrears. In sum, the first years of the Ghanaian ERP were hailed even by critics of SAPs as "remarkably successful, a classic example of 'adjustment with growth'".[36]

Critics of Ghana's experience with its ERP, however, point to a number of other factors. They cite the effect that the emphasis on export-oriented growth has had on the Ghanaian economy. Many critics have also raised doubts about the sustainability of World Bank policies and have questioned the programme's proclaimed benefits.

For a country embarking on an ambitious export-oriented economic programme involving agricultural products, the issue of land use is central: "Land use will be particularly affected since a country must decide how far cash crops for export should supplant farming for food."[37] In Ghana, the emphasis on growing cocoa for export has come at the expense of food crops. This is hardly discussed in the World Bank literature, except to note that market mechanisms will allow food prices to rise in tandem with export crops. In reality, however, the export orientation of the Ghanaian economy under the ERP has been at the expense of food producers, most of whom reside in the poorer Northern region; they have seen their terms of trade deteriorate relative to those of cocoa producers (Table 6.1).

This raises the question as to whether SAPs are meant to improve prices for all farmers, or only for export crop producers. If the latter is the case, then one of the key planks of SAPs is undermined with respect to its analysis that price is the key determinant of production and that SAPs are geared to overcoming the so-called urban bias by improving the prices paid to farmers. The case of Ghana also suggests that it is only the very large cocoa farmers that have benefited from SAPs, while smaller farmers have seen their conditions deteriorate:

Table 6.1: Relative prices of food: Ghana 1977-87 (1977=100)

	1977	1980	1981	1982	1983	1984	1985	1986	1987
Terms of trade food/ Non-food consumer items	100	96	91	112	138	86	60	57	55
Relative prices of food/ Cocoa production	100	131	92	125	184	136	64	51	42

(Source: Loxley, *Ghana*, p.33)

Just 32 per cent of Ghana's cocoa farmers – those with the largest operations – received 94 per cent of the gross cocoa income. The remaining 68 per cent – smallholders – received only 6 per cent of the income. Further, a mere 18 per cent of farming households in Ghana grow cocoa. The rest have seen their incomes continue to stagnate.[38]

Even cocoa production has fallen well short of World Bank expectations. Despite the price incentives offered to cocoa producers the increase in production has been short-term.[39]

In 1989 international cocoa prices began a severe downward plunge so that by 1990 prices were 54 per cent lower than their 1986 levels. As a result, Ghana's 33 per cent increase in the volume of cocoa exported over that period was wiped out by the drop in prices. By 1988 Ghana's terms of trade had fallen to 65 per cent of its 1980 level. Critics contend that the World Bank must take responsibility for this. As Loxley notes:

> The relationship between increased production amongst several cocoa producers in a short period of time was not adequately provided for in the programmes themselves when first conceived. Even as late as March 1987 the World Bank was forecasting a decline in world cocoa prices between 1986-90 of only 14 per cent.[40]

As it has turned out, the World Bank overestimated the price of cocoa by close to 50 per cent and did not foresee at all the dramatic price decreases that have occurred since 1989.[41] The World Bank did have at its disposal ample evidence of rapidly declining prices for cocoa during the 1980s. In 1983 two economists from the World Bank's Commodities and Exports Promotions Division published a study in a World Bank periodical forecasting a decline in both coffee and cocoa prices.[42] The analysts concluded that demand for cocoa would not grow in the foreseeable future. This trend, coupled with planned production increases by countries like Brazil and those of South East Asia, meant that "cocoa prices will fall even further than currently forecast".[43] The advice to producing countries is to "reduce production growth by diversifying out of coffee and cocoa".[44] And yet, in designing Ghana's SAP, the World Bank encouraged Ghana to base its recovery on expanded cocoa production.

However, other World Bank commodity price forecasts painted a much more optimistic scenario for cocoa. In 1989, as cocoa prices were beginning to collapse on world markets, the World Bank issued a major study entitled, *Recent Trends and Prospects for Agricultural Commodity Exports in Sub-Saharan Africa 1988-2000*. The report forecasted that cocoa prices would reach an all-time low in 1990 but that from that year onward they would experience a price increase of 7 per cent per year. This forecast has been far from accurate as cocoa prices continued to decline on world markets, reaching their lowest level in 19 years in 1992.[45] Combined with biotechnological advances to develop substitutes for cocoa butter and other cocoa-based products, the prospects for Africa's cocoa farmers are even more precarious.

It is only as a result of outside assistance that Ghana has avoided a total economic collapse in the wake of collapsing cocoa prices. Moreover, by 1990 the external debt of Ghana had reached over $3 billion. These debts were largely serviced through new medium- and long-term loans, and the doubling of official transfers. Development assistance transfers had grown from $211 million to an expected $600 million by 1990, a very rare exception in a world of shrinking aid allocations. By 1990 Ghana was able to finance only 53 per cent of its imports and net external service payments from its exports as compared to 73 per cent in 1986. In spite of huge increases in production, 1990 levels of export earnings barely reached those achieved in 1986.

An analysis of the export and food production sectors confirms that it is primarily large wholesale traders who have benefited from Ghana's SAP. Smaller food producers, in contrast, have seen their margins steadily eroded by falling real prices for their food in face of ever stiffer competition with cheaper imported food as well as competition over land and resources with large-scale cocoa producers. One of the stated goals of SAPs is to improve prices for all of the agricultural sector. The assumption is that improvements in the export sector will trickle down to the food sector. This has not occurred in Ghana. Production of basic food crops has fallen off since the introduction of the ERP and the terms of trade in comparison to cocoa producers have deteriorated dramatically (Table 6.1)

Even amongst cocoa farmers it has been a relatively small group of large-scale farmers who have benefited. A survey of one region revealed that only 32 per cent of cocoa farmers received 94 per cent of gross income while the remaining 68 per cent received only 6 per cent. In all of Ghana only 18 per cent of farming households cultivate cocoa, and the cocoa industry itself is male-dominated.[46] The rehabilitation of the cocoa industry has benefited a very small percentage of almost entirely male, large-scale traders and cocoa farmers to the detriment of the large majority of food producers who are mostly women. Marketed food production declined by over 20 per cent between 1984-86 during the rejuvenation of the cocoa industry.[47] As Francis Owusu notes, "The stagnating food crop economy is likely to have been especially harmful to poor women and children since many Ghanaian women rely on food producing and trading to meet many of their own needs and to enrich the diets of their children."[48]

A recent study examining the effects of Ghana's ERP on women traders notes how a variety of factors associated with structural adjustment has led to widening gaps between rich and poor traders, forcing a number of small traders into other activities in order to meet their survival needs. Also, contrary to the aims of SAPs, cheaper imports have succeeded in driving out locally produced goods such as rice, cooking oil and clothing, the common staples of trade for women.[49] The introduction of user services for health and education placed an even heavier burden on poorer women under the pro-gramme: "These women either never owned belts or have long since sold them to buy medicine."[50]

While Ghana entered its first ERP without much of a debt problem, it now has a serious one. Ghana's external debt has risen from $1.6 billion in 1983 to over $4.2 billion for 1992 (Graph 6.1, Table 6.2). In the first years of its recovery programme, Ghana relied heavily on expensive short-term IMF standby credits which quickly came due. Ghana also saw its debt servicing burden rise rapidly to approach 60 per cent of its exports by 1988. The IMF and World Bank have responded to this added burden by lending even more money on longer terms, in effect postponing the day of reckoning for their own unsustainable debt.[51]

During the late 1980s, Ghana was buffered from the effect of its

Graph 6.1: Ghana's Debt Profile 1982–92
(US$ millions)

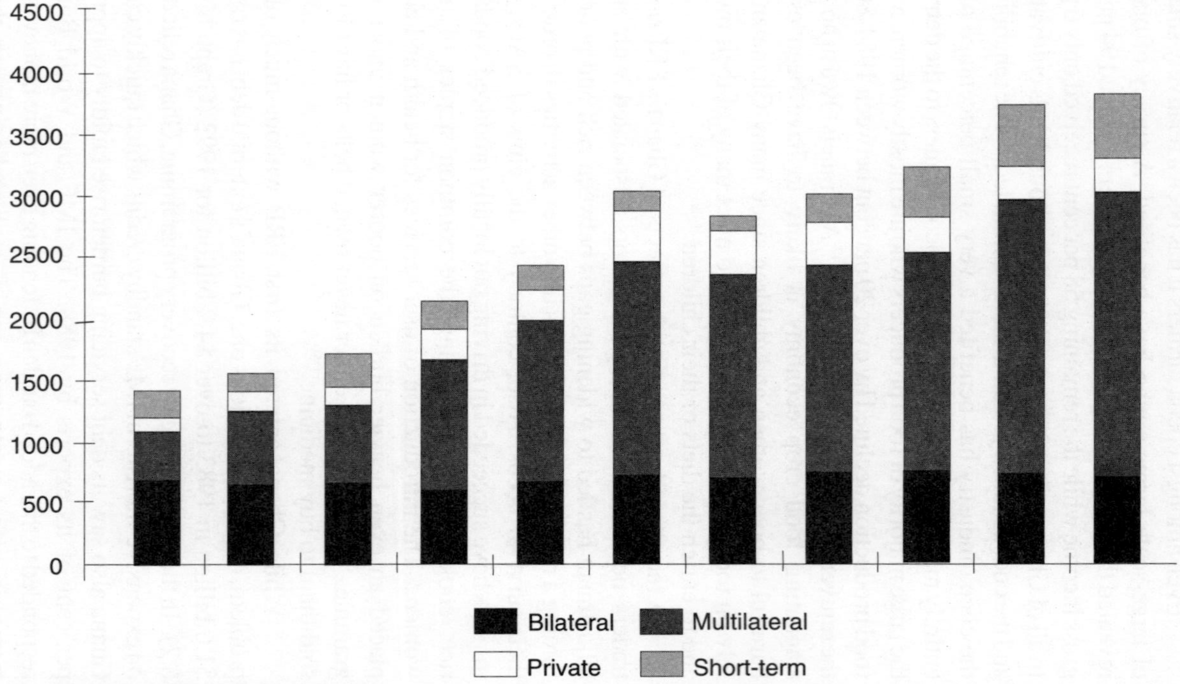

Bilateral / Multilateral / Private / Short-term

(Source: *World Bank Debt Tables*)

Table 6.2: Ghana's Debt Profile (US$ millions)

	1982	1983	1984	1985	1986	1987	1988	1989	1990	1991	1992	1993	TOTAL
TOTAL DEBT	1397	1598	1898	2227	2727	3263	3049	3295	3771	4209	4275	4590	
Bilateral	659	657	595	603	682	787	577	631	654	671	706	787	
Multilateral	425	703	917	1228	1568	2006	2078	2216	2583	2905	2928	3124	
Private	107	148	148	207	290	351	322	250	222	249	237	205	
Short-term	206	90	238	189	187	119	72	198	312	384	404	474	
DEBT SERVICE													**TOTAL**
Bilateral	42	63	53	51	54	55	58	37	38	37	49	44	581
Multilateral	29	51	51	76	122	284	377	283	215	185	168	163	2004
Private	4	17	23	20	43	68	109	123	91	57	64	49	668
Short-term	33	14	17	18	13	10	9	10	12	17	19	22	194
TOTAL	108	145	144	165	232	417	553	453	356	296	300	278	3447
NET TRANSFERS													**TOTAL**
Bilateral	-4	19	-26	-11	4	2	24	104	63	112	48	13	348
Multilateral	15	271	243	150	130	121	93	104	124	228	75	151	1705
Private	12	33	-3	28	63	-15	-42	-89	-47	-10	-5	-31	-106
TOTAL	23	323	214	167	197	108	75	119	140	330	118	133	1947
WORLD BANK/IMF													
DEBT SERVICE													**TOTAL**
IBRD	16	20	20	18	18	22	24	19	20	20	21	20	238
IMF	7	20	27	46	85	238	324	226	153	107	84	81	1398
TOTAL	23	40	47	64	103	260	348	245	173	127	105	101	1636
NET TRANSFERS													**TOTAL**
IBRD	-6	-14	-9	-10	-18	-22	-24	-19	-20	-20	-21	-20	-203
IMF	-7	262	192	76	-47	-91	-107	-49	-88	52	-84	-15	94
TOTAL	-13	248	183	66	-65	-113	-131	-68	-108	32	-105	-35	-109

(Source: *World Bank Debt Tables*)

skyrocketing debt because of the status it enjoyed in the eyes of the World Bank and the donor community as one of the committed adherents to structural adjustment. In 1987, for instance, Ghana received pledges of over $818 million from donor nations and agencies, well above the $575 million it had requested. Over the first two ERPs, Ghana received a total of approximately $3 billion in loans and grants from donors. These substantial increases in aid and concessional lending largely account for the increases in the growth rates which the country recorded during the first years of the ERP.[52]

The ecological impact of Ghana's outward-oriented policies is serious. Current projections estimate that the country could completely deplete its forests by the year 2000. The country's forests had already shrunk from 8.2 million square kilometres to 1.9 million square kilometres between 1900 and 1987. In the mining sector, the promotion of small-scale mining places mining in direct competition with food producers for land. While exports have been diversified to include a number of minerals such as gold, this has come at a high cost to the ecology of many regions through open-cast mining and the indiscriminate use of mercury.[53]

Ghana's experience with the World Bank also illustrates the high degree of intrusion by World Bank officials at every stage of its SAP. The fact that Ghana is currently ruled by a military government underscores the lack of accountability and democratic process involved in its structural adjustment experience. Hence, in Ghana's case, the World Bank has enjoyed a free hand. It is no secret, as Loxley notes, that the World Bank "crosses the t's and dots the i's" on every aspect of the Ghanaian economic policy:

> ...it is common knowledge that major agreements are typed in Washington for signature by the Ghanaian government and that often, because of bureaucratic delays in the government, the Bank will often draft responses to its own proposals on behalf of the government.[54]

In many respects the Ghanaian experience demonstrates how the adoption and implementation of SAPs produce a political structure where "decision-making becomes the prerogative of a few hand-picked elites in a 'parallel' government with external financiers".[55]

Another effect of Ghana's SAP has been the gradual collapse of industry, leading to the charge that under the ERP Ghana is becoming de-industrialized. Because manufacturing companies have found it extremely difficult to get access to foreign exchange, many viable government-owned industries were "divested". The public investment programme for 1986-88 allocated only 4 per cent of its funds for the industrial sector.[56]

Ghana faces a bleak economic future in the 1990s. Cocoa prices continue to fall and the country will be fortunate even to maintain existing levels of exports in face of stiff competition from Malaysian and Brazilian producers. Many of the structural adjustment loans that Ghana received from the World Bank and the IMF on hard, non-concessional terms will fall due during the 1990s. The effects of the ERP on the food producing sectors, on women and on the poor are becoming increasingly apparent. The environmental impact of the export-oriented development path will be felt for decades to come. As the glow from the Ghanaian success story begins to fade the World Bank has already begun to turn its attention toward other adjusting countries.

The case of Ghana provides an illustration of the many forces which an export-oriented growth model brings into play in an African context. Ghana's experience, while unique in many respects, has parallels in the experiences of a number of other sub-Saharan African countries. In spite of efforts to boost exports, which were successful in many countries, the region suffered a precipitous decline in export earnings due to falling commodity prices. There has been no serious effort by the World Bank to rethink their export-based strategy or to take responsibility for the harmful effects that it has had on both the people and the ecology of sub-Saharan Africa.

We now turn to considering Africa's future trade prospects under the latest round of the GATT.

The GATT Negotiations

The [Uruguay] Round is an attempt by transnational companies to establish sets of international laws that would grant
them unprecedented unfettered freedoms and rights to operate
at will and without fear of new competitors almost anywhere
in the world.[57]

The successful resolution of the current round of GATT talks is regarded by many as vital for developing countries' prospects of recovery as well as for promoting food security. The cause of developing countries will be enhanced with the removal of agricultural subsidies by the North, as well as the general removal of subsidies and marketing boards. Developing countries will be able to compete on fairer terms with their Northern counterparts once these changes have been made.[58]

The World Bank has consistently called for the global liberalization of trade as the best means of achieving the development goals of African countries. This is particularly true in the case of the recently ratified Uruguay round of talks for a new GATT. The GATT, established in 1948, is essentially a legal framework for the regulation of global trade. Its member countries meet periodically (in rounds) to remodel the agreement in response to changing conditions.

The World Bank claims to be championing the cause of developing countries by calling for the removal of agricultural subsidies by the North, as well as the general removal of subsidies and marketing boards. It argues that developing countries will be able to compete on fairer terms with their Northern counterparts once these changes have been made. A successful resolution of the GATT talks is vital for developing countries' prospects of recovery.

Behind this rhetoric lies a far more complex set of issues and interests which will not be of benefit to agricultural producers in Africa, let alone farmers in the North. The resolution of the current GATT round bodes increasing dependency of African countries on food imports, and makes the attainment of self-sufficiency an even more remote possibility. The new GATT will lead to increasing control of agricultural trade by agribusinesses, which already manage between 70-80 per cent of international trade in primary commodities.[59]

Many observers argue that the optimistic projections surrounding a successful GATT do not bear out, especially when its effects on poorer countries are studied.[60] The successful conclusion of the current GATT round is likely to undermine further the economies of countries which depend on primary products for export. The removal of export subsidies on Northern agricultural products will only begin to be reflected in prices beginning in the year 2000 and the full removal of restrictions on exports of clothing and textiles from developing countries is set to take effect only in 2006.[61]

Agricultural trade is an area of far greater importance to developing countries than to industrialized countries. As Chakravarthi Raghavan documents:

> In 1986, agriculture accounted for only 3 per cent of the GDP of the OECD countries and seven percent of the labour force. But in the Third World it accounted for 19 per cent of GDP and 60 per cent of the labour force. For the majority of Third World countries agricultural products account for 50-100 per cent of their total merchandise exports.[62]

The 1980s have seen the most protracted and deepest crisis since the Great Depression in the international agricultural trading system.[63] Prices for the major food staples plunged to their lowest levels since the Great Depression, precipitating record numbers of bankruptcies and foreclosures by farmers in North America.

The origins of this crisis, while complex, are not difficult to ascertain in view of the stated aims of the US' and European Community's agricultural policies. For the US the issue is clear and straightforward: it regards the export of farm surpluses as a means of consolidating its global market share in key commodities. This has been the over-arching strategy in post-World War II US agricultural policy.[64] Through a number of measures taken in the 1980s such as the Farm Act, the US has sought to increase its market share in farm products by flooding the world markets with cheap grains. In the words of one of the Republican senators who authored the Farm Act:

> ...if we do not lower our farm prices to discourage these developing countries from aiming at self-reliance now, our world-wide competitive position will continue to slide.... This [discouragement] should be one of the foremost goals of our agricultural policy.[65]

The Farm Act, while further impoverishing farmers by increasing their dependence on support payments, was a boon to corporate grain traders, who were able to purchase farm products at prices well below their cost of production as a result of overproduction and low prices.

Table 6.3: Net food imports of Africa and selected countries, 1983-85
(Annual average in US$ millions)

Region/country	Sugar	Live animals and meat	Cereals	Dairy products	Animal & veg.oils	Total Incl. sugar	Total Excl. sugar
AFRICA	827.3	1484.2	5498.3	1440.3	1280.4	10530.5	9703.2
Algeria	150.1	96.6	786.2	429.4	218.7	1681.0	1530.9
Angolia	16.8	55.0	75.4	42.4	24.9	214.5	197.7
Cameroon	0.1	10.7	50.3	10.0	5.1	76.0	76.1
Cote d'Ivoire	9.2	89.5	116.2	48.3	57.8	187.0	196.2
Egypt	162.8	481.2	1607.4	260.8	410.1	2923.3	2760.5
Ethiopia	3.4	11.2	112.3	17.6	23.9	139.2	142.6
Ghana	6.9	8.7	52.0	6.1	10.6	84.3	77.4
Kenya	0.1	14.8	57.1	5.9	56.5	104.8	104.7
Libyan Arab Jam.	41.1	286.3	244.4	128.2	77.2	777.2	736.1
Mali	13.7	106.9	65.7	4.2	0.0	23.3	47.0
Mauritania	11.5	33.7	54.5	25.1	5.2	62.2	51.1
Morocco	48.2	13.1	345.1	36.4	123.4	566.2	518.0
Mozambique	10.9	4.7	68.9	12.2	17.4	114.1	103.2
Nigeria	180.4	160.8	616.7	128.5	114.1	1200.5	1020.1
Senegal	4.8	21.1	105.2	21.1	33.7	118.5	113.7
Somalia	11.2	59.0	74.5	8.2	16.5	51.4	40.2
Sudan	17.0	66.3	68.2	26.5	21.9	107.3	90.3
United Rep. of Tanzania	0.7	0.6	68.3	10.7	13.3	92.2	91.5
Tunisia	34.5	42.9	155.5	37.1	12.5	282.5	248.0
Zaire	4.8	50.8	76.0	19.2	9.5	141.3	136.5

(Source: Raghavan, *Recolonization*, pp.164-5)

The overall impact of Northern countries' agricultural policies has been disastrous for African countries. Imports of food by African countries have steadily increased over the past two decades, largely as a result of food dumping. In spite of the fact that African countries export agricultural commodities, they are on the whole net importers of food, especially grains (Table 6.3). In effect, the "cheap food" policies of the past decade, while benefiting TNCs in the North and elites in the South, have severely disrupted any attempts to achieve food security in the continent. Rice and wheat imports have grown by over 6 per cent per annum over the past two decades in sub-Saharan Africa. These imports, combined with food aid, have not only fuelled a shift in consumer food tastes away from locally grown food, they have effectively priced domestic producers out of the market. In 1986, for instance, US maize dumping in Zimbabwe led to a drop in locally produced maize prices from $109 to $60 per tonne, and also left many producers stranded with a surplus. The US and the European Community were also dumping wheat in Mali and Burkina Faso for $60 per tonne while the cost of locally produced grains was approximately $100 per tonne.[66]

Some African countries have benefited from special arrangements like the Lomé Convention, which give them preferential access to European markets. Countries like Tanzania and Mauritius have benefited from the Sugar Protocol, while Botswana and Zimbabwe have been beneficiaries of the Beef Protocol. Overlooked is the far more detrimental impact that the American and European farm surpluses have been having on staple food production and food self-reliance in Africa and how this will be further entrenched in the new GATT.

The new GATT deals with surplus production through the removal of government agricultural subsidies. Yet, the evidence suggests that, in spite of the removal of subsidies, overproduction will continue well into the next century. While a ban on food dumping might have some impact, neither the European Community nor the United States is willing to agree to such a rule. Policies involving subterfuge, such as Deficiency Payments, already commonplace in the US and quickly being adopted in the European Community, effectively mean that, even with a new GATT, developing-country exporters and food producers will continue to face competition on world and local markets from those in the North eager to subsidize the corporate control of agriculture. This is part of the reality behind the rhetoric of the "level playing field".[67] As Canada's National Farmer's Union notes:

> This approach toward corporatization of agriculture relies on market forces to allocate production. It points unmistakenly in the direction of transferring more power over the lives of farm families into the hands of transnational corporations. It destroys the concept of self-sufficiency we strive to attain for many producers.[68]

Under the new GATT, developing countries will lose their present power to determine when temporary exceptions to a "free trade" regime would assist their economies. In GATT terminology this power was known as the "development principle". According to this principle, developing countries were given special privileges and exemptions in complying with certain GATT rules in recognition of their need to build up long-term economic capacity. In the current Uruguay Round this principle has been effectively abolished.[69] In effect, developing countries will be forced to liberalize their economies completely and remove all subsidies. The new GATT would make the structural adjustment of developing-country economies permanent, while Northern countries would continue to impose non-tariff measures such as anti-dumping regulations and "voluntary" export restraints on their trading partners.[70] Developing countries will, in turn, face higher prices for imported food as well as increases in the price of medicines due to the new rules governing intellectual property.

In the worldview of the World Bank, SAPs are the appropriate policy in a world of free markets predicated on comparative advantage. However, the real world is one where prices and trade flows are dictated by a country's capacity to subsidize its exports.[71] In this scenario, African countries are compelled to remove their own subsidies while allowing the subsidized goods from the North into their own countries without restrictions. The North, in turn, continues to discriminate against any efforts by African countries to process their raw materials by imposing duties on these goods. It has been and will continue to be a recipe for growing food insecurity in Africa and an important factor in the growing number of famines plaguing the continent.

Under the new GATT rules, it will be virtually impossible for poor developing countries to compete with the US and European Community countries which provide direct support payments to farmers as a tactic to by-pass subsidy regulations. The rules will also virtually prohibit any attempts by developing countries to achieve greater food self-reliance. For instance, Nigeria, which banned wheat imports from the US to encourage local production, would be prohibited from doing so under new GATT regulations.[72] As Brewster Kneen has noted, under the proposed GATT: "The possibility of building regional food systems dedicated to providing adequate nutrition for everyone would have become almost impossible, particularly for the deprived of the world."[73]

Making Structural Adjustment Permanent

> [A]griculture is not the issue... . Rather it is the linchpin to agreement on issues of greater magnitude, issues that really matter, like intellectual property protection, services, investment and subsidies.[74]

While the impasse over agricultural subsidies garnered the most attention during the Uruguay GATT round, it obscured the real and much more important international trade agenda. According to Chakravarthi Raghavan, the current GATT round is really about the reorganization of production on a global scale:

> The basic premise behind the Uruguay Round, and the new GATT that would emerge out of it, is that left to themselves private enterprise and Transnational Corporations (TNCs) function efficiently and for the benefit of all. Thus governments' powers to intervene and regulate need to be curbed.[75]

Raghavan argues that the current GATT negotiations are but a veil for the transformation of the global economy into a Free Trade Zone for TNCs. A coalition of the largest American TNCs and business associations has undertaken an intensive lobbying effort to ensure a successful resolution of the GATT, as well as its subsequent passage through Congress.

The new rules governing intellectual property rights and trade in services would provide a boon to countries like the US which currently claims to be losing between $50 and $100 billion per year through patent and copyright violations. They would also allow banks and other service-oriented TNCs unfettered access to developing-country markets (Table 6.4). At present only 1 per cent of patents are owned by persons or companies in the Third World and, of those, 84 per cent are owned by foreigners and less than 5 per cent are actually used for production in the Third World.[76] Any developing country which sought to protect its service industries, or develop its own pharmaceutical industry, as India has done, would face "cross-retaliation" from Northern countries against its goods. Because the new GATT is so comprehensive, it provides industrialized countries with an arsenal of retaliatory measures to counter any efforts of developing countries to establish their own development priorities. It is for this reason that many refer to the latest GATT as the attempt to make structural adjustment a global and permanent reality.

The proposed GATT rules for intellectual property rights in effect constitute a form of protectionism granted to TNCs who currently hold the majority of the world's patents. This will greatly benefit pharmaceutical companies and biotechnology firms seeking to monopolize global control over what they consider to be their intellectual property. Transnational drug firms will be granted 20 years of patent protection, with no exceptions, for basic medicines, food or living organisms.[77] The proposed rules are so comprehensive and intrusive that they would even place in jeopardy the rights of farmers to store seed from their harvest for the following season.[78] The enshrinement of intellectual property rights in a revised GATT will provide a powerful weapon for TNCs against recalcitrant developing countries. As the Ecumenical Coalition for Economic Justice notes: "A country denying a corporation its royalty claims could find itself punished by trade sanctions on its exports."[79] Not surprisingly, the TNCs favour a protectionist regime in the area of intellectual property rights, while arguing for the principles of free trade in the area of goods and services. As Martin Khor Kok Peng notes:

Table 6.4: Exports of Commercial Services

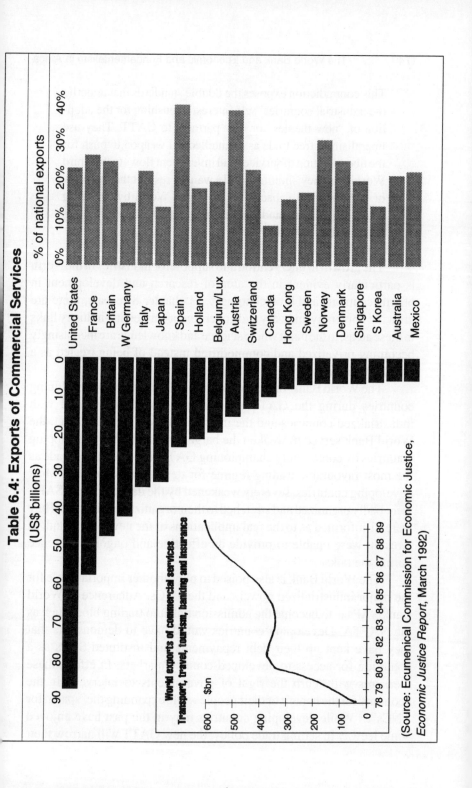

% of national exports

(US$ billions)

	40%
	30%
	20%
	0%

United States
France
Britain
W Germany
Italy
Japan
Spain
Holland
Belgium/Lux
Austria
Switzerland
Canada
Hong Kong
Sweden
Norway
Denmark
Singapore
S Korea
Australia
Mexico

0 10 20 30 40 50 60 70 80 90

World exports of commercial services
Transport, travel, tourism, banking and insurance

$bn
600
500
400
300
200
100
0

78 79 80 81 82 83 84 85 86 87 88 89

(Source: Ecumenical Commission for Economic Justice,
Economic Justice Report, March 1992)

This contradiction exposes the double standards that underlie the industrial countries' self-interest in pushing for the adoption of "new themes" or new partners to GATT. They use liberalism or free trade as an intellectual weapon to push for the liberalization of services and investment flows to the Third World; but they simultaneously want to restrict the free flow of technological capacity to the Third World by imposing patent obligations and intellectual property rights regimes onto the Third World.[80]

The growth in intervention and support for industries in the North is particularly evident in the area of research and development in pharmaceuticals and biotechnology. As chapter 8 reveals, there are growing university-industry and government-university-industry links in these areas, to the point where science and knowledge are increasingly becoming privatized and commodified instead of being treated as a common heritage for all.[81]

The World Bank, rather than promote the concerns of developing countries during the GATT negotiations, consistently sided with industrialized countries and the interests of the TNCs. In effect, the World Bank served to weaken the bargaining position of developing countries by consistently championing GATT and liberalized trade as the most favourable trading regime for developing countries. Most developing countries, severely weakened by the debt crisis and SAPs, were badly organized and stretched to their organizational limits. They were ill-informed as to the real implications of the new GATT and, as a result, were unable to provide an effective and ongoing presence during the talks.

The World Bank is also poised to play another important role for the major industrialized powers and the TNCs. Adherence to World Bank SAPs is to become the admission ticket to trading blocs such as the NAFTA. Developing countries would have to demonstrate that they have kept up their debt repayments and instituted SAPs as a condition for access to developed-country markets. In effect, these measures will "curb the right of governments to intervene in the economy for the benefit of their people while expanding the 'space' for TNCs".[82] While developing countries may in the past have enjoyed some leeway in setting trade policy, the new GATT will narrow their options to one: outward-oriented and completely liberalized economies. The Uruguay Round has paved the way for the GATT, the IMF and the World Bank to "combine forces in influencing trade and economic policy in the countries of the South".[83]

Conclusion

The main arguments of this chapter relate to the various impacts of the implementation of one of the key planks of SAPs: the need for countries to adopt export-oriented trade strategies. These arguments can be summarized in the following points:

- export-oriented growth has resulted in the increased alienation of land as the best land is allocated for the production of commodity crops, driving the poor onto marginal land. This process invariably leads to even greater concentration of control over resources;
- the expansion of commodity production at the expense of long-term food security and development rooted in the priority of agriculture;[84]
- growing urbanization;
- roll-back of attempts at redistribution and provision of social services;
- breakdown of local/regional/national social and political structures;
- increasing migrant labour;
- increased marginalization of women who have to cope with more work in the face of the loss of support for food crops and in health and education;
- the privatization of government industries and increased foreign ownership; the trade liberalization that accompanies the export-oriented thrust, "is conducive to the **decomposition** of the national industrial (import-substituting) sectors and their redirection towards the development of 'new' lines of production for the external market."[85]
- lower prices for commodities in the context of shrinking world demand and oversupply;[86]
- transnational banks and agribusinesses benefiting from low prices, secure supply and guaranteed minimum debt servicing.

In examining the impact of SAPs on trade in sub-Saharan Africa over the past decade, we must try to place short-run effects of SAPs in the context of long-term processes that stretch back to the colonial period. Many of the trading patterns currently practised were in place long before the implementation of SAPs. This chapter discussed how SAPs have intensified already existing inequitable trading patterns and have led to the consolidation of control over pricing and production by transnational interests. Many of these developments perpetuate processes that were in place during the colonial period. Other developments are rooted in changes in the global economy and the emergence of a global order based on transnational control of all aspects of production in the context of the dissolution of a nation's ability to set its own development priorities.

Increasingly, organizations and citizens' groups in the North and South are not only working towards launching international campaigns on the debt issue but are also forging alliances with environmental groups, church-based organizations, anti-free trade coalitions, women's and native groups, and anti-poverty groups. These alliances are becoming more cohesive in light of the growing recognition of the importance of understanding the integral connections among issues of debt, trade and structural adjustment. The next two chapters examine the impact of the current global order of debt, trade and structural adjustment from an ecological perspective, by examining the issues of land use and biotechnology.

Endnotes

1. Bruce Campbell, Chapter 1, Canadian Environmental Law Association, "The Environmental Implications of Free Trade Agreements," CELA, 1993, pp. 8-9.
2. C. Vaitsos, cited in Raghavan, *Recolonization: GATT, The Uruguay Round and the Third World*, (Penang: Third World Network, 1990), p. 94.
3. B. Balassa, *New Directions in the World Economy*, (London: MacMillan Press, 1989), p. 27.
4. Cheryl Payer notes how, in the early seventies, the World Bank financed a major campaign to discredit import-substitution development strategies. Major multi-volume studies were written by trade experts like Bela Balassa, Anne Krueger and Jagdish Bhagwati, all of which reached similar conclusions condemning import-substitution. See C. Payer, *Lent and Lost*, p. 28.
5. Many of the newly-industrializing economies in Asia also used massive state intervention involving subsidized credit, controlled interest rates, guaranteed internal markets and intellectual property borrowed and copied from abroad. These measures are no longer available to countries subject to SAPs, the GATT or NAFTA rules.
6. The example of cocoa production provides a good case in point. See C. Juma, *The Gene Hunters*, (Princeton: Princeton University Press, 1989), pp. 136-40.
7. M. Chossudovsky, "The Global Creation of Third World Poverty," p. 14. Samir Amin offers a similar perspective. What is important to consider, he notes, is the real rewards to labour in the Third World as compared to developed countries. It is these rewards that determine prices and not the other way around. Amin offers the example of coffee. Any devaluation intended to increase prices to producers would face a corresponding drop in the dollar price of coffee to maintain the minimal reward accruing to producers. "This is the lesson of history that the World Bank grandly overlooks." Amin, *Maldevelopment*, p, 38.
8. World Bank, *Africa's Adjustment and Growth*, p. 2. Ironically, this is precisely the strategy that lies at the heart of the World Bank's promotion of export-oriented strategies. As Kari Levitt observes, "...the pressure on indebted countries to adopt 'outward-looking' policies is primarily directed toward debt service. It is essentially a short-term policy having nothing to do either with static 'gains from trade', or with long-term strategies of development." K. Levitt, *Debt, Adjustment and Development*, p. 24.
9. Rau, *From Feast to Famine*, p. 84.
10. World Bank, *Accelerated Development*, p. 23.
11. Stephen C. Smith, *Industrial Policy in Developing Countries: Reconsidering the Real Sources of Export-Led Growth*, (Washington: Economic Policy Institute, 1991), p. 7.
12. United Nations Secretary General's Expert Group on Africa's Commodity

Problems, *Africa's Commodity Problems: Towards a Solution*, (Geneva: United Nations, 1990), p. 35.
13. A. Hewitt and H. Singer, "How to Foster Diversification, not Dependence," *Africa Recovery* 4/3-4 (October-December 1990), p. 37.
14. Cited in M. B. Brown and P. Tiffen, *Shortchanged: Africa and World Trade*, (Amsterdam: Transnational Institute, 1992), p. 19.
15. Helleiner, "Outward Orientation, Import Instability and African Economic Growth: An Empirical Investigation." Cited in Singer, "The World Development Report 1987," *World Development* (1988), p. 235.
16. Smith, *Industrial Policy*, p. 9.
17. See I. K. Otchere, "Exploring the Connection Between Export Promotion and Economic Growth: Evidence from Ghana," (paper delivered to the Canadian Association of African Studies Conference, Montreal, 1992), pp. 3-7, for a good literature review on this issue.
18. J. Loxley, "Crisis in Africa – Berg's Diagnosis and Prescription," in J. Barker ed., *The Politics of Agriculture in Tropical Africa*, (Beverley Hills: Sage Publications, 1984), p. 70.
19. P. Raikes, *Modernizing Hunger*, pp. 8-9.
20. Smith, *Industrial Policy*, p. 10.
21. H. Bienen, "The Politics of Trade Liberalization in Africa," *Economic Development and Cultural Change* (1990), p. 726.
22. Bienen, "Politics of Trade Liberalization, p. 727.
23. Bienefeld, *Structural Adjustment and Rural Labour Markets in Tanzania*, (Geneva: International Labour Organization, 1991), pp. 4, 73.
24. Bienefeld, *Structural Adjustment*, p. 72.
25. Smith, *Industrial Policy*, p. 35.
26. Smith, *Industrial Policy*, p. 36, ftnt. 34.
27. Loxley, "Crisis in Africa," in J. Barker, *The Politics of Agriculture in Tropical Africa*, p. 69.
28. Robin Broad, *Unequal Alliance: The World Bank and the Philippines*, (Berkeley: University of California Press, 1988), pp. 204-5 and note 1 pp. 321-2.
29. J. Barker, *Rural Communities under Stress*, p. 190.
30. J. Loxley, *Ghana: The Long Road to Recovery*, (Ottawa: The North-South Institute, 1991), p. 72.
31. Loxley, *Ghana*, p. 9.
32. Otchere, "Exploring the Connection," p. 2.
33. It is not unusual for the World Bank to press for marketing boards to be disbanded as a condition for receiving structural adjustment loans. In effect, farmers are left with no option but to sell directly to the multi-national trading companies or to chocolate companies which have established their own subsidiaries in West Africa. See M. B. Brown and P. Tiffen, *Shortchanged*, p. 76.
34. Loxley, *Ghana*, p. 17.
35. See Loxley, *Ghana*, pp. 25-7.

36. Loxley, *Ghana*, p. 25.
37. Brown and Tiffen, *Shortchanged*, p. 16.
38. "Farmers Adjust to Economic Reforms," *African Farmer* 3 (April 1990), p. 7.
39. Loxley, *Ghana*, p. 35.
40. World Bank, *Ghana: Policies and Issues of Structural Adjustment*. Cited in Loxley, *Ghana*, p. 81.
41. Toye *et al.*, *Aid and Power*, vol. 2, p. 196. The authors go on to note that providing such inaccurate forecasts "is a little hard to do, given that cocoa demand is not speculative and cocoa supply not greatly responsive to the vagaries of the weather".
42. T. Akiyama and R. C. Duncan, "Coffee and Cocoa Trends: An Unfavourable Outlook for Developing Countries," *Finance and Development* (March 1983), pp. 30-33.
43. Akiyama and Duncan, "Coffee and Cocoa Trends," p. 33.
44. Akiyama and Duncan, "Coffee and Cocoa Trends," p. 33.
45. Some of the working assumptions of the World Bank's forecasts bear mentioning here as well. The World Bank forecasts a 5 per cent annual growth rate in export earnings for Africa's primary commodities. This is based on the optimistic assessment that prices will rise by just over 3 per cent a year and that export volume will be increased by 1.5 per cent per year. World Bank, *Recent Trends and Prospects for Agricultural Commodity Exports in Sub-Saharan Africa*, cited in Brown and Tiffen, *Shortchanged*, p. 28.
46. Owusu, "Spatial Implications of Ghana's Structural Adjustment Programme," (paper delivered to the Canadian Association of African Studies Conference), Montreal, May 1992, p. 22.
47. C. Ahiadeke, "Cooperation or Isolation? A Review of Structural Adjustment Programmes in Sub-Saharan Africa, with Particular Reference to Ghana," (paper delivered to The Council for the Development of Economic and Social Research in Africa Conference), Dakar, September, 1991, pp. 34-5.
48. Owusu, "Spatial Implications," p. 24.
49. G. Clark and T. Manuh, "Women Traders in Ghana and the Structural Adjustment Program," in C. Gladwin, *Structural Adjustment and African Women Farmers*, (Gainesville: University of Florida Press, 1991), p. 232.
50. Clark and Manuh, "Women Traders," p. 233.
51. Loxley, *Ghana*, 46-7.
52. Otchere, "Making the Connection," p. 21.
53. Owusu, "Spatial Implications," p. 25.
54. Loxley, *Ghana*, p. 52. Also, E. Hutchful, "From Revolution to Monetarism: The Economics and Politics of the Adjustment Programme in Ghana," in B. Campbell and J. Loxley eds, *Structural Adjustment in Africa*, (London: MacMillan, 1989), p. 122.

55. Kofi V. Anani, "Transnational Elite Interests as Manifested in the Socio-Economic Recovery Programmes in Sub-Saharan Africa," (paper prepared for Ten Days for World Development), May 1992, p. 2.
56. Loxley, *Ghana*, p. 53.
57. M. Khor Kok Peng, *The Uruguay Round and Third World Sovereignty*, (Penang: Third World Network, 1990), p. 37.
58. A. Weston, "North-South Institute Briefing," (Ottawa: North-South Institute, June 1992).
59. Ecumenical Coalition for Economic Justice, "Collapse of GATT Talks: A Dangerous Opportunity," *Economic Justice Report*, II/I (March 1991), p. 2.
60. For a thorough analysis of the origins of and challenges to the optimistic projections surrounding a successful completion of the Uruguay Round see C. Raghavan, "Gains from the Uruguay Round: Facts, Myths and Faith," (Third World Network Features, Nov. 13, 1993).
61. C. Raghavan, "Uruguay Round Balance Sheet After Ten Years," (Third World Network Features, Dec. 17, 1993).
62. Raghavan, *Recolonization: GATT, the Uruguay Round and the Third World*, p. 163.
63. K. Watkins, "Agriculture and Food Security in the GATT Uruguay Round," *Review of African Political Economy* 50 (1991), p. 38.
64. P. Raikes, *Modernizing Hunger*, p. 120.
65. Sen. Rudy Boschwitz, cited in Watkins, "Agriculture," p. 41.
66. Watkins, "Agriculture," p. 46.
67. Watkins, "Agriculture," p. 47.
68. National Farmers Union, "NFU Statement on GATT Negotiations to the National Conference on International Trade and Agriculture," (Montreal, Dec. 2-4), 1988.
69. M. Khor Kok Peng, *The Uruguay Round and Third World Sovereignty*, p. 5.
70. Watkins, "Agriculture," p. 48.
71. K. Watkins, *Fixing the Rules: North-South Issues in International Trade and the GATT Uruguay Round*, (London: Catholic Institute for International Relations), p. 65.
72. Watkins, "Agriculture," pp. 49-50.
73. B. Kneen, editorial, *The Ram's Horn* 79 (Dec. 1990), p. 3.
74. William Brock, Chair, Multilateral Trade Negotiations MTN Coalition, in M. Khor Kok Peng, *The Uruguay Round and Third World Sovereignty*, p. 9.
75. C. Raghavan, *Recolonization*, p. 35.
76. M. Khor Kok Peng, *The Uruguay Round*, p. 30.
77. Ecumenical Coalition for Economic Justice, "US 'Trade' Strategy: 'Do as We Say; Not as We Do,'" *Economic Justice Report* 3/2 (May 1992), p. 6.
78. Pat Roy Mooney, cited in Raghavan, Recolonization, p. 45.
79. Ecumenical Coalition for Economic Justice, "Collapse of GATT," *Economic Justice Report* (March 1991), p. 6.

80. M. Khor Kok Peng, *The Uruguay Round*, p. 7.
81. Raghavan, *Recolonization*, pp. 92-3.
82. Raghavan, *Recolonization*, p. 40.
83. Raghavan, *Recolonization*, p. 60.
84. Rau summarizes this point nicely: "National infrastructure becomes designed to facilitate exports rather than respond to local needs, thus reinforcing the structures created by colonial regimes that discriminated against peasant farmers." Rau, *From Feast to Famine*, p. 103.
85. M. Chossudovsky, "The Global Creation of Third World Poverty," p. 16.
86. M. Chossudovsky, "Global Creation," p. 17.

—— CHAPTER SEVEN ——

Structural Adjustment and the Environment

> Indebtedness is not a curiosity of bad economic management, it is a symptom of a deeper malaise that equates "development" with the conversion of natural resources into consumable products, many of which we produce but cannot sell. Indebtedness makes claims on the environment which are insupportable and unsustainable. It is part of the motor of destruction that we see both in the developed world and in less developed countries, and to which an alternative is urgently required.[1]

The current imposition of SAPs serves to highlight the contradictions of an international system which is built on economic growth and inequality. This chapter highlights a number of perspectives that demonstrate how SAPs contribute to a global economy of increasing disparities which perpetuate poverty, starvation and the degradation of land. These processes are manifestations of debt-financed and export-oriented modernization patterns that continue to dominate development thinking and practice. The first section examines the relationship between debt and the environment. The second looks at how export-oriented growth strategies, as integral features of SAPs, have led to the intensification of land use and the over-exploitation of resources. Our third section examines some recent thinking on the inter-connectedness of gender, SAPs and ecology. The final section takes a critical look at the World Bank's recent attempts to integrate environmental concerns within the SAP paradigm.

Debt Financed Mega-Projects

Much of the money borrowed by developing countries[2] from the World Bank was used to finance large-scale mega-projects requiring a high degree of foreign involvement. The environmental legacy of the mega-project mentality, fostered by the World Bank, Western donor agencies, and private lending institutions, has become an issue of popular focus and attention. The depletion of the rainforest, forced resettlement, the genocide of indigenous tribes, flooding of immense expanses of productive land, and soil salinization are only a few of the horrific effects of a modernization mentality pursued by elites in developing countries who enjoy the blessing and backing of the international lending community.[3]

Not surprisingly, when debtor countries default on loan payments, many environmental groups have breathed a sigh of relief. When financing falters, the life-blood for these mega-projects is temporarily cut off. This should not be viewed, however, as a victory for sustainable development policies. The related social effects of SAPs and their impact on the environment must also be considered.

Social and Ecological Consequences

Agencies like the World Bank have used the debt crisis to impose SAPs on debtor nations so that they will reduce their tariffs on imports, cut government spending and increase exports. Adopting these measures is viewed by the World Bank as, "the most important ingredient in dealing with the debt problem", which will enable developing countries "to return to growth".[4]

However, SAPs have forced farmers in developing countries to operate as poor environmental managers. The massive deforestation taking place in Brazil and Ghana can be directly traced to these countries' attempts to service their debts by increasing their exports. Developing countries are exploiting their natural resources in order to finance a lifestyle for elites. Lumber and minerals have become the commodities that developing countries offer developed countries to finance their debt. And while the world market sets these commodities at ever depreciating prices, developing countries are forced to exploit their resources at a frantic pace.

A study commissioned by Friends of the Earth (Netherlands)

examined the effects of the debt crisis on the environment in a number of countries in the South. Ghana was one of the case studies. The report notes a variety of disturbing developments that have occurred since Ghana adopted a structural adjustment programme. Unprecedented deforestation and industrial water pollution were some of the effects cited. Ghana's push to increase its gold exports has led to cyanide poisoning of rivers and other water sources. It is estimated that the environmental costs of this degradation (not including the industry and mining sectors) amounted to roughly 4 per cent GDP, an amount higher than its rate of economic growth.[5] Ghana also passed a law which provided for numerous investment incentives. Between 1985 and 1989 the number of independent logging companies skyrocketed from 90 to over 800. If current trends continue, some estimate that Ghana will have depleted its forests by the year 2000.

Export-Oriented Growth and Land Use

An analysis of the goods that are protected in the North and those that are given preferential access reveals how land-use in the South is dictated primarily by economic forces in the North. For example, the importation of fodder crops (crops for animal consumption) by the European Community represents a displacement of over 10,000,000 ha. of land in developing countries. This highly inefficient diversion of food crop production for conversion to animal protein subsidizes the intensive livestock production practices in the North. Meanwhile, as land for food crops becomes more scarce in the South, poverty and land degradation increase. An examination of existing patterns of land use reveals how the international trading system works to meet the needs of rich consumers at the expense of poor farmers.[6]

Under the logic of the present international trading system predicated on structural adjustment, developing countries have been continuously pressured to increase exports in order to offset the continuously deteriorating terms of trade with the North. This forces producers to clear rainforests for export-led cattle production and increase the use of land for export crops rather than food crops. In Africa, nine countries rely on 3 commodities for over 90 per cent of their income (see Table 7.1). Meanwhile, *every* African country experiences a negative balance of trade with their former colonizers.[7]

What makes these figures even more disturbing is the fact that *imports* of staple food grains and processed food from industrialized countries have steadily increased. These have also had a marked impact on domestic food production and the prices of subsistence food crops. To comprehend the effects of deteriorating terms of trade at the local level we must examine the effects of export-oriented development on the terms of trade *at the producer level*. It is here that the devastating environmental impact of implementing SAPs can be assessed. From an ecological perspective, the international trading system is incapable of weighing the long-term environmental havoc wrought by continual resource exploitation for the purpose of earning scarce foreign exchange. This is largely due to the logic of the international trading system which dictates local level land-use policies in developing countries. In terms of policies and pricing, it has resulted in an even greater emphasis on export crops over crops oriented toward domestic consumption than occurred during the colonial period. This orientation towards extracting a surplus from the land has meant, "the predominance of forms of production in which the criterion of the economic yield of investment increasingly prevails over the ecological aspect".[8]

Land use is not dictated by basic needs in the developing world but upon consumer demand in the North. It has led to a situation where, for instance, the North American and European penchant for beef and cheaper hamburgers dictates land-use policies away from production for domestic consumption to the highly inefficient use of land for grazing or production of fodder crops.[9] In the process, subsistence farmers are forced to move to increasingly marginal land and to cultivate it more intensively to meet their basic needs.[10] This leads to overcrowding on land of low agricultural potential, increased landlessness and greater malnutrition. This, in turn, directly contributes to soil erosion, land depletion and rainforest destruction.

It is the producer and the environment which bear the brunt of export-oriented development models. Perpetually squeezed by lower prices and loss of control over production and inputs, producers are forced into unsustainable landuse. Soil erosion and deforestation are the inevitable results of this pauperization of rural areas.

In areas with fragile growing conditions, such as in Africa, the results have been disastrous. These results can be traced to the added

Table 7.1: Africa's Commodity Problems: Towards a Solution

Share of Three Leading Commodities in Total Exports by Country
(1983-84)

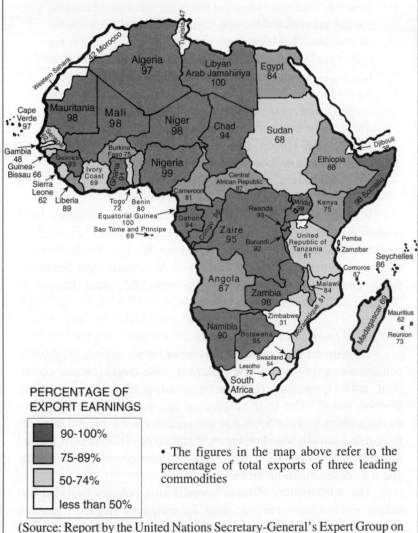

PERCENTAGE OF EXPORT EARNINGS

- 90-100%
- 75-89%
- 50-74%
- less than 50%

• The figures in the map above refer to the percentage of total exports of three leading commodities

(Source: Report by the United Nations Secretary-General's Expert Group on Africa's Commodity Problems, 1990.)

uncertainties that trade in an unstable global economy have brought to bear on farmers and pastoralists. This has set into motion processes that have, in large measure, led to the famines in these areas. Charles Perrings describes some of the consequences for agrarian societies of incorporation into the international trading system:

> Since certain input and output prices are set in world markets the link between real income, savings, and local environmental conditions has been partly severed. More particularly, the role of traditional institutions in regulating capacity utilization has been substantially weakened, with implications both for the incentive effects of traditional communal or common property, and for the way that uncertainty is accommodated. There are now two sources of uncertainty – the environment and the world market – and the behaviour of agrarian producers is very much a function of the methods chosen to minimize risk in both areas.[11]

Perrings goes on to remark how, under these conditions, local producers resort to drastically reduced time frames with respect to land and livestock management as survival strategies. It is "market forces", and not aggregate food production, which have made local producers more vulnerable to the exigencies of poverty and placed them on an "optimal path to extinction".

SAPs and the African Environment[12]

The current international division of labour casts most African countries as exporters of raw materials, cash crops (cotton, cocoa, sisal, coffee), minerals (oil, bauxite, coal, goal) and agro-forestry (timber, wood). The re-imposition of this pattern of development through the policies of SAPs has had serious environmental impacts. Export-led growth based on the exploitation of raw materials has led to creeping "savannization" of the forest, "sahelization" of the savanna and the "desertification" of the Sahel.

The introduction of trade liberalization policies has also had serious environmental implications. Essentially Africa has become a dumping ground for goods and services that are contaminated, expired and hazardous. Trade liberalization involves the removal of most restrictions on imports to facilitate foreign investment. In order to attract foreign business, many African countries have created free trade zones, simplified the process of investment, and introduced new industrial policies. Consequently, products that cannot meet Northern environmental guidelines are dumped in the continent and pollution-intensive production, like asbestos and pulp and paper, have shifted their base to Africa. Indeed, World Bank chief economist Lawrence Summer's suggestion that African countries import toxic wastes and polluting industries is already commonplace in many African countries.[13]

The dumping of toxic waste in the continent is attributable to the struggle to gain foreign exchange to make debt payments and the liberalization of trade which are the conditions of SAPs. In an environment of lax import controls and the virtual collapse of many governments, Africa has become the new site of toxic dumping. Although these products could be dumped more safely in the North, it is more costly to do so. It costs between $160 to $1000 per ton, and for the most dangerous between $2000-3000 per ton, to dispose of toxic wastes in the North. High temperature incineration costs between $500-$1,200 per ton, but Benin was offered $2.50 per ton to do the deed. Canada's Denison Mining Corporation entered an agreement with Gabon to dump its nuclear waste from its Colorado-based uranium mines.[14]

Cash-strapped African countries have become victims of toxic waste merchants because of the debt crisis. The Organization of African Unity passed a resolution banning the dumping of toxic waste in the continent. The question remains, however, whether countries in severe financial crisis would not be tempted to import toxic waste to earn foreign exchange.

Diversification of exports, which have become the catch-phrase in the era of SAPs, have also resulted in environmental abuses. In Cameroon, 150 licensed timber operating companies are involved in commercial logging, of which 23 are indigenous. Namibia's department of sea fisheries is involved in the large-scale harvesting of seals about to be exported to the Far East. According to the Namibia Animal Action Group, the first year mortality of seals is as high as 95 percent.[15]

The companies and governments involved are clearly preoccupied with the short-term benefits and do not take into consideration the sustainability of their activities. When the environment is abused beyond any profitability, the corporations pack their bags and leave. Poor farmers, whose lands were taken, have to contend with the menace of erosion, deforestation, drought, and famine. Pastoralists fight endlessly with peasant farmers over grazing lands.

Gender, Ecology and SAPs

Another area of growing concern is the gender-ecology-SAPs nexus. This approach attempts to integrate ecological concerns into gender-based analyses of the impact of SAPs.

A gender-ecology-SAP approach provides a framework for understanding the effects that the imposition of SAPs has on women and the sources of their livelihoods. It is women who are the most intimately involved with the land in developing countries. In Africa women grow over 90 per cent of the food domestically consumed. It is women, moreover, who most acutely bear the brunt of policies which wrest basic decision-making power from them and force them into unsustainable land practices in order to survive.

Assessing the role of women in shaping the environment is a complex task. Their role in contributing to environmental degradation is also the subject of often heated debates with arguments ranging from the simplistic neo-Malthusian explanations, which persist in World Bank thinking, to more nuanced approaches which embrace issues of political economy and gender.[16] Fiona Mackenzie argues that adopting a gender-ecology-SAP framework entails an assessment of the assumptions which underlie most impact studies on the effects of SAPs. To ask whether SAPs "cause" ecological degradation or the worsening of women's well-being is to adopt the dominant classical paradigm of causality which is always inconclusive, if not misleading. Robin Mearns calls for a shift from a reductionist scientific model of causality to an open system more akin to natural science feedback models or Quantum Physics. As Mearns points out about the normative models for impact studies on the effects of SAPs:

> ...those who construct the model do not recognize that the real world also includes complex, non-linear relationships... they believe them to be random, incidental and unimportant in aggregate.[17]

With the shift from food to commodity production women are "doubly-squeezed" by the increased labour required to grow these crops and the fact that it is the men who tend to appropriate the proceeds of this labour.[18] Mackenzie takes the results of gender impact studies on SAPs a step further to examine how women alter their land-management strategies. Many women are forced to forgo practices aimed at conserving the long-term sustainability of the soil for short-term survival purposes. By drawing together the results from two spheres of research – gender-based analyses of SAPs and geography studies of shifting land-use practices – Mackenzie demonstrates the connection between macro-economic policies such as SAPs and changes in sustainable resource management. Women have less time for these activities and are compelled to grow crops that require less time to cultivate on a more intensive basis.

Drawing on case studies from Ghana, Tanzania and Kenya, Mackenzie demonstrates how the squeeze on women's labour, access to land and income has resulted from macro-economic policies which have forced women to "violate their own knowledge"[19] by taking short-cuts with respect to land-management. While the ecological impacts of these kinds of changes in landuse practices are not imme-diately apparent or easily measurable, they form part of a range of processes that are contributing to the gradual deterioration of the soil, forests and waters of the continent.

The configuration of export-oriented trade policies must be considered along with the debt crisis in any examination of the impact of SAPs on African economies and environments. In doing so, we encounter the less obvious and long-term effects of the World Bank's development model for sub-Saharan Africa. These environmental concerns are also becoming effectively marginalized by the World Bank as it manoeuvres to become not only the African, but also the global, manager of the environment.

The World Bank and the Environment

It is only recently that the World Bank has become a convert to the virtues of integrating environmental concerns into its adjustment paradigm. As late as 1989, *From Crisis to Sustainable Growth* mentioned only in passing the importance of policies that protect the environment. In this report the World Bank notes, with some alarm, the looming environmental catastrophe: deforestation outstripping the rate of new tree planting by a ratio of 29 to 1; over 80 per cent of rangelands and dryland seriously affected by soil erosion; and pervasive declines in the fertility of cultivated land.[20] The causes of the crisis are attributed to overgrazing, overcultivation, and deforestation by farmers who do not have the required labour at hand to engage in conservation techniques. The root causes for this neglect of conservation on the part of the farmer are again attributed to low prices and land insecurity. *From Crisis* states confidently that adjustment-oriented policies would arrest this process and provide the needed incentives for conservation:

> A more prosperous rural environment – resulting from the removal of price, exchange rate, and fiscal and other distortions together with greater security of tenure and improvements in productivity – is necessary for farmers, forest dwellers, and pastoralists to have an interest in conservation. Conservation will fail unless it appeals to the farmer's self-interest.[21]

The approach suggests that a sound macro-policy environment incorporating liberalized trade and private property will offer the best future for Africa's fragile environment. Also emphasized is the need to reverse deforestation through such means as agro-forestry.

The 1991 *World Development Report* resorts to neo-Malthusian arguments in citing overpopulation as one of the sources of environmental degradation. This argument is based on what is described as the population-environment-poverty nexus. Sub-Saharan Africa, with its fragile soil base, cannot sustain the rates of population growth of the past two decades. Rapid population growth forces farmers to reduce fallow periods and to migrate onto more marginal lands.[22] Reference to this phenomenon is on the rise in World Bank literature, suggesting a return to the 1970s neo-Malthusian arguments surrounding the need for population control as the answer to Africa's crisis.[23] Nowhere in World Bank documents for Africa in the 1980s is a connection made between SAPs and ecological destruction.

1992 marked the year of the long-awaited UN Conference on Environment and Development (UNCED). Several years in the planning, this conference brought together business, governments, development and environment agencies, and NGO interests from the North and South to work out a global strategy for development and environmental protection. The World Bank has become a key player in UNCED and is still part of the manoeuvring that is taking place with regard to the programme of action that emerged from the conference. In 1990 the Global Environment Facility (GEF) was established largely through the initiative of a number of European countries. The GEF was envisioned as a pilot programme to provide grants or concessional loans to developing countries to help with projects and programmes designed to protect the environment. This programme was jointly administered by three UN agencies: the World Bank, the UN Development Programme, and the UN Environment Programme. However, it soon became clear that it was the World Bank which would be the chief administrator, with the other two agencies providing technical and monitoring assistance. According to a French delegate, the reason for handing over control of the GEF to the World Bank was simple: "There is no other institution which is capable of administering the GEF and capable of dealing with the huge amount of money that will be needed by the developing countries in the future."[24]

By effectively taking over control of the GEF, the World Bank has become the lead agency in implementing and administering the programme that emerged from the UNCED. NGOs have challenged the World Bank's control of the GEF. They are questioning the World Bank's environmental record which they see as one of the primary agents of environmental destruction. They also are wary of the bank's expertise, its undemocratic structure, and lack of accountability.[25]

To mark the occasion of the 1992 UN Earth Summit and to demonstrate its concern for environmental issues, the World Bank released its 1992 *World Development Report* which focused on the theme of the environment. The report, entitled *Development and the Environment*, makes a number of claims about the environmental problems facing developing countries.

According to the report, the most important and immediate problems facing developing countries are overpopulation, unsafe water, inadequate sanitation, soil depletion, indoor smoke from cooking fires, and outdoor smoke from coal fires. While these issues do figure in the environmental equation, the report virtually ignores the practices of industrialized countries which have contributed to the present crisis: carbon dioxide emission, depletion of the stratosphere and ozone layer, water pollution, deforestation, photochemical smog, acid rain, soil erosion, and hazardous waste management.

The report fails to discuss the relationship between current economic development policies of developing countries and their environmental impact. Rather than address the fundamental disparities between rich and poor countries or the need for a fundamental redistribution of the world's assets, the report simplistically implies that overbreeding by uneducated women and deforestation by ignorant farmers are the major environmental problems besetting developing countries.

The World Bank sees population increase as one of the root causes of environmental degradation. In short, African women, according to the World Bank, are having too many babies. Such a perspective neglects the fact that while Third World nations consume only 20 per cent of world resources, Western countries, which make up only 16 per cent of the world's population and 24 per cent of its land, consume approximately 80 per cent of the world's resources. In fact, the average North American consumes more energy commuting to work in a week than the average African does for all uses in an entire year. Furthermore, Western countries are responsible for producing over 75 per cent of the world's environmental pollution. The World Bank's single-minded emphasis on overpopulation as the culprit distracts attention away from the more pressing issue of the North's over-consumption.[26]

The report also erroneously blames the destruction of precious vegetation solely on the peoples of developing countries. It is not the Third World peoples who are destroying their vegetation for the construction of large-scale industries; it is the multinational corporations who are looking for cheaper and greener pastures to exploit for maximum capitalist gains. A recent study conducted by the UN Centre on Transnational Corporations (which was recently abolished during the US-inspired restructuring of the United Nations) concluded that the activities of TNCs generate over half of the greenhouse gases emitted by the six industrial sectors having the greatest impact on global warming.[27]

The World Bank's Environmental Solution

The World Bank resorts to its standard menu of market-oriented solutions to solve the environmental crisis. Its key policy advice to developing countries is to continue to implement SAPs. The key recommendations of the report are aimed at increasing the role of the market, privatization of land ownership and increased efficiency of labour. By liberalizing their economies, the report argues, poor countries will be able to increase their output dramatically. While greater pollution will occur at first, "rising income will make environmental protection affordable and such protection will enable future income growth".[28]

An Alternative Approach

It is clear that the interests of the global environment will not be well served by the World Bank. The countries of the South and their allies in the North must continue to lobby hard for the democratization of the World Bank and the GEF. In its present form, the World Bank cannot and should not be allowed to control an agenda on which the entire fate of the world depends.

Rather than promote hi-tech, market-oriented solutions to the environmental problems facing African countries, we need to support approaches which will enhance the role of small-scale farmers. These include the transfer and support of appropriate technology such as fuel-efficient stoves, waste-to-fuelwood schemes such as biogas, and solar energy. Most important is the just resolution of the debt problem facing all developing countries, since it is the single-most important cause of environmental destruction and poverty. In resolving the debt issue we recognize the close relationship that exists between our global economic system, the environment, the protection of indigenous peoples, and the satisfaction of our basic needs.

Churches, in the North and South, are active in movements and coalitions that are forming to speak out against the injustices of the current global economic order predicated on debt and unjust trading relations. Chapters 9 and 10 focus on the response of the churches in sub-Saharan Africa to the crisis of structural adjustment.

Endnotes

1. M. Redclift, *Sustainable Development: Exploring the Contradictions*, (London: Methuen, 1987), p. 72.
2. For instance, between 1983-85, fully 70% of Latin American loans of the big ten debtors was repatriated abroad. The Stockholm International Peace Research Institute estimates that 20% of Third World debt can be attributed to arms purchases. See S. George, *A Fate Worse than Debt*, pp. 20-22.
3. P. Adams and L. Solomon, *In the Name of Progress*, (Toronto: Energy Probe, 1985), pp. 37-57; also Susan George, *A Fate Worse than Debt*, pp. 156-63; and B. Rich, "Multi-lateral Development Banks: Their Role in Destroying the Global Environment," *Ecologist* 15 no.1/2 (1985), pp. 56-68.
4. World Bank, *World Development Report* 1989, pp. 19, 22.
5. Friends of the Earth (Netherlands), *Debt and Development in the Third World*, (Netherlands: Friends of the Earth, 1991), p. 11.
6. Redclift, *Sustainable Development*, p. 94.
7. B. Dinham and C. Hines, *Agribusiness in Africa*, (Trenton: Africa World Press, 1984), p. 11.
8. O. Sunkel, "The Interaction Between Styles of Development and the Environment in Latin America," *CEPAL Review* 12 (1980), p. 33.
9. For instance, cattle farms for the European market thrive in famine-stricken Sahel. 800-900 kilograms of grain are used per capita in the industrialized countries to fatten cattle per year while 150–200 kilograms would be sufficient to feed a Third World resident and his or her chickens. A. Gorz, *Ecology as Politics*, (Montreal: Black Rose Books, 1980), p. 96.
10. O. Sunkel, "The Interaction between Styles of Development and the Environment in Latin America," p. 28.
11. C. Perrings, "An Optimal Path to Extinction? Poverty and Resource Degradation in the Open Agrarian Economy," *Journal of Development Economics* 30 (1989), p. 5.
12. This section and the section critiquing the World Bank's 1992 *World Development Report* adapt material from an article co-written by Patience Elabor-Idemudia, John Mihevc and Kole Shettima entitled "World Bank Takes Control of UNCED's Environment Fund," *Economic Justice Update*, (Summer 1992).
13. "Leaked World Bank Memo Sparks Debate," *BankCheck* (Winter 1992) pp. 1, 6.
14. Elabor-Idemudia *et al.*, "World Bank", p. 4.
15. Elabor-Idemudia *et al.*, "World Bank", p. 4.
16. A. Salau, "Environment and Gender: Ecological Crisis, Women and the Quest for Sustainable Development in Africa," (paper prepared for the Council for the Development of Economic and Social Research in Africa Workshop on Gender Analysis and African Social Science, Dakar (September 1991), p. 10.

17. R. Mearns, *Environmental Implications of Structural Adjustment: Reflections on Scientific Method* (IDS Discussion Paper No. 284, University of Sussex, 1991), p. 24.
18. F. Mackenzie, "Exploring the Connection" (unpublished draft, 1991), p. 5.
19. B. Kettel, "Women and Environments: Challenging the Myths," (Environment and Women Session, CIDA, 20-21 June, 1990), cited in Mackenzie, "Exploring the Connection," p. 5.
20. *From Crisis*, p. 101.
21. *From Crisis*, p. 101.
22. *World Development Report* 1991, p. 61.
23. For instance see K. Cleaver, "The Population, Agriculture and Environment Nexus in Sub-Saharan Africa," (World Bank, Draft Discussion Paper, May 1990).
24. S. Elegant, "NGOs Concerned Over World Bank Role in 'Green Fund'," *Third World Economics* (16-30 September 1991), p. 7.
25. V. Shiva, "Why the World Bank Should Not be the Guardian of the World's Environment," *Third World Economics* (1-15 October 1991), pp. 18-19.
26. Elabor-Idemudia *et al.*, "World Bank".
27. M. Khor, "UN Restructuring against South's Interests," *Third World Economics* 42 (1-15 June 1992), pp. 19-20.
28. World Bank, *World Development Report* 1992, p. 1.

— CHAPTER EIGHT —

The Ambiguous Promise of Biotechnology

The fact that micro-organisms, as distinguished from chemical compounds, are alive is a distinction without large significance. (Chief Justice Warren, Diamond vs. Chakrabarty, 1980)[1]

The 1980 landmark US Supreme Court case of Diamond vs. Chakrabarty stands as a watershed in the process by which biogenetic material and processes can be privately owned. The case involved the application for patenting a bacterium which can literally digest oil slicks. In its decision the Supreme Court broke with its longstanding principles in these matters, i.e., "if it is living, it is not patentable".[2]

In 1985, the US Patent and Trademark Office granted the first patent for a plant. In 1988, a patent was granted for an animal, a mouse, which had been genetically altered to render it susceptible to breast cancer. The real significance of the genetically altered mouse for Harvard University and Monsanto, the corporation to which it licensed the production rights, is that they can collect royalties on the offspring of the original mouse for 17 years. One need only apply the same process, notes Brewster Kneen, to the cattle or poultry industry to realize the potential profits that lie in store for universities and corporations engaged in this type of research.[3]

A mere four months after the Supreme Court decision of June 1980, Genentech, one of the first biotechnology firms, offered its stock for sale. Within minutes the stock soared from $35 to $89 a share and the company was able to raise $55 million within a few hours. The company did not, as yet, have a single product on the market.[4] In early 1990, a controlling share (60 per cent) of the company was purchased by the Swiss pharmaceutical giant, Hoffmann-La Roche, for $2.1 billion.[5]

There is great optimism surrounding the many diseases and deficiencies of nature which biotechnology is on the verge of solving. Popular magazines and newspapers herald the exciting discoveries in the field of biotechnology in areas such as AIDS vaccines, cancer treatment, cystic fibrosis, and other infectious diseases. As an adjunct to curing diseases, biotechnology supporters claim that it may solve the global food crisis and eradicate hunger permanently. For developing countries, biotechnology is promoted as the solution to the persistent problems of low productivity, hunger, poverty, and health.[6] As Michael Apple notes with great optimism:

> We are on the threshold of the transformation of plants into novel varieties with important new properties. By adding new genetic information to plants and by altering the genetic information they already contain, the possibility of creating food plants which can overcome the barriers we now see as constraining our food supplies is evident... .[7]

In agriculture, genetic manipulation is on the verge of artificially controlling the ripening of apples, developing frost-resistant citrus fruits and super-ovulating cattle, as well as producing genetically engineered chocolate, coffee, maize and vanilla. The benefits of these technologies are proffered as a panacea to developing countries which will be able, finally, to conquer the problems of hunger and disease. These new technologies of food production are less dependent on petroleum-based agriculture. They would also help to solve the problem of land scarcity since, theoretically, production would be partially removed from the land and into laboratories.

In 1990, total Research and Development (R&D) in biotechnology amounted to roughly $11 billion.[8] Between two-thirds and three-quarters of this research is privately funded and increasingly concentrated, as multi-national pharmaceutical, chemical and seed companies scramble to buy out each other and the smaller biotechnology firms. Almost all of the previously independent biotechnology companies are currently under the control of the TNCs, as subsidiaries or through joint ventures (Tables 8.1 and 8.2). This consolidation and increased monopolization has taken place alongside an unprecedented explosion of biotech research carried out by universities under contract to TNCs.

Table 8.1: The 'True' New Biotechnology Firms

NBF	Activity	Founder	Comment
Agrisense	AgBiotech	Provesta and Dow Corning	Joint venture of the two corporations
Beghin Meiji	Sweeteners	Beghin-Say and Meiji Seika Kaisah	
Biocode Ltd.	DiagKits	Shell	Full subsidiary
Bionks Co.	AgBiotech	Kyowa Hakko Kogyo and NPI	Joint venture, Sumitomo Corp. also involved
Chembred	AgBiotech	American Cyanamid	Fully owned
Clause Genetic System	AgBiotech	Clause and PGS	50-50 joint venture
Danisco	AgBiotech	DD-Sukker, DD-Sprit and Danisco	Fusion of the three companies, $1.8 billion estim. turnover
Diaplus	DiagKits	Hoffm.-La Roche and NPA Biotechnologia	Joint venture of the TNC & USSR company
FloriGene	AgBiotech	Sandoz, DNAP and others	Sandoz involved via Zaadunie
Fresh World	AgBiotech	DuPont and DNAP	Joint venture
Gene Shears PTY	AgBiotech	Limagrain and CSIRO	$20 million investment by Limagrain in this Australian project
Grand Biotech. Co.	AgBiotech	Miyoshi, Tokyo Menka Kaisha and KYS	Joint venture of the two Japanese companies and a seed company from Taiwan
Huale Seeds	AgBiotech	Sapporo Breweries & National Seed Corp.	Joint venture of Japanese & Chinese groups
Keygene	AgBiotech	Rabo-Biotech Venture Fund	Rabo is large bank in the Netherlands
Mecor Inc.	BioFood	Meiji Seika Kaisha	Fully owned by the Japanese TNC
Micro-Bio Rhizogen	AgBiotech	AGC and RhizoGen Corp.	Joint venture
Oxford Glyco-systems	Carbohydr.	Monsanto and others	Also involved: Adven Ltd., Alafi Capital Corp. and Univ. of Oxford
SDS Biotech KK	AgroChem	Sandoz and Showa Denko	Joint venture of Swiss and Japanese groups
Valent USA Corp (USA)	AgBiotech	Sumitomo & Chevron	New American subsidiary of the two TNCs

(Source: Hobbelink, *Biotechnology*, p.35)

Table 8.2: Investments in Food- and Agriculture-Related Biotech Companies
(Take-overs and equity investments, 1988-90, selected cases)

Company	Partner	Activity	Comment
Biotechnica (USA)	Molecular Genetics (USA)	agbiotech	Biotechnica buys MG's germplasm and plant breeding divisions for some $4 million
Biotechnica (USA)	Several	seeds	The agricultural division of the American biotech company bought four US seed companies: McAllister Seed, Horizon Seeds, Plant Science Research, Flanagan Soybean Research Co.
Booker	Daehnfelt (DK)	seeds	Controlling interest acquired in Feb. 1988; planned to bid for remaining shares
British Am. Tobacco	Twyford Int'l (UK)	agbiotech	The TNC buys the UK biotech research centre of Twyford
Calgene (USA)	Desert Cotton Co.	seeds	Desert Cotton bought by Calgene's subsidiary, Stoneville Pedigree Seed
Calgene (USA)	Plant Genetics Inc. (USA)	agbiotech	Calgene takes over Plant Genetics
Danisco (DK)	Three Danish companies	food/seed	Danske Sukkerfabbrikker Danske Soritfabbrikker and Danisco fuse into a new company: Danisco. Strong in agricultural biotech, seeds and food processing
DNAP (USA)	AGS (USA)	agbiotech	DNAP buys Advanced Genetic Sciences
ICI (UK)	Contiseed (USA)	seeds	ICI buys Contiseed from Continental Grain for $50 million. Strong in Latin America, Australia and Thailand

(continues on pps 203 & 4)

Japan Tobacco (J)	Plant Genetic Systems(B)	seeds	Japan Tobacco buys 25% of PGS ($6 million)
Kirin Brewery (J)	Tokita Seed (J)	seeds	Kirin buys 20% of Tokita Seed, currently No. 11 in Japanese seed production
Kubota (J)	Mycogen (USA)	biopestic	Kubota intends to buy 14% of the US biotech firm Mycogen, specialized in the field of biopesticides
Limagrain (F)	Picard & Co. (UK)	seeds	The French leader in seeds strengthens its position in the UK through this acquisition
Limagrain (F)	Shissler Seed Co. (USA)	seeds	Limagrain buys the seeds division of Shissler
Lubrizol (USA)	Sungene (USA)	agbiotech	The TNC, already big in seeds, buys Sungene
Mitsubishi/ Meiji (J)	Bio-Isolates (UK)	food	The two Japanese firms bought 22% of BI's capital (for $3.7 million) and obtained exclusive rights to market BI's products in Japan
Mitsubishi (J)	Nestlé (CH)	food	The Japanese TNC buys two companies from Nestlé: Trex (fats) and Princes (canned food). This is considered the first move to strengthen its food and biotech operations in Europe
Procter & Gamble (USA)	Calgene (USA)	agbiotech	P & G buys over 700,000 common shares of Calgene for $5 million
Rhône-Poulene & Orsan (F)	Clause (F)	seeds	Orsan (daughter of Lafarge-Coppee) and Rhône-Poulene buy 45% of Clause seed company. Lafarge already had 10% and the two TNCs have now majority control. All seeds interests were put together in one new company: Aritoris, 50:50 owned by the two TNCs

Rhône-Poulene (F)	Nordica Int'l Inc (USA)	food	R-Poulene buys Nordica, a US company specialized in milk and cheese
Sandoz (CH)	Coker's Pedigree Seed (USA)	seeds	Sandoz's US subsidiary Northrup King buys Cocker's Pedigree Seed Co.
Sandoz (CH)	Hilleshög (S)	seeds	Sandoz buys Hilleshög from Volvo. Buyout includes 10% equity in PGS (Belgium) and 15% in Advance Genetic Science (USA)
Sanofi (F)	King Group (CDN)	seeds	Sanofi is full daughter of Elf-Aquitaine (F), already a major seed company with 1988 turnover of $107 million. With the acquisition of King Group, it further strengthens its seeds interests
(USA)	Biotech-nica (USA)	agbiotech	State Farm Life Insurance Co. increases its investment in Bio-Technica Int'l with $23 million) and now owns 67% of its shares
Shell (UK/NL)	Maxell Hybrids (USA)	seeds	Shell's subsidiary Nickerson Seed buys Maxell. More recently Shell announced that it intends to sell Nickerson
Unilever (UK/NL)	Barenburg Seeds (NL)	seeds	Unilever buys 60% of the Dutch seed company
Unilever (UK/NL)	Biocom Bio-chemicals (IRL)	food	Unilever buys 74% of the Irish company specialized in enzymes and food colorants
Unilever (UK/NL)	Distillers Yeast Ltd. (UK)	food	Distillers Company Yeast Ltd. bought from Guinness for 26 million pounds sterling. Important for fermentation technology

(Source: Hobbelink, *Biotechnology*, pp. 37-39)

And yet the brave new world which biotechnology heralds contains many hidden perils, especially for small-scale farmers. A closer examination of the forces involved in the development of these new technologies for food production reveals many very disturbing features which do not bode well for African countries. Furthermore, the risks these technologies carry for the unleashing of unmitigated ecological disasters is also of considerable concern. This chapter examines *how* these new technologies are likely to impact on agriculture in Africa in the context of structural adjustment.

The World Bank's Biotechnology Vision

As with the Green Revolution, which it played a major role in supporting and implementing, the World Bank is keen to spread the good news of biotechnology to developing countries. In a major report published in 1988 applauding the success of the Green Revolution, the World Bank points to the future successes that lie ahead in the field of biotechnology.[9]

The World Bank sees great opportunities for African countries occuring through biotechnological innovations. According to *From Crisis to Sustainable Growth*, greater productivity, drought- and disease-resistant crops are only a few of the benefits that lie in store for African farmers. The report suggests an exciting set of new marketing opportunities in this field:

> A flexible African response to these competitive dynamics must be based on a close monitoring of biotechnological trends, more joint research and development partnerships with Western companies, and the development of substitute products.[10]

During the UNCED process, the World Bank promoted the granting of Intellectual Property Rights (IPRs) to international agricultural research centres. Such a scheme would enable these centres to enter into joint ventures with transnationals which would gain access to the centres' stocks of germplasm and subsequently apply for control over the genetic manipulation of these public resources. The World Bank also played a key role in transforming the UNCED treaty on biodiversity into a tract supporting the basic principles of biotechnology.

The Appropriation of Creation

> I think that the world seed trade figure is probably something like $30 billion annually. And this number, if you stop to think about it, simply represents a heck of a lot of DNA, the primary genetic input into the agricultural sector. Numero Uno. Not exactly a discretionary item. No agriculture without seeds.[11]

Often ignored in the optimistic literature on biotechnology are the global economic forces that are shaping the kinds of innovations that are developed. A more comprehensive evaluation of this technology considers biotechnology, not merely as an innovation, but as a revolution in the very way the processes of life itself are understood, appropriated and marketed. Unlike the Green Revolution which had only limited application, the bio-revolution has the capacity of radically transforming *every* aspect of food production as well as the international structures involved in determining the production, processing and distribution of these products.

What also distinguishes the bio-revolution from the Green Revolution, and must be included in any analysis of it, is the thrust towards privatization which is geared to guaranteeing the private profitability of biotechnology research. Biotechnology is geared towards privatized research driven by TNCs which are aided by the patent protection of their products. This process has occurred alongside the rapid accumulation in recent years of seed companies by multi-nationals largely involved in the chemical and pharmaceutical industries. This movement toward vertical integration ensures that these multi-nationals have virtual control over every stage in the production of food, including the type of seed developed and the types of fertilizers and pesticides to which a particular crop will respond.

The control over the means of food production right down to the level of the gene has profound implications for local producers. Not only is this technology beyond the reach of local producers, it threatens to appropriate from local producers what is left of their ability to benefit from nature's own self-reproduction of seeds as part of the fruit of its bounty. As J. Kloppenburg notes, biotechnological processes can be viewed as,

...part of the continuing process of primitive accumulation, for they function to uncouple agricultural producers from the autonomous reconstitution of their own means of production.[12]

From the perspective of local producers, there are three noteworthy features of biotechnology which augur not only for their increasing marginalization and dependency, and for an increasing loss of ecological diversity, the traditional bulwark against diseases and pests. These three features of the bio-revolution, which will be considered separately, are: 1) the privatization of biogenetic property; 2) the increasing privatization of R&D; and 3) the *socialization* of plant genetic resources. All three of these features define a context where the powerful manipulate and create institutions which define ownership, private property and the "legitimate" operation of the market.

The Privatization of Biogenetic Property

Allowing the manipulation of life's processes to fall under the absolute control of the private sphere has profound ramifications for our conception of nature's processes and for our understanding of life itself. The very information encoded in the DNA is falling under private control, to become a means of production.[13] In biotechnology, it is not the production of a particular gene or process that holds the greatest potential for profit, but the *ownership* of the genetically altered product that makes it so lucrative.[14] Through these decisions, the US has set in motion a global trend towards the "discovery" and subsequent patenting of any of life's processes having potential for profit.[15]

For instance, Canada has passed legislation that will facilitate the patenting of genetically altered plants and animals; and the US is pressuring other countries to pass similar legislation protecting the creators of these "new" life forms.[16]

It is the prospect of adding value at the most basic level of life's processes that is luring investors into the biotechnology industry and is one of the driving forces behind the explosion of take-overs that have occurred in the past few years. In the process, the role of labour in food production is being transformed by capital which, through the private ownership of manipulated biological processes, is able to control every aspect of food production. Poorer countries will increasingly become dependent on basic research performed in the North, for which they will be forced to pay annual royalties.

The Privatization of Research:
The University-Industrial Complex

> Biotechnologies are making the hitherto hidden convergences between knowledge, power and profits explicit.... . No more will the separation of science and profits work as a patriarchal fiction because the universities, the modern intellectual "commons", are being totally "corporatised" and privatized. Companies are buying up scientists and entire departments and programmes with multi-million dollar, multi-year contracts.[17]

The high cost of R&D in biotechnology, and the increased capital-intensive nature of this kind of research, has led to an ever-increasing association between universities and biotechnology firms. The major sources of investments in biotechnology come from venture capitalists who organized companies like Genentech, Genex, Biogen, and Cetus. These companies turned to the skilled scientific sector in universities, offering high salaries and multi-year contracts to carry out applied research. The biotechnology firms, cash-hungry from the outset, also looked for linkages with the large multi-nationals in search of particular products or research. Multi-nationals like Ciba-Geigy, Monsanto, DuPont, Sandoz, Hoechst, fresh from their acquisition of major seed companies, are banking on their ability to transfer quickly to the global market the fruits of any marketable discoveries made in university laboratories.[18] It is estimated that by the year 2000 between 10 and 20 TNCs will control the entire global seed market.[19]

Not only do the prohibitive start-up costs preclude developing countries from conducting this type of research, public agricultural research institutions in developing countries are also rapidly being squeezed out of performing basic research or being privatized with the support and urging of the World Bank. That leaves a very small group of research institutions and universities, funded by corporate sources, as the avant-garde to carry out R&D in biotechnology. This growing link between universities and corporations raises a number of disturbing implications for the future direction of scientific research (Table 8.3).

Basic research geared towards the public good or for the benefit of smallholder agriculture is being increasingly abandoned in favour of research dictated by the availability of corporate funding. This shift flows from the recognition among scientists and researchers that the primary goal of biotechnology research is profit and not public interest.[20]

Research conducted on malaria vaccines illustrates the implications of this more explicit link between universities and corporations. Research by scientists at New York University aimed at developing a malaria vaccine is geared primarily toward meeting the high income market of tourists and military personnel, and not towards the general populations of developing countries.[21] Genentech refused to release the vaccine for more general use in the Third World because the World Health Organization has refused to give it an exclusive licence, which would enable Genentech to collect monopoly rights on the production of malaria vaccine.[22]

In agriculture, biotechnology research is not primarily geared toward developing pest- or disease-resistant strains of crops. Instead, it is directed toward injecting herbicide-resistant genes into crops. For instance, researchers at Calgene, a major biotechnology firm, have implanted into cotton a gene that is resistant to Roundup, a herbicide which it also markets. Hence, the trend of biotechnological research is toward developing crops that will tolerate *increased* applications of herbicides and pesticides.

The ecological implications of this chemical assault on the land are not factored into a consideration of the consequences of these "new" techniques.[23] In fact, the $2 million cost of developing a herbicide-resistant crop is a good investment considering the $40 million estimated cost of developing a new herbicide. The same is true in the case of pesticides. Developing chemical-adaptable plants will increase sales considerably and is currently the route seed and biotechnology firms are vigorously pursuing.[24]

University researchers are also increasingly compelled to keep secret their research findings because they are potential trade secrets. Not only does corporate rivalry render exchange between colleagues

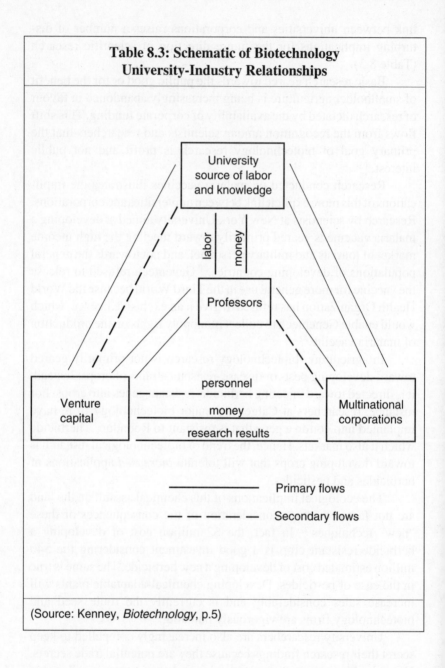

Table 8.3: Schematic of Biotechnology University-Industry Relationships

University
source of labor
and knowledge

labor   money

Professors

Venture
capital

personnel

money

research results

Multinational
corporations

—————— Primary flows

— — — — — Secondary flows

(Source: Kenney, *Biotechnology*, p.5)

increasingly rare, students and faculty from foreign countries more often than not find themselves completely excluded from this kind of research. The thrust toward research to develop marketable products in the universities is, in effect, leading to greater fragmentation, secrecy and the stifling of creative interaction among departments. Universities are increasingly finding their entire agenda being dictated from outside sources. Martin Kenney warns of the implications for the university of its collaboration with the biotechnology industry:

As the university is bought and parcelled out, basic science in the university will increasingly suffer. The speculative, non-commercial scholar will be at a disadvantage, and the intellectual commons ... will be eroded and polluted. Industry will then discover that by being congenitally unable to control itself and having no restraints placed on it by the public sector, it has polluted its own reservoir.[25]

The Socialization of Genetic Resources

It is estimated that over 95 per cent of plant genetic resources are located in the world's poorest countries.[26] It comes as no surprise, then, that genetic resources are the only aspect of biotechnology where the trend is toward socialization rather than privatization.[27] Plant genetic resources are the raw materials for biogenetic manipulation. It is precisely for this reason that the institutions and corporations in the North are eager to ensure that they continue to be considered as the "common heritage" of humankind. Such an arrangement gives biotechnology firms unlimited and, for the most part, free access to the labour and research which is devoted to collecting, screening and maintaining the huge range of plant species. This work is carried out by the International Board of Plant Genetic Resources (IBPGR) which was established in 1974 to collect, maintain and exchange plant genetic resources.

The maintenance of these resources has proven to be a very useful safety valve for misguided agricultural practices in the North. Examples abound of situations where strains or germplasm from developing countries have rescued crops in the North from serious diseases. Pat Roy Mooney notes the profound reality that often escapes notice in the North:

> ...the so-called "bread basket" nations may be grain-rich but they are gene poor and wholly dependent upon the Third World for the long-term survival of Western agriculture.[28]

In effect, the IBPGR performs a vital service for biotechnology firms by facilitating their access both to the germplasm and labour power of developing countries. Once turned over to the North, the plants and germplasms are manipulated and patented, to be sold back to the South where exorbitant prices are paid for what in effect belongs to them without any hope of their ever gaining access to the technology and skills by which these "improved" varieties are developed. Estimates of the potential global sales of biotechnology-based agricultural inputs range between $50-100 billion per annum.[29] What J. Kloppenburg predicted in 1984 is already occurring with great rapidity:

> The gene revolution in the Third World will probably involve the extraction of genetic resources from the LDCs, their incorporation into commercial plant and animal varieties in the corporate laboratories of the advanced industrial nations, and the reintroduction of these improved varieties into the LDCs via an expanding factor market. Once again, biotechnology may well reflect the historical experience of hybrid corn by generating not a reduction in regional disparities, but the intensification of existing inequalities.[30]

Consequences for Local-Level Agriculture

The transformation in small-scale agriculture resulting from the bio-revolution is difficult to predict. However, the trends that are already apparent are quite disturbing. It is no exaggeration to claim that biotechnology represents the final blow to the survival of smallholder agriculture. In agro-industrial terms, rural small-scale agriculture, primarily carried out by women, is considered as a passive residual left behind by the Green Revolution.[31] The fruits of the bio-revolution are completely out of reach of the smallholder because it will be necessary for the state to reorganize agriculture to provide sufficiently large enough units to accommodate the new technology. Vandana Shiva warns that biotechnology will dramatically intensify the disparities first wrought by the Green Revolution:

> While the Green Revolution and the Bio-revolution differ in scope and impact of control, they share the logic of commoditization and demand-led growth in agriculture. If the package is technologically and financially beyond the access of the ordinary cultivator and people by its research and resource intensity, biotechnologies will breed new inequalities and new ecological hazards.[32]

The shift towards large-scale farming estates is already occurring in many developing countries. The debt crisis and the implementation of SAPs are facilitating this transformation. Developing countries scrambling to restructure their economies to meet IMF and World Bank demands are rapidly eliminating what little support they gave to small farmers and abolishing marketing boards. The completion of the Uruguay GATT Round effectively sealed the demise of marketing boards and supply-management systems.

The burgeoning biotechnology industry also threatens to wipe out the primary sources of foreign exchange for many developing countries. A return to our case study of Ghana and cocoa provides a good case in point.

Biotechnology and the Future of Ghana's Cocoa Industry

> It might seem elaborate and clumsy to first extract genes from plants and animals, then incorporate them into something else, only to produce substances that have to be further modified to resemble the food we used to eat. But the detour is logical if one takes into account by and for whom the technology is being developed. Under the control of the food processors and chemical industries, biotechnology creates a new comparative advantage, this time of industry over agriculture.[33]

Cocoa production is carried out largely in West Africa, Brazil, Ecuador and Malaysia. These are the only climatic regions that can grow this sensitive crop. Over half of the world's cocoa is grown by smallholders but the international trade is dominated by state farms. Production shifted significantly from Latin America in the early 1900s to West Africa, which, by the 1960s, produced about 75 per cent of the world's cocoa. Since then, countries like Brazil and Malaysia have moved in to increase their share of global production significantly. Malaysia, for example, quadrupled its cocoa plantations in the 1980s through the introduction of higher-yielding varieties which increase output per hectare considerably (up to six times more than Ghana). Ghana's global market share has shrunk dramatically from about 27 per cent in 1970 to only 10 per cent for 1990 (Graphs 8.1 and 8.2).

The impact of developments in biotechnology has already been severely felt by African producers of cocoa like Ghana. Newer producers like Malaysia have been able to introduce these higher-yielding cocoa hybrids into the large-scale plantations, both cutting significantly into the market share of African producers as well as resulting in overproduction and a significant lowering of prices. Advances in biotechnology are expected to increase cocoa output from the present level of 150-200 kilograms per acre to about 1400 kilograms per acre.[34]

The other major development which threatens the cocoa industry in Ghana is the search by TNCs to develop cocoa substitutes through biotechnology. The US, by far the largest importer of cocoa, has not been able to monopolize control over the price of cocoa successfully over the years because of the narrow range of suppliers. Biotechnology, however, holds out the prospect for the chocolate firms to completely transform the global cocoa trade. In collaboration with universities such as Cornell, Pennsylvania State and Reading, and biotechnology firms such as Genencor, multi-nationals such as Hershey's, Cadbury-Schweppes and Nestlé are attempting to produce higher-yield cocoa plants and cocoa butter through various forms of enzymatic processing or protein engineering. Success has already been achieved in this latter area, although at an uncompetitive cost. A low-cost, laboratory produced cacao butter is, however, imminent, as are a number of other processes that will enable the production of cocoa from other vegetable oils and by micro-organisms, virtually eliminating the need for

Table 8.4: Cocoa Production, Yield, Exports and Dependency

	Production 1987 (1000 MT)	% change[1] 1980/87	Yield 1987 (KG/HA)	Exports 1987[2] (MIL.$)	Dependency on cocoa exports[3]
Cameroon	120	0%	267	237	52%
Ghana	210	-22%	175	489	99%
Ivory C.	570	21%	543	1084	57%
Nigeria	130	-23%	186	168	73%
Brazil	405	23%	622	606	7%
Malaysia	175	361%	1072	344	9%
Other Third W.	392	32%	308	867	1%
Third W. total	2002	18%	369	3795	5%

Notes:

1 Refers to change in total cocoa production since 1980
2 Export income includes (semi-) processed cocoa products
3 Dependency is measured export income from cocoa per income from export of all agricultural products

(Source: FAO, *1987 Production and Trade Yearbooks*, FAO, Rome, 1988)

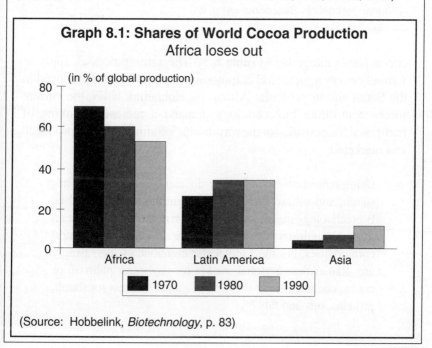

Graph 8.1: Shares of World Cocoa Production
Africa loses out

(in % of global production)

Legend: 1970, 1980, 1990

(Source: Hobbelink, *Biotechnology*, p. 83)

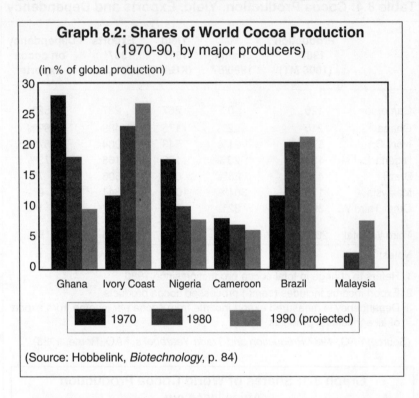

Graph 8.2: Shares of World Cocoa Production
(1970-90, by major producers)

(in % of global production)

Ghana   Ivory Coast   Nigeria   Cameroon   Brazil   Malaysia

■ 1970   ■ 1980   ■ 1990 (projected)

(Source: Hobbelink, *Biotechnology*, p. 84)

cocoa plants altogether[35] (Table 8.5). The same processes apply to virtually every agricultural commodity, especially those produced in the South and in particular Africa. As Hobbelink notes, the current forces controlling biotechnology demand a radical rethinking of traditional frameworks for the way in which commodities are produced and marketed:

> Using biotechnology, all these different sources of protein, starch, and oil are increasingly becoming interchangeable. Biotechnology makes food production more and more like an assembly industry. Crops as such are no longer agricultural commodities, but their molecular components increasingly are. Rather than a global market for soybeans, palm-oil or cocoa, one has to start thinking of global markets for starch, proteins, oils and fats.[36]

Table 8.5: Biotechnology Research on Cocoa

Research by	Type of Research	Comments
Penn State Univ. (USA)	Tissue culture for HYVs, increasing fat content, incorporating 'sweetness genes'. Also rDNA work on cocoa tree	$1.5 million budget, co-funded by industry
DNAP (USA)	Tissue culture for new varieties	Joint venture research with Hershey Foods, EPO patent application filed for cocoa TC technique
Cadbury-Schweppes (UK/USA)	Tissue culture and rDNA. Also work on improving fermenttation of cheap cocoa	With University of Reading (UK). Tissue culture research has stopped recently
Ajinomoto (Japan)	CBS from cheap oils	Licensed patent from Tokyo University
Fuji Oil (Japan)	CBS from olive, safflower or palm-oil	Processes patented. Company claims the CBS has good properties for chocolate
CPC Int'l (USA)	CBS from yeasts	Process patented
Genencor (USA)	Enzyme techniques to convert palm-oil in cocoa butter	Patent application for process filed
Cornell Univ. (USA)	Cell culture to produce CBS	Research started in 1987
Nestlé (CH)	Enzyme techniques to improve fermentation of of cheap cocoa	Focus on cheap cocoa from Malaysia
Mars (UK/USA)	Enzyme techniques to improve taste of Malaysian cocoa, including fermentation techniques	Joint research with Malaysian government
KAO Corp. (Japan)	rDNA enzymes to produce CBS	Two patent applications EPO
Unilever (UK)	Enzyme technology to convert several oils and fats into CBSs	Unilever currently controls 50% of global CBS market

(Source: Hobbelink, *Biotechnology*, p. 87)

The impact of these developments on the African countries which rely on cocoa production are profound. First and foremost, since the new technology will only fit into large, mechanized estate-farming techniques, the inevitable result will be substantial losses in foreign exchange earnings, eliminating most of the smallholders engaged in cocoa production. Prices will continue to tumble and the position of suppliers will become increasingly insecure as TNCs will have a variety of sources from which to choose. Another development, which has already been borne out in the cases of coffee and cocoa, is the permanent collapse of international agreements of agricultural commodities. Buyers have no interest in guaranteeing prices in such a volatile market. The Northern industrialized countries, scrambling to capture their share of R&D and to keep up in the biotech race, are blind to the impact that these developments are having in the South.

The Uruguay GATT round clearly demonstrated the aggressive stance of Northern corporate interests in controlling all aspects of the bio-revolution. TNCs engaged in a very intense lobbying campaign to persuade or bully countries into accepting the validity of intellectual property rights. This turned into a moral crusade with recalcitrant countries being charged with theft and piracy of valuable R&D belonging to the TNCs. This was coupled with claims, such as those put forward by US TNCs, that they are currently losing between $50-100 billion annually due to patent and intellectual property violations.

The countries of the South find themselves in an increasingly weak position to benefit from biotechnology. In effect, biotechnology spells the further marginalization of smallholder agriculture; farmers will be pushed further onto marginal land and forced into unsustainable practices in order to survive. Furthermore, in the current global economic context, biotechnology only portends reinforced inequality and dependencies, and enhanced ecological degradation.

The ecological effects of biotechnology are only vaguely understood and extremely difficult to predict. Some dire warnings have been issued about the potential effects of introducing new life forms into the environment. For instance, the newly introduced herbicide-resistant crops can easily hybridize with their wild relatives which, as weeds, will then carry the herbicide-resistant gene. The consequences of spreading foreign genes into new lineages (for the purpose of marketing a particular herbicide more effectively) will certainly be enormous, if not catastrophic.[37] Although biotechnology may herald the development of pest-resistant plants, the current drive is to produce pesticide- and herbicide-resistant plant varieties. This is already issuing in an even greater chemical assault on the environment as TNCs rush to develop seeds that are resistant to their own pesticides and herbicides. According to a DuPont executive the current research is toward developing seeds that have a trait which says: "I don't care how much chemical you throw at me, it doesn't faze me." The development of a soybean strain resistant to the herbicide atrazine is estimated to be worth over $120 million in increased sales annually.[38]

The Counter Bio-Revolution

It is primarily through the research and networking efforts of NGOs that public awareness has been raised regarding the implications of the bio-revolution. These groups have forged international links and have succeeded in influencing policy-makers and in forcing governments in the North and South to take a closer look at conventions such as the GATT as well as to resist attempts to repeal laws which protect local seed and pharmaceutical industries in countries like India, Sri Lanka, Brazil, Nigeria as well as Canada. This is being complemented with efforts carried out by a variety of NGOs to support and encourage the re-introduction of local plant varieties and genetic diversity into agricultural practice.

Southern countries are beginning to assert their proprietary claims over genetic resources. Recently, attempts have been made to assert Farmer's Rights. As a counter to the attempts to usurp control of global genetic resources, coalitions from developing nations are putting forward proposals that would recognize the centuries of informal innovation by farmers that have gone into producing present-day plant cultures. As Pat Roy Mooney notes, one of the features of this informal innovation system suggested by groups in the South is that these innovations are not produced in laboratories but "arise from informal (often cooperative) efforts which are purposeful and creative as any similar efforts in more formal or 'western' models of innovation".[39] Groups proclaiming Farmer's Rights are pressing for conventions which would impose a tax on all internationally traded biological products originating from the South and Automatic Licensing Rights to all Third World countries for any patents based on genetic material derived from the South.[40] Vandana Shiva reminds us of the crucial role that women play both in the conservation of resources and also in organizing to resist against efforts to usurp control:

> Because of the fact that the germ plasm of the world lies in the forests and the fields of the Third World... the conservation of genetic resources lies in the hands of Third World women, tribals and peasants. As in all other attempts to protect the sources of life and to conserve the feminine principle, women peasants will probably again take the lead in the politics of seeds.[41]

NGOs, in the North and South, are active in movements and coalitions that are forming to speak out against the injustices of the current global economic order predicated on debt and unjust trading relations. These dynamics have produced struggles throughout the South which revolve around the democratization of control over resources. Filipino farmers are rejecting the green revolution seeds that indebted them to pesticide and fertilizer companies and, instead, are planting traditional rice varieties that do not require chemical inputs. In October, 1993, over 500,000 farmers rallied in India to protest against the GATT and the patenting of seeds. Women in Kenya and Mozambique have organized greenbelt movements to reclaim parts of cities for vegetable gardens and to experiment with sustainable agro-forestry techniques. Other alternatives include the promotion of South-South trade and regional trade arrangements.

Many NGOs are also involved in the provision of capital goods and technology within their development projects in the Third World, either through very soft loans, or more frequently, through grants. In these situations, the NGOs themselves are able to get supplier credits for their purchases on terms which can benefit the recipients if they involve sales which might otherwise have been handled under commercial terms.[42] These initiatives point to the variety of alternatives to the export-oriented SAP model that are already being practised and suggest sustainable long-term models which should be pursued and supported by governments and multilateral organizations.

Endnotes

1.   Cited in Redclift, *Sustainable Development*, p. 193.
2.   J. P. Berlan, "The Commodification of Life," *Monthly Review* 41 (1989), p. 24.
3.   Brewster Kneen, *From Land to Mouth*, (Toronto: New Canada Publications, 1989), p. 98.
4.   C. Juma, *The Gene Hunters: Biotechnology and the Scramble for Seeds*, (Princeton: Princeton University Press, 1989), p. 110.
5.   H. Hobbelink, *Biotechnology and the Future of World Agriculture*, (London: Zed Books, 1991), pp. 30-1.
6.   See for example, E.C. Wolf, *Beyond the Green Revolution*, (Washington: Worldwatch Institute, 1986), pp. 30-35, wherein he provides a rather optimistic assessment of the possibilities of biotechnology for the Third World and its ecologically beneficial characteristics.
7.   M. Apple, cited in Redclift, *Sustainable Development*, p. 189.
8.   Hobbelink, *Biotechnology*, p. 32.
9.   J. R. Anderson *et al.*, *Science and Food, the CGIAR and its Partners*, World Bank, 1988, cited in Hobbelink, *Biotechnology*, p. 10.
10. World Bank, *From Crisis*, p. 31.
11. David Padwa, Agrigenetics Corporation, 1982, cited in J.R. Kloppenburg, *First the Seed: The Political Economy of Plant Biotechnology, 1492-2000*, (Cambridge: Cambridge University Press, 1988), p. 191.
12. J. Kloppenburg, *First the Seed*, p. 281.
13. Kloppenburg, *First the Seed*, p. 97.
14. Kenney, M. *Biotechnology: The University-Industrial Complex*, (New Haven: Yale University Press, 1986), p. 241.
15. Brewster Kneen's wry comment on this development captures the arrogant presumption that lies behind the patenting of life: "In other words, everything in the world– Creation itself – is private property waiting to be discovered, to be owned. The Creator God, then, will have to argue the case in patent court." *From Land to Mouth*, p. 99.
16. In fact, the introduction of legislation in Canada to reform its intellectual property law was one of the less-publicized requirements of the Free Trade Agreement between the US and Canada. This legislation, Bill C-15, will ensure that US investments and products from biotechnology research will be protected. This will serve to privatize the plant breeding process which hitherto has been carried out in public institutions in Canada. C. Juma notes that while legislation to privatize plant breeding will protect and enhance a few firms eager to exploit the potential market for these products, "in the long run it is likely to lead to the control of the seed market by large US and European firms. In addition, Canadian firms will have to work much harder to be able to sell their seed in the US. Possibilities exist for the US to use

intellectual property law as one of the NTBs (non-tariff barriers) against Canadian seed and other biotechnology products". Juma, *The Gene Hunters*, p. 168. See also, *Genetic Resources for Our World* (GROW) 2 (1989).

17. V. Shiva, *Staying Alive: Women, Ecology and Development*, (London: Zed Books, 1988), pp. 135-6.

18. F. Buttel and M. Kenney, "Biotechnology: Prospects and Dilemmas for Third World Development," *Development and Change* 16 (January 1985), pp. 63-5.

19. Hobbelink, *Biotechnology*, p. 45.

20. M. Kenney, *Biotechnology: The University-Industrial Complex*, p. 113.

21. Juma, *The Gene Hunters*, p. 126.

22. F. Buttel, M. Kenney, and J. Kloppenburg, "From Green Revolution to Bio-Revolution: Some Observations on the Changing Technological Bases of Economic Transformation in the Third World," *Economic Development and Cultural Change* 34 (1985), p. 50.

23. Buttel and Kenney, "Biotechnology: Prospects and Dilemmas for Third World Development," p. 67.

24. Juma, *The Gene Hunters*, p. 113; also Hobbelink, *Biotechnology*, p. 61.

25. Kenney, *Biotechnology: The University-Industrial Complex*, p. 246.

26. P. R. Mooney, "Law of the Seed," *Development Dialogue* 1-2 (1983), p. 26; also see Juma, *The Gene Hunters*, p. 21.

27. K. Meagher, "Institutionalizing the Bio-Revolution: Implications for Nigerian Smallholders," (unpublished), 1990, p. 15.

28. Mooney, *The Law of the Seed*, p. 11.

29. Buttel and Kenney, "Biotechnology: Prospects and Dilemmas for Third World Development," p. 66.

30. J. Kloppenburg, "The Social Impacts of Biogenetic Technology in Agriculture: Past and Future," in *Social Consequences and Challenges of New Agricultural Technologies*, eds. G. M. Bernard and C. C. Geisler, (Boulder: Westview Press, 1984), p. 318.

31. D. Goodman *et al.*, *From Farming to Biotechnology*, (Oxford: Basil Blackwell, 1987), pp. 162ff.

32. V. Shiva, *The Violence of the Green Revolution: Third World Agriculture, Ecology and Politics*, (London: Zed Books, 1991), p. 215.

33. Hobbelink, *Biotechnology*, p. 72.

34. Vaino P. Shivute, "Agricultural Production: From the Green Revolution to the Bio-Revolution," in M. Suliman ed. *Alternative Development Strategies for Africa*, vol. 2, (London: Institute for African Alternatives), p. 67.

35. Juma, *The Gene Hunters*, pp. 136-40; also Hobbelink, *Biotechnology*, p. 88.

36. Hobbelink, *Biotechnology*, p. 95.

37. Juma, *The Gene Hunters*, p. 131, Shiva, *The Violence of the Green Revolution*, p. 207.

38. Hobbelink, *Biotechnology*, p. 54.

39. P. R. Mooney, *Genetic Resources for Our World* 2 (1989), p. 7.

40. Pat Roy Mooney has estimated what a hypothetical royalty payment back to

the South to compensate for the appropriation of biological germplasm would be: "If Third World guardians of biodiversity were remunerated at royalty rates similar to those claimed by chemical and pharmaceutical companies, then the original stewards of precious biological resources would collect US$302 million a year from global seed vendors and US$45 billion a year from world pharmaceutical sales." ECEJ, "Which Way for the Americas", Canadian Centre for Policy Alternatives, 1993, p. 46.

41. V. Shiva, *Staying Alive*, p. 140.

42. Robert Thompson, "Canadian Trade and Aid Relations with Nicaragua," Canada-Caribbean-Central American Policy Alternatives, 1984.

—— CHAPTER NINE ——

African Churches and the Crisis of Structural Adjustment

A theoretical impasse persists in social scientific considerations of the role of religion and the church in Africa. Most studies tend to overlook the role of religion and the churches, dismissing the churches as conservative or neo-colonial obstacles to democracy and popular participation. African writers also tend to be suspicious of religion and the churches because of their legacy in the colonization of the continent. Few consider the important role that churches are playing in recent and current liberation and democratization struggles in countries like South Africa, Kenya, Zimbabwe, Malawi, Madagascar and Zaire.

A closer examination of the African reality reveals the very powerful role that religion plays in the development process. Churches have been at the heart of the political upheavals sweeping through Africa. These momentous changes can, in part, be traced to a fundamental theological re-orientation on the part of churches in Africa. This can be seen in the re-affirmation of liberation theology rooted in prophetic discourse condemning corrupt leaders and calling for elections. A key constitutive element in this re-orientation has been the churches' response to the effects of the debt and SAP crisis. This new focus, however recent, points unmistakably to a fundamental shift in the churches' role in political processes in Africa. The churches are demonstrating a more activist role both in their relations with the state and in terms of their position towards international agencies like the World Bank and IMF, Northern church partners and NGOs. However, by focusing only on the more liberating and prophetic discourse, one risks ignoring another important role that religion and the churches continue to play in Africa of upholding the status quo and as a reactionary force.

This chapter examines some of the key features in the development of African churches' position on the debt crisis and structural adjustment. In particular, the work and ideas of African church leaders who are actively engaged in mobilization efforts at the grassroots are highlighted. Many of these recent developments indicate a number of emerging trends in African churches on important economic and political concerns. In the past, churches in Africa have spoken out on political matters. What is unique about recent developments and statements is the increasing attention being accorded to economic concerns, especially those related to the international financial system. These must be considered together with positions being articulated by churches on political issues. It is the explicit integration of a political economy analysis within a theological framework which is of particular interest.

The issues are organized around the following concerns:

1)   How have churches in Africa responded to the debt and SAP crisis? What are some of the key theological issues that are emerging? How are the churches in Africa reflecting on the SAP crisis as a theological issue.

2)   How are church organizations responding at the grassroots level? This section looks in particular at grassroots initiatives which attempt to enhance the understanding of the economic crisis.

The Theological Response of African Churches to SAPs

This section considers the issues that are being raised by African Church bodies and individual theologians through an analysis of recent statements, documents, and articles. The themes being discussed in the wake of the SAP crisis can be organized around five key areas:

a)   the root cause of the present crisis as rooted in unjust international and national structures dating back to the colonial period. Related to this is the recognition of maldevelopment as a pattern of global development instituted during the colonial period that has been perpetuated after independence. As such, the church must come to terms with its role as an agent in this process of maldevelopment and be a force for liberation from it;

b)   an upsurge in biblical and ethical perspectives on the debt crisis and structural adjustment;

c)   a more outspoken criticism of political and church leadership as co-opted agents of maldevelopment. This includes openly challenging corrupted national elites;

d)   self-reliance and delinking as the alternative path for Africa's development;

e)   the need for churches to be agents of advocacy, mobilization and conscientization at the grassroots.

Maldevelopment

In the mid-1980s the All African Conference of Churches (AACC) commissioned a long-term study to examine the root causes of drought and famine in the continent. In its conclusions, the report offers an explanation of the economic crisis in sub-Saharan Africa. This analysis of the churches stands in stark contrast to the World Bank's findings. The focus of the African churches is primarily on Africa's position in the global economy and the model of development it has been forced to adopt. Drought and growing food insecurity are seen as the result of environmental destruction, the shift from food to cash crop production and the appropriation of the best land by settlers, large landowners and multi-national corporations. The institution of wage labour in the mines and fields is cited as the greatest cause of social dislocation and the breakdown of the rural economy.[1] The report refers back to the pre-colonial period where various mechanisms were in place to ensure enough reserves in times of drought. The current pattern of development has led to the disintegration of these protective mechanisms in favour of an economy geared toward wage labour and the production of cash crops.[2] Independence did not bring about a radical re-orientation of these development patterns: "The economic mechanisms of exploitation and oppression once set in motion are difficult to reverse and this is the problem that all of Africa is facing."[3]

The report also concluded that the intractability of Africa's problems is further exacerbated by the analytical framework of "crisis". This has precluded a more profound and comprehensive analysis and has led to the outpouring of epitaphs describing Africa as the "doomed", "bankrupt" or "lost" continent.

Colonialism and Neo-colonialism

> ...the central issue is not that of hunger but that of overcoming poverty and underdevelopment. These two are a result of the international links between Africa and the Western world. Links that have turned Africa into a raw material producing continent for the Western world. This international link has alone produced structural relationships internally that reproduce poverty and underdevelopment. One has therefore to act at these two levels – internal and international.[4]

The crisis in Africa is analysed by this current in the African churches in terms of the connection between internal and external forces shaping the continent's development. Unlike some of the dependency critiques of the 1960s and 1970s, theological critiques are turning their attention to the logic of the international financial system and the local and national interests that uphold neo-colonial development patterns in Africa.

This has resulted in increasing collaboration in research projects, consultations and conferences. In 1989, a conference in Luanda, Angola, brought together theologians, economists, social scientists and grassroots workers from a number of African countries to examine the root causes of the economic crisis. The basis of their declaration is "to challenge the assumptions that economic issues should be left to the experts and those in the state responsible for socio-economic planning".[5] What is most striking about this declaration is the unitary discourse that is achieved in the analysis of Africa's problems. It succeeds in focusing the machinations of national governments, transnational corporations, and the multilateral banks through the theological lens of idolatry:

> We observe in the working of the present international economy a firm, almost religious commitment to an economic system based on the accumulation of power, wealth, property and capital at any cost: even the misery and death of others.

Today, the international economic system functions as a "golden calf" which promises economic salvation defiling itself, teaching an ideology of material consumption, in place of the Word of God. This system substitutes luxury for human needs.[6]

African church leaders have become far more outspoken in criticizing the national elites who have actively participated in a model of development that has led to greater impoverishment and the repression of basic human rights. The grace period indicative of the 1960s and 1970s where churches also subordinated issues like democracy and human rights to the more pressing problem of development has given way to a spate of harsh indictments of the political elites who have profited from this model of development at the expense of the poor. The theme of flight capital is increasingly addressed by churches as a symbol of a corrupted elite that has lost the respect of the people and must give way to its will through elections. It is indicative of a planned usurpation of capital and resources out of Africa. As Aaron Tolen describes:

> Africa's crisis was thought out and planned. Contrary to what the World Bank and the International Monetary Fund or the Organization of African Unity would have us think, it is the outcome of deliberate and consistent action.[7]

The Luanda Declaration describes the crisis of leadership gripping Africa in even harsher terms:

> Our intellectuals, experts, politicians and administrators in both church and state have mostly been bought through bribery, corruption and wanton greed for power, wealth and participation in the idolatrous consumption, materialistic lifestyles of the world's privileged few who, and on whose behalf, the WAR AGAINST THE DISPOSSESSED is being perpetrated.[8]

The attention given by church leaders to the national character of the crisis has led to a rising number of church-supported and -inspired democratization movements currently sweeping Africa. This is a significant departure from earlier analyses which tended to blame Africa's problems exclusively on the legacies of colonialism. Many of these movements focus on a critique of the state and in particular the one-party system, leaving aside any consideration of the international dimensions. A pastoral statement issued by Zambia's Catholic Bishops in September 1990 focuses exclusively on the role of the Zambian government in the food riots that had ensued after the removal of subsidies on mealie-meal, the staple food of the majority in the country. The bishops' letter does not, however, consider the role of the World Bank and IMF in laying the responsibility for the riots at the feet of the government:

> What is not clear, however, is why a decision of such major importance – the raising of [the price of] our basic commodity – should have been imposed upon the people without any public discussion and in a way which placed an intolerable burden upon those already struggling to survive.[9]

The statement goes on to note that the one-party system, with its lack of accountability, has led directly to the increase in the gap between rich and poor.[10] This lack of accountability has also meant that the burden of economic restructuring programmes has fallen on the backs of the poor. Coming as it did just prior to the referendum which paved the way for multi-party elections in the country, the Bishops' statement was a clear indication that the church was no longer willing to support a single-party system.

After multi-party elections were held in Zambia and the Chiluba government adopted SAPs the Bishops were again outspoken in condemning the government, this time for its implementation of SAP policies. In a pastoral letter entitled "Hear the Cry of the People", issued in August of 1993, the bishops criticized the SAP measures "whereby the gap between the rich and the poor appears to be widening".[11]

Similar developments have taken place in countries like Malawi and Kenya. In Malawi, it was a Lenten Bishops' Pastoral Letter denouncing human rights abuses, poor standards in health and education and other shortcomings of the government which touched off a number of demonstrations calling for the removal of President Banda and the holding of elections. Banda moved swiftly in denouncing the bishops, confiscating the letter and even considered having the bishops killed.

Multi-partyism is not regarded as the solution to all of Africa's ills by a number of African church leaders. The General Secretary of the AACC, Jose Chipenda, warns against the false promises of multi-partyism. The forces calling for multi-partyism are the same ones who have divided up African countries to their own ends already. He sees lurking behind the call for multi-parties the designs of the transnationals:

> These (TNC) forces are ready to do anything to establish a geo-political hegemony favourable to their expansion and prosperity. In Western countries, these transnationals are concretely committed in politics, giving financial backing to parties which they deem better suited to their interests.[12]

Chipenda goes on to warn how in rural Africa it is those who have the financial power backed by foreign interests who dominate in a multi-party system.

The Churches as Instruments of Recolonization

One of the more pressing issues in Africa is the debate over the proper role of Christians in the political arena. This debate directly confronts the general crisis of legitimacy in many of the post-colonial African governments. Many writers cite the failure of the churches to mobilize Christians to call the leaders to account as indicative of the general crisis in the churches in Africa. They regard this failure as due to the perpetuation of the "two kingdom" thesis, essentially emphasizing the separation of church and state, which prevailed during the colonial period. By letting their political leaders off the hook, as it were, the churches have allowed them to become corrupt and unaccountable to the people. This has resulted in an understanding of religion as a force, as J. H. Boer notes, which is "expected to produce a people with high personal morality, a great sense of duty and obedience, but certainly not inclined to radical social thinking, let alone action".[13]

Boer challenges churches in Africa to draw on their religious resources to effect social change.[14] The two kingdom theology of the colonial period has persisted in the post-independence period, because the church did not redefine its role in relation to the emerging states.[15]

Perhaps the most urgent issue facing the churches today is the role they are playing in the areas of health and education. As these services are being cut back, it is the churches, in concert with Northern donors, who are stepping into the breach. This raises some very disturbing questions for churches who are being called on to provide the same services they did during the colonial period:

> ...the education given was intended to convert Africans to Western thinking and civilization. In the same line of thinking, medical services. Thus from the starting point, medical services were used also as a demonstration of the superiority of Western civilization.[16]

It is during this period of adjustment, where churches and NGOs are becoming more involved in providing basic services that serious questions are being raised: "Are the Bible and the Cross now preceding the new imperial flag – thus allowing for the total economic domination of the world by the Western industrial powers?"[17]

Biblical and Ethical Perspectives on Debt and Structural Adjustment

The struggle for the moral high ground in the debt and SAP crisis has led to a proliferation of statements with highly charged biblical and ethical arguments. This has come not only from church and solidarity groups in the North, invoking biblical or theological arguments favouring the cancellation of the debt. This type of invocation is also becoming more commonplace in the literature which upholds the status quo as divinely blessed. Theologians and churches in the South have also turned the issue of debt and SAPs into a profoundly theological problem invoking basic biblical principles calling for cancellation or repudiation.

In the African churches a number of noteworthy responses to the debt and SAP crisis have been especially attentive to the theological and biblical characteristics of the dominant model. Unlike many of the statements issued by Northern church agencies, the responses emerging from Africa almost uniformly consider the debt and SAP crisis as symptomatic of a much more deeply-rooted global crisis with theological implications. This section highlights some of the emerging biblical and ethical responses to the debt and SAP crisis in Africa.

From Exodus to Exile

> *I plead sickness*
> *I am an orphan*
> *I am diseased with*
> *All the giant*
> *Diseases of society,*
> *Crippled by the cancer*
> *of Uhuru*
> *Far worse than the jaws of Colonialism,*
> *The walls of hopelessness*
> *Surround me completely*
> *There are no windows*
> *To let in the air*
> *Of hope!*
>
> (Okot P' Bitek, *Song of Prisoner*)

A number of important shifts have taken place in African biblical perspectives on the economic crisis. During the nationalist anti-colonial struggles the predominant biblical motifs were of liberation from slavery. As the economic and political crisis deepened in the 1980s this gave way to a greater theological pre-occupation with the prophetic literature. At the grassroots level, however, it is the apolcalyptic literature that predominates in reflections on the current crisis.

The shift to a greater attention on the prophetic literature stems from the increasing restiveness of church leaders towards the corruption of its leaders and lack of accountability to its people.

The Luanda Declaration draws on the idolatry motif which runs through the writings of prophets like Amos, Micah, Hosea, Obadiah and Isaiah. The declaration accuses the leadership in Africa of becoming enslaved by the idolatry of material luxuries proffered by the international financial system: "The worship of material wealth, status and power enslaves the African elite to the bribery and corruption of the TNCs which are the instruments of the gods of capital accumulation."[18]

The following passages from Amos and Micah are used in the declaration to capture the growing antagonism of Africans towards their leaders:

> *because they sell the righteous for silver*
> *and the needy for a pair of shoes*
> *they that trample the head of the poor into*
> *the dust of the earth*
> *and turn aside the way of the afflicted*
> *they lay themselves down beside every altar*
> *upon garments taken in pledge*
> *and in the house of their God they drink*
> *the wine of those who have been fined.* (Amos 2: 6-9)

> *Listen, you leaders of Jacob, rulers of Israel,*
> *should you not know what is right?*
> *You hate good and love evil,*
> *you flay men alive and tear the very flesh from their bones;*
> *you devour the flesh of my people,*
> *strip off their skin,*
> *splinter their bones;*
> *you shred them like flesh into a pot,*
> *like meat in a cauldron.*
> *Then they will call to the Lord, and he will give them not*
> *answer*
> *when that time comes he will hide their face from them,*
> *so wicked are their deeds.* (Micah 3: 1-5)

The favoured passages from the New Testament are those depicting the Gathered Community: "For where two or three are gathered in my name, there am I in the midst of them" (Matthew 18: 18-20). This vision of community delegated to take charge of God's creation is contrasted to the "materialistic and individualistic life-styles, the by-product of Africa's socio-economic integration into the international economic system of alienation".[19]

One of the major factors in the democracy movements currently sweeping through the African continent has been the openly critical stance of the churches towards the political regimes. This can be seen in the theological shift that has occurred and the reference to passages like those cited above. This shift has played an important role in the mass demonstrations that have occurred in a number of African countries, supported by the churches. It signals a profound political change on the part of the churches which have, in comparing their political leaders to the corrupt leaders denounced by the prophets, in effect served to unleash the momentous political upheavals occurring in many African countries.

Another important gathering of theologians, church leaders, social scientists and economists was held under the auspices on the All Africa Conference of Churches in late 1990 under the theme "The Debt Crisis as it Affects Human Rights". The conference statement describes the debt crisis as a theological crisis rooted in the "diabolic and unjust financial and economic systems based on the lust for power and the greed for wealth – Idols – that require the lives of women, children and men with their perverted morality and structural evil".[20]

The political-economic analysis of the document is also comprehensive and analyses the debt and SAP crisis in terms of its local, national and international actors. It examines the effects that the debt crisis has had at all of these levels and sets out a programme of action for local, national and international churches. The statement declares that the:

> ...disastrous effects of the payment of the African debt be compared to a low intensity war which brings death, hunger, malnutrition, sickness, unemployment, homelessness and loss of dignity and personal worth to millions of children, women and men, young and old.[21]

In its analysis of the debt crisis, the conference admits to "the abdication by the church of its responsibility to train, teach and nurture the continent and its people in responsible citizenship... and to challenge Christians of the North on the realization of a just and equitable international financial, monetary and economic order".[22]

The biblical re-orientation that is suggested by this call to lead is rooted in the prophetic tradition. It is only by drawing on the richness of the prophetic tradition in the Bible, as one of the conference speakers noted, that the structural roots of the economic crisis can be attacked. This includes a re-orientation of relationships with Northern churches from one of donor and recipient "into the aggressive prophetic role that brings about repentance, transformation, justice and sanctity in relationships".[23] This again marks the call for a new role for the churches in Africa in moving to the forefront of the voices condemning the corruption in the current economic order and calling for radical change. The political power that lies behind this re-orientation cannot be overestimated as the number of political upheavals currently sweeping through Africa can attest.

The current economic crisis and the imposition of SAPs have also given way to a proliferation of apocalyptic motifs to describe the disintegration at the socio-economic and cultural levels. A note of despair prevails in many African countries at the grassroots level. We are no longer in the desert, noted one church leader, but in the end time. Women in Africa euphemistically refer to SAPs as Satan Amongst the People.[24] Biblical phrases are turned around to describe SAPs as in the following: "To those who have more, even more will be given to them; and those who have little, even the very little that they have will be taken away."[25]

The economic crisis and massive social, economic and cultural disintegration have given rise to the spread of Northern-based right-wing fundamentalist churches taking advantage of this prevailing worldview amongst people. The influence of these churches and movements has been rapid and constitutes a serious threat not only to the mainline churches and to Christian-Muslim relations in many African countries. Paul Gifford has provided a number of detailed accounts of the operations of these churches and the biblical motifs which are used to capture the hopes (and wallets) of desperate Africans.

Structural Adjustment and the Apocalypse

The doctrines promoted by the fundamentalist churches, often backed by large sums of money in their missionary work in Africa, together offer a powerful religious explanation for the poverty and misery of the majority of Africans. As Gifford explains:

> Since these apocalyptic passages give great prominence to plagues, famines and disasters of every kind, these Christians tend to see all kinds of hardship and deprivation as foretold for what they think are these "end-times".[26]

The success in spreading the "good news" among Africans that the current state of affairs is all part of God's plan for humanity has had a profound effect in engendering passivity and resignation amongst Africans towards the prospects of effecting social and political change. The preaching of this form of dispensationalism is accompanied by the promotion of the "gospel of prosperity". Prosperity is offered as a simple matter of faith. Stories abound of examples where people offer a preacher everything they own based on the promise (Mark 10:29-30): "There is no one who will not receive a hundredfold here in this life."[27] The distortion of these passages conveniently diverts attention away from an examination of the social, political and economic dimensions of the crisis. As Gifford notes:

> ...any brand of Christianity that insists that wealth is not something to be guilty about but on the contrary is to be enjoyed as God-given has considerable appeal. In as much as it diverts attention from the present economic system and merely fosters the determination to be among those who benefit from it, this gospel of prosperity is the polar opposite of liberation theology.[28]

While it is tempting to dismiss these church movements as irrelevant in the more important discussions around economic and political questions, one risks neglecting what has become a very potent political and economic force in Africa today. It poses a fundamental challenge not only to the mainline churches but to all groups and social movements struggling for change. In ignoring these movements, one ignores the fundamental reality of religion as the single-most important force in the life of Africans, grounding their worldview and conditioning their struggles for social change.

The Economic Crisis and the Crisis of Faith

    I have often raised the question as to how we can explain the apparent contradiction, that contemporary Africa continues to be, perhaps, the most "religious" continent in the world, and yet its peoples remain the most abused of all in history. How could it be that the peoples who continue to call on God most reverently are the ones that God seems to neglect most vehemently? Could it be that irreligion is the key to success, and that religion is the key to backwardness?[29]

In the wake of the precipitous decline in Africa's standard of living in the 1980s, the questions raised here by J. N. K. Mugambi have begun to take on a special significance. The Jobian characteristics of Africa's plight have moved to the forefront as the key challenge to the churches in Africa in the 1990s. They have led many to wonder whether it is precisely the slowness with which Africa is secularizing that keeps it in its "backward" state. This assumption continues to persist in anthropological and development-studies debates on the so-called "backwardness" of Africa.[30] According to Mugambi, the secularized view sees Africa as a continent of "lazy, helpless beggars who are unable to repay their debts... . Their cultural and religious heritage is measured against the standards of those who believe that Heaven is north of the Equator and Hell is another word for the southern hemisphere".[31]

Mugambi is quick to point out, however, that the pessimism about Africa and its prospects are largely driven by negative myths generated by the religious and secular press in the North. He proposes that Africans themselves must replace these negative myths with positive myths of their own:

    The myth of a vanishing people must be replaced by the myth of a resurgent, or resilient people. The myth of a desperate people must be replaced by the myth of a people full of hope. The myth of a hungry people must be replaced by the myth of a people capable of feeding itself... .[32]

The most important theological shift now taking place in Africa, according to Mugambi, is from the theme of liberation to one of social transformation. During the anti-colonial liberation struggles, the theme of liberation dominated both the political and theological discourse. Nonetheless, there was a remarkable coherence in both the political struggles for independence from colonial rule and the religious discourse proclaiming liberation from sin, especially in the immediate post-independence period. But, as Mugambi points out, the theological discourse, along with the political discourse that accompanied it, became locked into a liberation framework without taking it a logical step forward, the struggle for new forms of social organization that liberation implied:

> Christian theology in Africa, particularly during the 1960s and 1970s, emphasized very much the theme of liberation as Exodus from colonial bondage, without highlighting the transformative and reconstructive dimensions. The exodus motif was so dominant that there was hardly any other biblical texts that could be associated with African Christian theology.[33]

This oversight, or lack of attention to the need of putting forward new forms of social organization, was based on the assumption that the removal of colonial administrations would automatically result in new forms of social organizations, once Africans were in charge. Now that the last colonial regime has disappeared the task at hand, in Mugambi's view, is to shift gear "from an emphasis on liberation to engagement in social transformation and reconstruction. This can either be based on the post-Exodus model or the exile motif of Ezra, Haggai and Nehemiah".[34]

Most important, for Mugambi, is the need for this alternative social reality to be worked out by Africans themselves, based on a multi-disciplinary analysis:

> The resources for this re-interpretation are multi-disciplinary analyses involving social scientists, philosophers, creative writers and artists, biological and physical scientists.[35]

Some of the features of these new forms of social organization include a withering away of what Mugambi describes as "denominational self-centredness" on the part of churches before the latter can play a serious role in offering alternative models. Also important is the need to re-appropriate Christianity in a uniquely African light and greater attempts at conciliation with non-Christian religions.

These new, more hopeful images of Africa must be communicated in an effective and popular campaign which includes the media and the power of oral tradition in African culture.[36]

African Reflections on the Debt Crisis

Throughout the 1980s one of the most popular themes in the theological literature on the debt crisis was that of the year of jubilee. It formed the basis of a wide variety and number of campaigns in the North and South using the biblical precept calling for the cancellation of all debts, or in the words of Jesus, a year of grace (Lev. 25; Luke 4:18-19). A powerful moral exhortation usually accompanied the claim that the debts could no longer be repaid and that the biblical precept of jubilee applied in the case of Third World debt.

This appeal to the jubilee ethic was ignored or co-opted by those who represented the interests of creditors, and those concerned with the stability of the international financial system. Critics insisted that the jubilee principle simply did not apply in the age of accrued and compound interest, and those who advocated debt relief were naive about its possible deleterious effects on the health of the whole, that is, the global financial system.

Theologian Godfrey Mwereria lists a number of other theological concerns which have prevented African theology from critical reflection on the debt crisis. The first is the "religiosity of poverty" which pervades theological thinking in Africa especially in fundamentalist churches. The second is what he calls the "theology of apartheid" which allowed Western Christianity to become both oppressor and evangelizer. The third he describes as the theology of passivity or the culture of silence. It is these theological tendencies that must be overcome if there is to be any possibility of "adequately responding to the debt crisis with a liberating and transforming spiritual energy".[37] Over and against this theology he offers a transformative theology which places the poor who are marginalized by the debt crisis at the centre of all theological reflection and mobilization. Mwereria is convinced the solution to Africa's debt crisis rests upon a theological transformation:

> Paradoxically, the most powerful instruments that Africa has in the resolving of the debt crisis are theological instruments rather than economic instruments. The crucial agenda implied in this theological task is a reconstruction of an African political theology that becomes the basis of African normative political economy, collective self-reliance and theology of development. This political theology should be based on African people's history, culture, anthropology, ontology and praxis. The essential elements and structures in the process of reconstructing African political theology should include:
> • Rediscovery of the popular religiosity of the African people that transcends institutionalized and denominationalized religion. • Rediscovery of critical and political theology and faith that will bring about the birth of a new consciousness of faith, the true metanoia which stems from solidarity with people's praxis. • Rediscovery of the theology of development which becomes the basis of people's struggling, mobilizing and renewing faith.[38]

Mwereria expands on these ideas by putting forward a comprehensive programme built on grassroots community self-reliance delinked from the international economy. According to Mwereria, it is the vision of "community wholeness" which should be the key principle behind all development efforts, including those involving churches and NGOs. Mwereria's vision is a radical one which rejects the piecemeal approach often taken by churches and NGOs to the crisis in Africa. Only a radical alternative or a "historico-breaking" process will be adequate to achieve the necessary transformation towards a just development for Africa.[39]

At the National Church Council and denominational levels, popular education materials are being produced which provide a comprehensive analysis of the root causes of the debt crisis. While many of these reflections place the blame on an unjust international economic system, increasing attention is also being accorded to corruption and mismanagement at the national and local levels. The reference to the prophetic literature to depict these abuses is having a significant political impact, especially in countries with authoritarian regimes.

The National Council of Churches of Kenya (NCCK) has issued a number of studies and reflections on the debt issue. It went so far as to commission a play on the origins of the debt crisis which was subsequently banned, but was eventually performed in a number of churches. The position of the NCCK on the debt crisis has shifted from one advocating debt forgiveness to one which is openly critical of the Moi regime and calls for the debts to be paid by those who incurred them. At the same time, the connection is established between corrupt domestic leadership and its alliances with international capital.[40]

Jephthah Gathaka also draws on the analysis of the debt and SAP crisis provided in the papal encyclical *Sollicitudo Rei Socialis*.[41] As Gathaka notes in commenting on the encyclical's analysis, "if anybody needs to be forgiven it is certainly not the poor in the villages or urban areas of Africa who do not know what happened to the money".[42]

Gathaka conducts an exegesis of Nehemiah, chapter 5 and finds that it resonates powerfully with the present crisis in Africa. What is interesting for Gathaka about Nehemiah is that the historical period is post-exilic, much like the post-colonial period in Africa. The debt crisis is threatening the community life of the people. Nehemiah demands that the rich creditors absolve the loans in order to restore the community. What Gathaka finds most striking is the description of the effects of the debt crisis as closely parallel to the impact of SAPs. Women are most affected and, therefore, it is the duty of the church "to mobilize women in the cry against injustices created by the debt crisis".[43] Just as the situation in Nehemiah's time provoked an outcry from the people, the current situation calls for an outcry from the people and the churches.

While the complaint in Nehemiah is against richer Jews exploiting poorer Jews, Gathaka extends this to include all of humanity. "Therefore our brothers and sisters in the North cannot dismiss us and watch as we crumble, with the debt burden a cross that Africa carries crawling."[44] Furthermore, the imposition of SAPs is akin to the selling of children to service the debt mentioned in Nehemiah. "When our leaders agree to SAPs which have no value for human dignity and which affect the most disadvantaged in the community, women and children and poor are they not actually selling their brethren to foreigners?" [45] Gathaka concludes his exegesis by advocating a multi-dimensional approach be taken to the debt crisis rooted in the suffering and outcry of the people.

This kind of analysis demonstrates the tremendous evocative power of the Bible for African theological reflection on the debt crisis and SAPs. Rather than viewing this kind of theological reflection in terms of the "traditional" vs. "modern" conception of African culture, the contextualization of the debt crisis and the drawing upon biblical themes presents more of a challenge to Northern theologies that do not engage in contextual analysis. The use of biblical sources combined with socio-economic analysis provides a more unified approach which helps to identify and lay bare the personal and structural forces involved in the perpetuation of the debt crisis. Far from being reductionist, this kind of appeal is built upon a vision of humanity as the community of peoples. The community breaks apart when some members enrich themselves at the expense of others. The African theological responses to the debt and SAPs regard the crisis as a crisis of the global community, the entire people of God. It is a framework which also provides the grounding for mobilization, the "cry for justice", a cry which God does not ignore and which forms the basis for social transformation.

African Churches and Northern Partners

In large part, the churches in Africa, through their relationships with Northern donors, have perpetuated dependent and disarticulated forms of development. Present at most national council levels as well as at the local level are mechanisms for attracting funding for projects from Northern donors, but few strategies for developing long-term programmes rooted in a vision of social transformation:[46]

> The churches are just following policies which lead to dependency on outside assistance. Because of this dependency and present lack of structures and infrastructure necessary to engage in the development process, there is no elaborated church development policy at the national level.[47]

In response to this, greater independence and financial autonomy on the part of local churches is called for, as is greater coordination by the various churches working in a given country; for Northern donors are asked to adopt a much more long-term approach in their relationships with African churches.[48]

The Crisis in Leadership in the Churches

The shift towards a more openly critical stance with respect to the political leadership has also been turned inward. This has resulted in a number of self-critical evaluations about the lack of prophetic church leadership during a time of crisis. Some feel that, because the church has been caught napping while significant upheavals have occurred, the church has awakened only to react and not to lead.[49] This growing recognition is accompanied by the perception that church leaders simply are not theologically or politically equipped to comprehend the root causes of the crisis let alone respond effectively. It is this kind of leadership that is felt to be critical in any effort toward social transformation. For Ben Masilo, efforts at social transformation "will be in vain as long as these centres and church leaders are not willing to face justice and peace issues".[50]

Self-Reliance and Delinking

African church leaders are also increasing the call for Africa to disassociate itself from the current global economic order. Reminiscent of campaigns which were part of the anti-colonial struggle, the analysis which accompanies current delinking strategies is based on a more sober reflection on the failure of modernization and the possibilities that present themselves in the current "new world order".

For writers like Godfrey Mwereria, the option to delink is rooted in an analysis of the current global order which does not offer a just resolution to the debt crisis. This entails a turning inward, requiring "an alternative political, cultural and economic orientation".[51] In many respects, these appeals parallel those made by African political economists, like Samir Amin, who has consistently called for Africa to delink from the global economy. As Amin notes, the concept of delinking is frequently confused with autarky. Amin defines delinking as the submitting of economic relations to the inward logic of the national economy and not to the external logic of the global economy. This concept has been widened and been applied by theologians to issues of culture and religion. For them, delinking also embraces the struggle for a new education which will reorient African society to embrace its own religious and cultural forms. Like Amin, theologians argue that this does not mean a closing off of African culture and religion from outside relations.

> As in traditional societies, the new education through a liberating and integrated development should be that which must put emphasis on the need to get away from the outward-oriented economy in favour of a more inward-looking production for self-help, self-identity and self-improvement and esteem.[52]

> Various strata of Africa's population are waging a struggle for survival wherever they resist the multiple forces of humiliation and death; the Church in Africa can only side with them and lead their struggle in the light of the Gospel.[53]

Lay Centres in Africa: Training for Transformation

In responding to the debt and SAP crisis, African churches have found that their work is simply tending to the casualties of SAPs. Recently, however, many church-based communities are organizing themselves on principles of popular participation toward social transformation. For instance, the Zimbabwe Christian Council sponsors a Learning for Transformation Course where participants learn to see themselves and their communities not as passive victims of social forces but as their own agents for social change and transformation. Similar Workshops for Social Transformation are taking place in other African countries. The participants engage in theological reflection on the economic crisis and study the logic behind the global economy's thrust toward capital accumulation. This logic is countered with the Christian principle that stresses community welfare as the primary goal of all goods, services and human labour:

Is the present crisis not a *"KAIROS"*, a moment most favourable for the creation of purely African political options, apt to
channel our energies to serve each and everyone's welfare?[54]

The Training for Transformation Workshops (which adapt Paulo
Freire's ideas on education to an African context) enable church
leaders and workers to grasp and to make the connections between
their own context and the injustices of the global economy.

The lay centre movement in Africa also provides a significant
"social space" for the church. The Training for Transformation programmes, which are gradually becoming integrated into the programmes of lay centres, provide a renewed vision of Christians in
society as instruments of justice. These seminars provide the opportunity for consciousness-raising, mobilizing action groups and, most
importantly, overcoming the fear and lack of confidence among lay
people at the grassroots. Jonah Katoneene, Director of the Association
of Christian Lay Centres in Africa (ACLCA), regards the Training for
Transformation model as the lifeblood of the churches in Africa in the
1990s.

It is this re-orientation which has enabled the lay-centre
movement in Africa to grapple with issues of economic justice.
Katoneene emphasizes the importance of providing a theological basis
for economic justice work. The traditional dichotomy which has
obtained between spiritual commitment and social responsibility must
be overcome and these issues brought together into a unified vision. It
is this unity which has become the driving force behind the response
to the intolerable burdens imposed by SAPs. For this reason, study of
the root causes of poverty and the economic crisis is crucial and must
be integrated into theological training. It is this gospel towards the
marginalized which should be the driving force behind economic
justice. The renewed goal of the lay centres is to transform those
educated into "prophet/teachers" who realize that their role in society
is not only a matter of speaking out against evils in society but, more
significantly, a question of seeking to transform the present oppressive
structures into humane and just relations among the children of God.[55]

More recently the ACLCA has begun to integrate ecological
issues into its Training for Transformation programme. A recent
publication, *The Taproot of the Environmental and Development*

Crisis in Africa, examines the crisis in Africa from a variety of perspectives. Of particular interest is the theological stance adopted by the book's author J. J. Otim. It is not Christian Theology or the Industrial Revolution which has been the major culprit in the eco-imperialist attitudes of the colonialists and present-day leaders in Africa, but what he terms

....the theology of conquest, the promised land, individualism, chosen people, abundance and of *laissez faire...* . It is the theology that destroyed African traditions, value systems and cultures, plundered the resources of the continent and set not only Africa but the whole world on a collision course with nature.[56]

To this attitude he contrasts the religious outlook of traditional African culture of sustainable co-existence, which is still deeply rooted in the minds of traditional indigenous Africans.[57] Hence a theological approach can provide a useful analytical framework to analyse the "socio-political and economic roots of the continent's problems and help create political conditions that make ecological responsibility possible... . The theological basis for such participation stems from the fact that nature, socio-economic development and the spiritual aspect of human beings are intertwined".[58]

The development vision offered by the lay-centre movement in Africa is one of delinking and self-reliance. It consists of arresting dependent development models, of which the debt crisis and SAPs are only symptoms, and promoting self-reliant development rooted in African cultural and religious traditions.

Advocacy, Mobilization and Conscientization

The African churches' alternative development path is rooted in grassroots education and conscientization. These include efforts at promoting economic literacy and an understanding of the operation of the global economy. This is achieved by producing literature at a popular level and providing courses for animators.[59] Most importantly, information is aimed at promoting programmes rooted in self-reliance at the grassroots level. Not only should this conscientization process occur at the local level, the churches argue, it must become an international effort:

> To support this development the Christian community in the rest of the world should adopt as its first priority the conscientization of the population in order to awaken public opinion which can put pressure on their governments, transnational corporations and other powerful institutions to induce them to cease their misuse of the world's natural and human resources uniquely for their own ends.[60]

This vision of solidarity, many writers point out, is already being lived out in the daily survival struggles of many Africans. As Tolen points out, it is only as a result of adopting alternative strategies that people have managed to survive and a basis for a more comprehensive alternative been laid:

> It is through solidarity that, despite the crisis, the children continue to go to school, some of the sick are cared for and hope is still alive. When the day comes that African governments at last give priority to inter-African relations, then we shall see African integration taking place.[61]

Many communities have identified and are implementing need-oriented, self-reliant, indigenous, participatory and sustainable development practices. As Godfrey Mwereria, a member of the AACC's Development Network, confirms:

> This is basically an intellectual and spiritual effort, an involvement to rediscover the truth and reality of the situation which is always with the people in their praxis and culture. In this perspective development is with the people, not as something that arrives with the *expert*.[62]

The vision of pan- or integrated Africanism is being revived as the only viable alternative to the current development model. The churches are playing an important role in mediating civil conflicts in many regions in an attempt to help bridge regional differences and build towards a model of intra-African solidarity. This is accompanied by the growing conviction that, while Africa's economic problems are rooted in an unjust international economic order, the solutions and alternatives can be found within the continent. There is a growing recognition that the present global system no longer considers Africa of any strategic importance. In many ways this provides the continent with a *kairos,* a critical opportunity to embark on a course of self-reliance. This vision is rooted in an economic model based on the use and management of resources to satisfy the basic needs of Africans first. This vision, many writers and church leaders contend, is only possible by means of a "second revolution" or "second liberation" which would lay the basis for true social transformation.

Conclusion

This chapter has provided a very brief overview of the variety of emerging trends in African theological responses to the debt and SAP crisis. It has focused on the ideas and concerns that have been raised by African church leaders who are actively involved in organizing and mobilizing responses to economic justice issues at the grassroots level. One of the key moments in this emerging discourse is the call for the indigenization of Christianity and the re-appropriation of African culture as a necessary precondition for achieving economic and political independence. This represents a significant development on the dependency debates of the 1960s and 1970s which focused primarily on the need for economic independence. In collaboration with social scientists in Africa, the dependency debate is moving in new directions. It is explicitly recognizing the religious character of dominant models of economic development and responding with alternatives that integrate the cultural and spiritual dimensions of development.

The strategy of delinking has been dismissed as a pipe dream by many who regard it as an illusory throwback to the independence struggles of earlier decades. In Latin America the themes of delinking and self-reliance have receded into the background in face of the realities of the new world order. In Africa, partly as a result of the growing recognition that the global economy has very little need for the continent, the debates about delinking and self-reliance are experiencing a resurgence. African theologians and social scientists are putting forward these alternatives for self-reliant development at a time when much of the South is moving toward greater integration into the global economy. The current collaborations that are occurring amongst theologians and social scientists in Africa provide a much more optimistic social scientific vision of religion as a powerful force in the struggle for social transformation.

The next chapter continues our discussion of some of the emerging theological responses to the debt and SAP crisis in Africa by focusing on women.

Endnotes

1. Churches' Drought Action in Africa, *Report on the Root Causes of Hunger and Food Insufficiency in Africa*, (Nairobi: All Africa Conference of Churches, 1986), p. 24.
2. *Root Causes*, p. 27.
3. *Root Causes*, p. 30.
4. *Root Causes*, p. 40.
5. African Network of the Churches Participation and Development, "Luanda Declaration: Our Christian Response to the 'War Against the Dispossessed,'" (Luanda, May 1989), p. 1.
6. "Luanda Declaration," pp. 5-6.
7. A. Tolen, "Africa Through New Eyes," (Geneva: World Council of Churches Central Committee, September, 1991), p. 3.
8. "Luanda Declaration," p. 2.
9. Catholic Bishops of Zambia, "Economics, Politics and Justice," (Pastoral Statement, September 15, 1990), p. 12.
10. Catholic Bishops of Zambia, "Economics, Politics and Justice," p. 12.
11. Zambia: Churches Confront Government, *(Africa Information*, Aug. 17, 1993).
12. All Africa Conference of Churches, "The Right Time for Change: What Hope for A Crisis Stricken Africa?" (Nairobi: All Africa Conference of Churches), p. 19.
13. J. H. Boer, *Christians and Mobilization*, (Jos: Christian Council of Nigeria, 1989), p. 3; see also D. M'Passou, *Towards a Theology of Development*, (Chilema: Christian Communication Programme, 1987), p. 23.
14. Boer, *Christians and Mobilization*, p. 7.
15. L. Imunde, *Salt in the Stew: Theological Basis for Christian Participation in Social Transformation*, (Nairobi: All Africa Conference of Churches, 1989), p. 30.

16. *Root Causes*, p. 33.
17. *Root Causes*, p. 46.
18. "Luanda Declaration," p. 6.
19. "Luanda Declaration," p. 8.
20. All Africa Conference of Churches, "Maseru Declaration on the Debt Crisis," (Maseru, Lesotho, September 1990) p. 23.
21. All Africa Conference of Churches, "Debt Crisis," p. 20.
22. AACC, "Debt Crisis," p. 22.
23. AACC, "Debt Crisis," p. 9.
24. Conversation with Omega Bula, October, 1991.
25. World Council of Churches, "Testimony of Mr. Cosmas M. Musumali and Mr. A. J. Annorbah-Sarpei for the Ecumenical Hearing on the International Monetary System and the Churches' Responsibility," in World Council of Churches' Commission on the Churches Participation in Development, *Debt Resource Materials* 2, 1988), p. 16.
26. P. Gifford, *Christianity: To Save or Enslave?*, p. 4.
27. Conversation with Omega Bula, October, 1991.
28. Gifford, *The New Religious Right*, p. 24.
29. J. N. K. Mugambi, "Problems and Promises of the Church in Africa," (paper prepared for the All Africa Conference of Churches, Kanamai, November, 1991), p. 1.
30. See P. Ufford and M. Schoffeleers, *Religion and Development*, p. 6.
31. Mugambi, "Problems and Promises," p. 3.
32. Mugambi, "Problems and Promises," p. 5
33. Mugambi, "Problems and Promises," p. 6.
34. Mugambi, "Problems and Promises," p. 7.
35. Mugambi, "Problems and Promises," p. 7.
36. Mugambi, "Problems and Promises," p. 10.
37. G. Mwereria, *The Root Causes of Debt Crisis in Africa: An Agenda for Continental Collective Self-Reliance*, (Nairobi: Southern Network for Development, 1990), p. 16.
38. Mwereria, *Root Causes*, p. 17.
39. Mwereria, *Root Causes*, p. 28.
40. K. Kanyinga and J. Gathaka, "In Search of Debt Crisis' Solution: Structural Adjustment Programmes (SAPs); Recolonization or Liberation and Alternatives?" (Paper presented for the National Council of Churches of Kenya Workshop: The Debt and Economic Crisis in Africa, Nairobi, March, 1991), pp. 17-8.
41. The relevant passage from the encyclical reads as follows: "[T]he debtor nations, in order to service their debts, find themselves obliged to export the capital needed for improving or at least maintaining their standard of living. It is also because, for the same reason, they are unable to obtain new and equally essential financing. Through this mechanism, the means intended for the development of peoples has turned into a brake upon development instead, and indeed in some cases has even aggravated underdevelopment"

(Par .9). As Gathaka points out this analysis is set against the background of an analysis of the structures of sin described in the encyclical as, "those economic, financial and social mechanisms which, although they are manipulated by people, often function almost automatically (thus) accentuating the situation of wealth for some and poverty for the rest. These mechanisms, which are manoeuvred directly or indirectly by the more developed countries, by their very functioning favour the interests of the people manipulating them. But in the end they suffocate or condition the economies of the less developed countries" (Par. 16). See J. Gathaka, "Sounds from the African Churches", (paper presented at the Institute of Church and Society Conference on Nigeria's External Debt, Jos, November, 1990), pp. 4-5.

42. Gathaka, "Sounds," p. 5.
43. J. Gathaka, "Economic and Social Problems Created by Debt and Economic Crisis: Biblical Exposition on Nehemia 5:1-13," (paper delivered to the All Africa Council of Churches International Affairs Conference on The Debt Crisis as it Affects Human Rights, Maseru, September, 1990), p. 6.
44. Gathaka, "Economic and Social Problems," p. 7.
45. Gathaka, "Economic and Social Problems," p. 16.
46. *Root Causes*, p. 17.
47. *Root Causes*, p. 18.
48. *Root Causes*, p. 20-1.
49. T. Njoya, *ACLCA News*, 3/2-3, (1991), p. 5.
50. B. Masilo, *ACLCA News*, 3/1, (1991), p. 16.
51. "Delink with West, Africa Urged," *ACLCA News*, 1/2 (1989), p. 7.
52. *Root Causes*, p. 33.
53. All Africa Conference of Churches, "The Right Time for Change," p. 24.
54. "The Right Time for Change," p. 3.
55. Katoneene, "Social Transformation," p. 12.
56. J.J. Otim, *The Taproot of Environmental and Development Crisis in Africa*, (ACLCA Publication No. 2, Nairobi, 1992), p. 63.
57. Otim, *The Taproot*, p. 62.
58. Otim, *The Taproot*, p. 64.
59. *Root Causes*, p. 74.
60. *Root Causes*, p. 75.
61. Tolen, "Africa Through New Eyes," p. 5.
62. Mwereria, "The Debt Crisis in Africa," p. 7.

— CHAPTER TEN —

Structural Adjustment and Women: The Response of the Churches

During the 1980s, social scientists turned their attention increasingly towards the impact of structural adjustment on women. While there are significant variations in the positions adopted by various writers on the issue of gender and adjustment, most studies reach the conclusion that women are bearing a disproportionate share of the burdens imposed by SAPs. The most widely publicized study, conducted by UNICEF, looked especially at the increased burdens imposed on women in the areas of health and education.[1] The UNICEF report called for adjustment programmes which included a human face, and programmes specifically targeted to groups most adversely affected by SAPs.

Another report conducted by the Commonwealth Expert Group on Women and Structural Adjustment came to the following conclusion:

> The economic crisis of the 1980s, and the type of stabilisation and adjustment measures taken in response to it, have halted and even reversed the progress in health, nutrition, education and incomes which women had enjoyed in developing countries during the previous three decades. In the 1980s, despite greater national and international commitment towards gender issues, most women have suffered disproportionately during the widespread economic and social disruption that has occurred in much of the developing world.[2]

Inherent within examinations of the gender impact of SAPs are a number of theoretical debates concerning the efficacy of various approaches to the issue. This field of research is especially sensitive in uncovering the assumptions in various approaches to the studies of women and development. This is especially true with respect to the growing understanding of male-bias that is endemic to development thinking. As Diane Elson notes in her introductory chapter to the volume of studies entitled *Male Bias in the Development Process*, gender-based approaches must seek to move conceptually from traditional women and development approaches, which attempt to integrate women into existing development patterns and to improve their overall position. Such an approach targets women (often as a development problem) as a homogeneous group with undifferentiated interests. What is needed, Elson argues, is a shift to an approach which emphasizes gender relations and how specific policies have differential impacts on existing gender relations.[3] Only by adopting a gender analysis can SAPs be critically assessed in terms of their impact on women.

This chapter examines some of the recent attempts to analyse the gender impact of SAPs in sub-Saharan Africa. The major strength of gender analysis is its ability to uncover the male-bias assumptions contained within the policies and prescriptions of SAPs. Its other strength lies in its appreciation of grassroots organizations as possessing real transformative potential. However, some of the current gender and development literature on SAPs continues to neglect the role of religion and of the churches in response to SAPs. A corrective to this conceptual hurdle is attempted by examining the contribution that the churches in Africa have made in terms of gender analysis and responses to SAPs. This is done by looking primarily at the work of the Women's Desk of the All Africa Conference of Churches on issues of economic justice.

The World Bank and Women in Development

In all of the major World Bank documents pertaining to Africa, barely a mention is made of the gender implications of SAPs. In fact, until 1987 the issue of women in development hardly warranted any attention by the World Bank, either in its documents or in its projects. By and large, any project-specific programmes to assist women were restricted to family planning, health and nutrition programmes.

In 1987, the World Bank launched a major initiative intended to integrate attention to women by establishing a Women in Development (WID) Division. This initiative was geared to expanding women's opportunities by enhancing their productivity and earning potential.

The programme was designed to improve women's economic opportunities by overcoming some of the traditional obstacles they faced. In the World Bank's view these included excessive fertility, lack of education opportunities, the male bias to extension programmes, access to credit and secure land tenure.

By 1990, in a special report entitled *Women and Development*, the World Bank could boast of important progress in its project orientation to address women's concerns. In agriculture, projects with specific actions to help women had jumped from nine out of 56 in 1988 to 22 out of 53 in 1989.[4] Lending which would assist women jumped from 10 per cent to 20 per cent of all projects between 1988 and 1989.[5]

What is curiously absent in this assessment is any serious consideration of how women were being specifically affected by SAPs. This imperviousness to the connection between SAPs and the growing impoverishment of women is startling in light of the numerous campaigns which focused on this concern, such as the one launched by UNICEF. While it is theoretically possible to separate the imposition of SAPs from the issue of women in development, it is practically impossible to do so. In Africa SAPs have radically altered the behaviour and survival mechanisms of women, a problem that the World Bank continues to view with the categories of "excessive fertility" or barriers to entrepreneurial opportunities.

In a similar vein, the World Bank's 1989 major document on sub-Saharan Africa, *From Crisis to Sustainable Growth*, mentions women's special development concerns only in passing, devoting roughly a total of one page out of 194 to the issue. The obstacles to women's development potential are seen to be caused solely by internal factors or "tradition":

> That women play a central role in development is becoming increasingly recognized. They are the principal producers of food, the managers of household resources, and the custodians of family welfare. This is a case in which tradition and development do seem to clash. African women face a variety of legal, economic and social constraints.[6]

In following this logic, *From Crisis* blames population pressures and shrinking farm sizes through inheritance as the causes for men leaving the land in search of wage-labour and women being called upon increasingly to manage farms. The effects, however, are accurately described:

> Women's agricultural workload grows while their traditional work burden in childcare, wood gathering, water fetching, and staple food pounding remains the same – or grows too. The burden on women means that land preparation, planting, and weeding are often delayed, which depresses yields.[7]

Again, no mention is made of other factors such as higher prices for inputs, user fees for health and education, lower prices for commodities as factors which contribute to the effects described above. The solution offered is to privatize land and ensure women security of tenure, along with improving their access to credit and education.[8] By identifying the problem in reference to a theoretical world of free markets, the *solution* is identified through the measures of SAPs that will release the entrepreneurial potential of women. In the World Bank's view SAPs can enable women to move from what the head of the Bank's WID Division describes as unproductive to productive work:

> In this area, the fundamental task is to switch labour and resources from less productive to more productive lines of work. The Bank's women-in-development strategy emphasizes the types of investments (education, health/family planning, credit, extension) that can help women make this switch faster and more effectively. In the meantime, special efforts may be needed to tide over the poorest women until they can produce more and earn more.[9]

The World Bank's 1991 *Annual Report* claims a deepening commitment to integrating women into its operations. The basis for this claim is its own studies and reviews which reveal that over 62 per cent of its economic and sector reports "contained substantive discussions or recommendations on WID issues as compared with 41 per cent in 1990".[10]

UNICEF: Adjustment with a Human Face

While UNICEF has openly criticized SAPs, it has itself been criticized for a tendency to regard women as a homogeneous target group which is being adversely affected by SAPs in the areas of health and education. While UNICEF's country studies provide important statistical analysis on the deteriorating conditions of health and education, its analysis does not examine many other gender-related impacts of SAPs. UNICEF accepts the basic premises of SAPs in proposing "adjustment with a human face", and specific poverty alleviation programmes that would target women, children and sectors adversely impacted by SAPs.

The UNICEF approach has been criticized on a number of fronts. Elson notes how its approach takes little account of the increased time and costs that the decentralization of health care means for women.[11] Rudo Gaidzwana points out a number of other deficiencies in UNICEF's human-face approach to SAPs. The human-face approach perpetuates the basic attitude of women as welfare recipients to be targeted with specific programmes to ease their transition into more "productive" forms of labour, much in the way the World Bank advocates. By advocating programmes like feeding supplements, Gaidzwana argues, the solutions perpetuate the perception of women's work as unpaid labour and increases their dependence on men.[12]

Gender-based Research on SAPs

Gender-based analyses of the impact of SAPs have been helpful in overcoming the conceptual barriers of the more traditional WID approach. Gender-based analyses seek to uncover the gender bias implicit in official development theories such as those put forward by agencies like the World Bank. What are presented as gender-neutral economic prescriptions to improve the overall welfare of people are in fact rooted in a number of assumptions, the impact of which is the further marginalization and super-exploitation of women as a result of the adoption of these policies.

A gender and development approach examines the role that women are being forced to play in the era of SAPs and WID. According to Janet Bujra, both approaches share the axiomatic view of development as the promotion of capitalist relations of production. Hence the feminization of poverty associated with SAPs and feminization of development indicative of the WID thrust are flip sides of the same coin which perpetuates and intensifies the exploitation of women. For African women in the 1980s this meant entering the migrant labour force and being compelled to produce cash crops. Gender analysis exposes the myth that women have been excluded from "development" and examines how women's labour has subsidized both the local and global economy. The WID approach serves to integrate women further into this process, perpetuating the fiction that women (like developing countries) need only "catch up" to their more prosperous counterparts. As Erika Marke notes:

> Therefore, we have to realize that emancipation will only be possible for a minority of privileged middle and upper class women in the North and in the South on the backs of the poor, especially poor women, who will continue to be structurally disadvantaged and exploited. This means that if we follow the Northern emancipation strategy, we help to stabilize the status quo and to divide the feminist movement into winners and losers.[13]

A gender-based analysis not only focuses attention on the direct and measurable impacts of SAPs on women, it also examines many of the gender-based assumptions of SAPs and their effects on gender relations. The macro-economic thinking on which SAPs are based, while couched in gender-neutral language, takes little account of the sexual division of labour, the inter-changeability of labour and resources within the household, and how shifts in entitlements and incentives have a dramatic impact especially in terms of women's labour. The most glaring assumption of the typical SAP recipe lies in its view of labour as a costlessly transferable factor of production.[14] In the worldview of World Bank economists, the problem is reducible to one in which the production of non-tradables outstrips production of tradables due to price distortions. The solution involves shifting price incentives toward the production of tradables by removing subsidies on non-tradables. The so-called non-tradables include locally produced food, and government services such as health and education.[15]

Elson perceptively notes the range of assumptions implied in this analysis. First, the model suggests that all that is required is a simple shift in the allocation of labour in a typical household and not an overall increase in labour time as the above citation from the director of the World Bank's WID Division suggests. Even more insidious are the assumptions about the gender shifts in the allocation of labour that SAPs imply, the shifts of labour to the "hidden" sphere of domestic labour that are brought on as a result of SAPs, and finally, the kinds of assumptions about what could be described as the "fungibility" of resources and labour within the household.[16]

The shift from non-tradable to tradable crops invariably results in a loss of control over the proceeds of the sale of these crops, since it is usually men who control this sphere of production, even though women may contribute significantly to the crops' production.[17]

Increased efficiency in government expenditures on health and education or overall balance of payments is largely due to the shifting of costs from the paid to the unpaid "domestic sphere".[18] Here, the assumption of the World Bank, and of UNICEF, is that domestic unpaid labour is "infinitely elastic". Not only is it assumed that women can take on the added burden of health care and added labour for the provision of school fees, women are also called upon to provide their added labour to community projects such as road-building, water and housing projects.[19] The result is becoming increasingly apparent: women are being stretched beyond their limit, leading to the disintegration of the household and of the community.[20] The survival strategies that women are being forced to adopt are quite drastic, as the survey of Nigerian households in one district demonstrates (see Table 10.1).

**Table 10.1:Survival strategies of
Nigerian households under SAPs**

Measure Adopted	No. of Households	% of Total (Total=180)
Reducing meal frequency from 3 to twice/day	153	85
Reducing meal frequency from 3 to once/day	54	30
Reducing the quantity of meals per intake	180	100
Elimination of food groups from diet:		
Fish	108	60
Beef	153	85
Chicken	162	90
Egg	171	95
Milk	171	95
Sending children out to work for income	45	25

(Source: Elabor-Idemudia, "Women and Economic Reforms," p. 11)

Finally, the SAP model assumes that households operate on the principle of the pooling of resources. Hence, a re-allocation of incomes in favour of males will not have a negative impact on the household if the overall income level of the household is maintained. This assumption has proven to be false in a number of studies.[21] Women's incomes tend to be allocated toward overall household needs while men retain a considerable amount for personal uses. As Elson notes in summarizing her critique of SAPs:

Models of structural adjustment which depict the problem as something that can be solved by changing relative prices so as to switch resources from non-tradables to tradables in fact rely on an increase in the provision of a non-tradable that is not explicitly included: an increase in women's time and effort in the reproduction and maintenance of human resources.[22]

Church-based Women's Organizations in Africa

It is surprising that most of the gender-based analyses of SAPs make no reference to the role of the church-based organizations. Women's organizations are viewed to be moving beyond the issues of meeting basic survival needs to embrace broader social and economic issues. As a result, they possess a transformative perspective in the areas of gender discrimination as well as in issues of social and economic justice at the national and international levels.[23] In spite of this recognition of the crucial role that local organizations play in responding to SAPs, church-based efforts are largely overlooked.[24]

In her overview of women's social movements in Africa, Rhoda Reddock notes that the study of women's grassroots organizations is largely ignored by social scientists. Even the women's organizations whose major *raison d'être* lies in meeting basic reproductive needs possess transformative potential by the very fact that they posit alternative social forms to those of existing power structures. Because many of the day-to-day activities of these groupings seem trivial and uninteresting, they are not considered to be the stuff of social scientific research.[25] Ayesha Imam points to the persistent neglect of gender issues in widely regarded treatments of issues of political struggles, agriculture and social movements.[26]

And yet, neither writer accords any significance to church-based organizations. In her call for multi-disciplinary research of social movements in Africa, and especially with respect to gender-related concerns, Reddock subsumes the study of religiously-based organizations under the heading of "Historical Studies". As for present-day religious-based organizations, Reddock asks:

> ...how can such a large body of women organized in these at best reformist organizations be mobilized to become part of a movement for positive social change, on their own and their societies behalf?[27]

It seems that even social scientists who advocate a gender-based analysis of the impact of SAPs, and who see the transformative potential that exists in social movements, nonetheless do not regard church-based organizations as falling within the category of social movements worthy of serious consideration or research. While they are regarded as serving the important purposes of solidarity, community-building and distraction from the worries of the home, they are not generally regarded as the sites for mobilization or social transformation. A corrective to this relative neglect (bordering in some cases on disdain) for the work of women's church-based organizations in responding to the SAP crisis in Africa is urgently needed. The following section highlights the work of the AACC's Women's Desk since 1989 in responding to the SAP crisis.

The All Africa Conference of Churches' Women's Desk

In January 1989, the Women's Desk of the All Africa Conference of Churches embarked on a programme targeting economic justice issues. Previously, the concerns of its Family Life Division were restricted to traditional programmes considered to be the domain of women, such as primary health care, nutrition and education. The shift in emphasis resulted from the growing awareness that the impact of the debt crisis was far more deleterious than any of the programmes could adequately address. Adopting popular education techniques and placing greater emphasis on political and socio-economic analysis, the Women's Desk launched an ambitious campaign aimed at educating and mobilizing women around issues of food security, the marginalization of women's issues in the churches, community-based health education, women and economic justice, and child survival and development. Since that time, conferences and workshops have been organized focusing on these themes.

The Consultation on Women and Economic Justice was held in June of 1990 in Zambia. The consultation was devoted to examining the role and contribution of women in the economy, especially during a time of economic crisis. The emphasis was on helping women to become literate about the magnitude of the debt crisis and the impact of adjustment programmes on their lives. As Omega Bula, director of the Women's Desk, describes:

The explanations on how this [the impact of SAPs] happens were not hard to find in our own lives. We were challenged not only to address symptoms, but causes of the economic crisis by first reclaiming the economy as a woman's domain.[28]

The issues raised at this conference and the themes presented by speakers were comprehensive and far reaching. The approach was multi-disciplinary, with an emphasis on the connection between theology and economics. The clearest challenge provided by many of the conference speakers was for the churches in Africa to reform their own unjust structures which oppress women. These themes were woven into a reflection on the effects of SAPs from a political and economic, as well as biblical and theological, perspective.

The Church as Oppressor of Women

Theologian Mercy Odudoye directly challenges the assumptions about women prevailing in church structures that reflect those of governments and other institutions. The church not only neglects to examine its own structures, notes Odudoye, it also discounts the unpaid labour of women: "Has the Church a voice where it is women who become poorer and poorer in the unjust wage structure, and as a result of their struggle to feed their families while society and Church continue to put the honourable label of 'bread winners' on men? It is about time the Church stood up for and by women."[29] Dr Agnes Aboum is far more blunt in her own assessment of the churches' attitudes towards women:

Despite the hardships women face, pastors insist on being served special food on their pastoral visits. They know very well that these poor women need the money and food for the family or do not even have it. Is this what we understand by the Churches' solidarity with women and the poor to mean? It would seem that instead of the church hierarchy being in solidarity with women, it is instead oppressive.[30]

Aboum's critique of church structures extends also to church women's organizations which continue to represent a welfare mentality on issues of social and economic justice. A co-requisite for social transformation is the democratization of unjust structures which include the church. What is required, notes Aboum, is a strategy of democratization which builds on women's own capacity to resist and mobilize to bring about more just political and ecclesiastical structures.

Theology and Economics

Women in the churches in Africa bring a unique perspective in their reflection on the theme of theology and economy. As Odudoye declares:

> What has economics to do with Christianity? some may ask, forgetting that God is an economist. We are part of God's household and elements in God's housekeeping. Indeed as stewards of creation we cannot separate economics from theology... . The least in God's economy is always at the centre. In God's economy the margins are more important than the centre. Should the Churches of Africa not take up the economic concerns of women and other church people?[31]

This approach stands in contrast to the dominant approach of male theologians in Africa who remain caught in refuting the "two kingdom" thesis in providing justification for the Church's involvement in politics. In very important respects, the focus on the economy marks a significant theological movement. The recognition of the inseparability of theology and economics forms the starting point of a critique of unjust economic structures. It is based on the conviction that, in God's economy, the resources of the earth belong to all equally.[32] The modern economic system which allows the obscenely rich to co-exist beside the starving person is described in theological terms as the "reign of Baal and not Yahweh".[33] The conference's final statement regards the economy as one of the central issues for the churches in Africa:

> Economy is defined as a process of managing resources, e.g. power, time, money, production and whatever is at human-kind's disposal towards the benefit of all God's people (creation).

Theology and economy are related just like the soul is part of the body; when the body is nourished the soul remains alive in the body. We cannot separate theology and economy.

Theology is the backbone which illumines our management of the economy; therefore, economy should become one of the aspects of the ministries of the church.

The Church is called to be involved in economic justice in the same way she has been involved in social justice.

In the African culture we express ourselves: I AM BECAUSE WE ARE – whatever I have belongs to us. Our communities sustain us and give us life in relation to God.[34]

By reading the Bible from this critical perspective what emerges is the conviction that the experience of the women in the Bible is closely akin to what African women experience today. This has moved women to respond, as theologian Nyambura Njoroge declares, to "capture Jesus' teaching and practices in regard to the women who were oppressed, rejected and non-recognized in the Bible".[35] This is in contrast, according to Njoroge, to traditional African readings of the Bible which ignored its teachings about the poor and oppressed and passed over the many positive stories of women.

Theology and Structural Adjustment

By affirming the inseparability of theology and economics as their starting point, the Women and Economic Justice consultation focuses on structural adjustment as one of the most important theological issues facing women in Africa. Not only is the economic crisis viewed as an issue for women, what is also integrated is a class, cultural, political and social analysis:

The economic crisis we are talking about is very much political, social and cultural. It is moreover systemic from the old model to the new model. The way it affects women is not uniform: it has different manifestations for different women depending on their social background/class.[36]

The analysis of SAPs, their impact on women, and what the response to them should be, is clear and unequivocal:

> Evidence shows, however, that women are more affected by the crisis than men. Whilst Structural Adjustment Policies talk of restructuring with a human face, there is little tangible evidence towards that direction. It would seem that one of the attempts of this emphasis is to silence strong resistance by people and therefore the need to relax somewhat the most stringent conditions. But the fact remains that international capital has to make a profit with or without a human face... that is the more reason why we in the Church need to scrutinize such policies in order that we are not deceived or seen to be endorsing them. We should call for the scrapping of Structural Adjustment Policies.[37]

Njoroge writes of the devastating effect that the economic crisis has had on women in Africa:

> As a result of the gruesome economic crisis in Africa, the majority of African women are pushed onto the margin of all these basic needs. In the process, the African woman is rendered malnourished, powerless and most vulnerable to poor health. The fact that the woman has to walk long distances for these basic needs leaves her exhausted, aged and weak. At the same time, the same bodies are required to spend so many hours in a day, *bent over* in the fields, weeding, planting, harvesting etc. Worse still, these are the African women who bring forth in the world between seven and ten children in their lifetime. Finally, we find that the plight of the African woman is not only non-recognized, but she has become the "rejected of history".[38]

One of the most pressing issues that church-based women's networks have addressed is the growing inability of women to meet the basic survival needs of their families. Church-based programmes are not able to cope with the effects of policies like the removal of subsidies on health care and education. In the wake of this, women are increasingly forced into activities such as smuggling, prostitution, brewing and selling alcohol. This brings many women into conflict with their own religious beliefs. The other effect is the growing hopelessness of women who blame themselves for their inability to cope. The increase in spousal abuse, suicide and alcoholism are only some of the often unreported results that women's networks seek to address. It is with this recognition that the AACC Women's Desk recently launched a continent-wide programme for economic literacy.

It was largely through the analyses and experiences of church women at the continental Consultation on Women and Economic Justice that the decision was taken to focus on economic literacy. The goal is to organize workshops for women church leaders at the national church-council level to give them functional literacy on economic issues and to train them in appropriate methodologies for training women at the grassroots.

While it is difficult to gauge the potential impact of such a programme, it will undoubtedly provide an important space for women to analyse the root causes of their problems, reflect theologically, and to organize and mobilize for change. As Omega Bula notes, one of the already visible effects is the confidence that women build up for themselves in overcoming their own "blame the victim" tendencies, and in recognizing the real sources of their problems and how to overcome them. A training video on the effects of SAPs on women was produced and distributed throughout the continent. These initiatives by the Women's Desk of the AACC point to a movement away from traditional welfare-oriented programmes to programmes rooted in a vision of social transformation.

Women's Resistance

To develop a vision of stewardship for modern life there is a need for a public theology of the political economy.[39]

Women are at the heart of the resistance movements opposed to SAPs. Throughout the continent, it is the churches which are at the forefront in organizing seminars and workshops devoted to understanding the economic crisis and the response of women. An important component of the struggle of women in Africa lies in engaging in critical reflection on the legacy of theological discrimination against women. It is precisely because of the traditional role that has been assigned to women by the churches and economy that women are uniquely placed to provide transformative alternatives:

> From women's perspective, a new understanding of development has to follow the vision of a just, peaceful and sustainable society whose primary concern is to care for the integrity of creation. As a result of their specific history, the gender-related role assigned to them by patriarchy, and knowledge and experiences gathered from that, women can take the lead in concretizing this vision.[40]

In seeking to understand more clearly the roots of women's resistance to oppression, social scientists tend to overlook the religious dimension. This is especially the case in Africa where religion is either viewed as a barrier to modernization or the handmaiden of colonialism. Yet, by overlooking this crucial dimension, what is missed is one of the constitutive elements not only of women's resistance and liberation but of other movements as well. As Njoroge points out:

> [I]t is crucial to note that the African woman's ethical vision is rooted in African culture and spirituality which helps Africans to organize attitudes of resistance to oppression and rejection. It is within these organizations or basic communities that we find "little steps of liberation".[41]

The analysis of gender-based approaches to SAPs and the contribution of church-based women's networks points to the need for greater collaboration amongst women's groups opposed to the SAP agenda and for strategic alliances with anti-poverty, trade union, environmentalist and native groups. A gender-based analysis provides insights which facilitate the linking of issues and of movements among feminists, ecologists and liberation theologians. It reaffirms the conviction that the impetus for transformation must come at the local level from those who now bear the brunt of environmental degradation and poverty. It places the struggles of the marginalized to regain control over their land and development at the forefront.

The Story of Women

The story of women and economic justice
is a story of life and death
A story about endless agonies

A story about managing the unmanageable
A story of endless hours of work and toil

A story of sleepless nights
A story about destitution, squalor and neglect

A story of hearing about policies
that determine our lives but never being
there to participate

A story of the voiceless and powerless

A story of trials and temptations
A story of lost personalities and dignity

A story of survival behind battle fronts
as women and children flee bomb raids

A story of structural, emotional and physical violence.

A story of struggle and humiliation
A story of dreams and visions unfulfilled

A story of hope

A story of combat and resistance
A story of withdrawal from structures of exploitation

A story of innovation and creativity
A story of breaking new frontiers for survival

A story of heroic people marching to
the future with new alternatives for
the survival of the human race.

Agnes Chepkwony Aboum[42]

Endnotes

1. A. C. Cornia, *et al*, eds., *Adjustment with a Human Face*, vols. 1 and 2, (Oxford: UNICEF, 1987).
2. Commonwealth Expert Group on Women and Structural Adjustment, *Engendering Adjustment in the 1990s*, (London: Commonwealth Secretariat, 1990).
3. D. Elson, *Male Bias in the Development Process*, (Manchester: Manchester University Press, 1991), p. 1.
4. World Bank, *Women and Development*, (Washington: World Bank, 1990), p. 10.
5. *Women and Development*, p. 14.
6. World Bank, *From Crisis*, p. 60.
7. *From Crisis*, p. 103.
8. *From Crisis*, p. 104.
9. B. Herz, "Bringing Women into the Economic Mainstream," *Finance and Development* 26/4 1989, p. 25, cited in Elson, *Male Bias*, p. 206.
10. World Bank, *Annual Report* 1991, p. 55.
11. Elson, *Male Bias*, p. 178.
12. R. Gaidzwana, "Structural Adjustment and Debt," (paper prepared for the European Debt and Development Network, Munich, July 1992).
13. Erika Marke, "The Nineties: The Decade of Women's Development," in All Africa Conference of Churches Women's Desk, *Church Women's Consultation on Economic Justice*, p. 57.
14. Elson, *Male Bias*, p. 165; J.Vickers, *Women and the World Economic Crisis*, (London: Zed Books, 1991), p. 22.
15. Elson, *Male Bias*, p. 167.
16. Elson, *Male Bias*, p. 168.
17. P. Elabor-Idemudia, "Women and Economic Reforms," (unpublished, 1992), p. 3; N. Kanji, "The Gender Specific Effects of Structural Adjustment," (paper for the workshop on Economic Policy, Equity and Health), Harare, Feb. 1991, p. 18; Elson, *Male Bias*, pp. 173-4.
18. Elson, *Male Bias*, p. 24.
19. N. Kanji, "The Gender Specific Effects," p. 21.
20. Elson, *Male Bias*, pp. 25, 179.
21. See Idemudia's survey of Nigerian households which indicated that almost 40% of women surveyed had no access at all to their husband's income while in only 17% of cases was money management jointly carried out by husband and wife. Elabor-Idemudia, "Women and Economic Reforms," p. 9.
22. Elson, *Male Bias*, pp. 185-6.
23. Gaidzwana, "Debt and Structural Adjustment"; Elson, *Male Bias*," p. 192-3.
24. Elson, *Male Bias*, p. 187.
25. R. Reddock, "Towards a Framework for the Study of Women, Gender and

Social Movements in Africa," (Draft Working Paper prepared for Council for the Development of Economic and Social Research in Africa Workshop on Gender Analysis and African Social Science) Dakar, Sept. 1991, p. 11.

26. A. Imam, "Gender Analysis and African Social Sciences in the 1990s," *Africa Development* 3/4 (1990), pp. 5-6.

27. Reddock, "Towards a Framework," p. 20.

28. All Africa Conference of Churches Women's Desk, *Final Report: Consultation on Women and Economic Justice*, (Nairobi: AACC, 1990), p. 1.

29. M. Odudoye, "To Deal Justly," in *Final Report*, p. 4.

30. A. Aboum, "Women and Economic Justice: The Invisible Victims," in *Final Report* p. 7.

31. M. Odudoye, "To Deal Justly," p. 5.

32. A. Shipman, "Theology and Economy," in *Church Women's Consultation on Economic Justice*, (Nairobi: AACC Women's Desk, 1990), p. 9.

33. E. Musau, "The National Council of Churches of Kenya is in the Forefront in Promoting Women's Activities," in *Church Women's Consultation*, p. 41.

34. *Final Report,* pp. 20, 22.

35. N. Njoroge, "Theological Reflection on the Effects of the Economic Crisis on Women in Africa," *Church Women's Consultation*, p. 5.

36. A. Aboum, "Women and Economic Justice," p. 6.

37. A. Aboum, "Women and Economic Justice," p. 10

38. Njoroge, "Theological Reflection," p. 4.

39. E. Musau, "The National Counci,l" p. 43.

40. Erika Marke, "The Nineties: The Decade of Women's Development", p. 59.

41. Njoroge, "Theological Reflection," p. 5.

42. A. Aboum, in *Final Report,* p. 27.

Conclusion

> As theologians, ethicists, sociologists, feminists, ecologists
> etc. we have not done enough to stop the market from being
> treated as something sacred and put an end to the sacrifices
> required in its name of the poor sectors of our countries.[1]

Julio de Santa Ana's challenge vividly captures the ideas and analysis presented in the preceding chapters. The issues raised in this book all point to the need for greater collaboration, not only amongst social scientists and theologians, but among the many social movements and grassroots organizations committed to social, economic and political justice.

This book has highlighted the variety of challenges that have been directed at the World Bank's structural adjustment agenda over the past decade. A key operating principle throughout has been to consider the SAP project as a religious vision imbued with a coherent theology and value-system. As such, it can be placed on the same terrain of analysis as the alternative visions of development promoted by churches and grassroots organizations.

Over the past decade structural adjustment has taken a heavy toll in sub-Saharan Africa. Structural adjustment policies succeed in maintaining and enhancing the wealth and power of elites in the North and South, taking no serious account of the vast majority of the world's inhabitants. The ideology of SAPs is one which calls on African countries to continue to sacrifice their dwindling resources and labour on the altar of the global market in the hope that one day their economies will recover. SAPs move us towards a global market where corporations, without national or community allegiances, control every aspect of production. It is this reality, as John Cobb Jr. and Herman Daly observe, that lies behind the rhetoric of trade liberalization:

Free traders, having freed themselves from the restraints of community at the national level and having moved into the cosmopolitan world, *which is not a community*, have effectively freed themselves of all community obligations.[2]

The corporate free-trade development model has begun to eclipse the debt-financed developmentalist model. This model allowed industrialized countries, banks and corporations to export their surpluses to the South as the South fell into an abyss of debt to finance the imports that were to place them on the road to modernization. This experiment failed, not because of an unexpected rise in oil prices or interest rates, but simply because it was unsustainable in that it served the short-term interests of banks, transnationals and elites in poorer countries. It was not a model of development rooted in respecting or considering the voices that were killed, left homeless, landless and impoverished in the name of development and modernization.

The recognition that the theology of SAPs is essentially community-destroying and death-dealing[3] lends an urgency to the ethical task of linking issues of participatory and self-reliant development, ecology, feminism, peace, and other social justice movements. When a global perspective is adopted the integral relationship among these issues is illuminated, along with some indices for common action. This global perspective is *physically* rooted in the concerns and struggles of local communities, the poor and the marginalized in Africa. It is only by examining development through these lenses that it has become possible "to corrupt the self-evidence of development in its masquerade as natural law".[4]

One of the fundamental features of present global development policies is the process by which basic livelihood decisions are increasingly being wrested away from the local and community levels and ceded to the "impersonal" forces of the market. The kind of analysis which focuses its attention on the interface between global economic structures and local-level concerns is gradually emerging as a trend in the alternative development literature. A social analysis which considers the interface of the global economy and local-level processes holds the most promising prospect for alternative social spaces to emerge.

There is a growing sense of hope among academics and those in social movements that the SAP agenda can be successfully resisted and overthrown. Henry Bernstein is convinced that SAPs will fail in Africa: "trying to coerce African states into basic policy 'reform' does not confront, hence cannot resolve, the contradictions of 'agricultural modernization' in the face of the environmental conditions, social processes of peasant farming, and historical patterns of commodification in Africa."[5] Gerald Helleiner states categorically that "it is time to call an end to the decade of 'structural adjustment'".[6]

In place of SAPs, the option of self-reliant patterns of development is gaining prominence, not as a decision between two models of development, but as a necessity for survival. Africans, to the extent that they become increasingly marginalized and irrelevant in the global economy, can move in the direction of delinking with the global economy. Many regard this as a positive affirmation of the values of self-reliant, participatory and sustainable development which affirms the diversity of Africa's peoples and traditions. A vision of development that is about people, their goals and aspirations, persists in Africa, in spite of the countervailing forces which attempt to impose a value-system which reduces all human activity to self-seeking individualistic "rational" choices.

The alternative development perspectives put forward by churches and other grassroots organizations stress participatory self-reliance, basic human needs, and long-term sustainability in their attempts to respond to the impact of the current SAP agenda. The final chapters of this book have provided a glimpse of the vitality of analysis, debate and concrete action that is emerging from the churches in Africa at the grassroots level as well as at the institutional level. These efforts are evidence of the serious reflection that is taking place in the churches in Africa struggling to respond to the SAP crisis in a way that bears witness to a liberative transformative model of the church. Noteworthy in this process is the increasing collaboration between church agencies, and groups, and other grassroots organizations as well as the attempts to integrate social analysis and theological reflection. This is accompanied by an analysis which is also grappling with the ambivalent history of Christianity in Africa, and which seeks to uproot theologies which have been oppressive, racist and destructive of the indigenous cultural traditions of its people. These oppressive theologies persist in Africa and are reinforced by revived attempts to "evangelize" the continent currently waged by a number of fundamentalist religious groups. This suggests the need for an analysis which reflects upon religion and religious-based movements in terms of both their liberative, transformative as well as their reactionary, oppressive features. As Jean-Marc Ela suggests:

> We must rethink our basic faith because it has failed to enter genuinely into African life and root itself there, and because its claim to universality has been destroyed. As we bring Christianity face to face with the African reality, we must rethink God.[7]

Women in the churches in Africa are increasingly voicing their opposition to the gender bias which continues to persist in church structures. Many women regard this as the key locus in the struggle for social and economic transformation. The economic and theological analysis developing under the women's church network provides a very valuable contribution to gender analysis on SAPs. Women's organizations in Africa offer the greatest transformative potential for participatory, self-reliant and sustainable forms of development. An important component of this struggle lies in reflecting critically on the transformative potential of women and women's networks and supporting these initiatives.

These emerging voices and perspectives in the African churches provide a powerful challenge to Northern churches and to theology and ethics. They specifically challenge theology and ethics to become more integrally involved in issues of the economy. They call for a widening of current understandings of economics to embrace ecology, gender, culture and religion as integral aspects of economy. They view ethics and theology not simply as a realm of discourse that provides the basic principles and ideals on which social and economic policy is built. This kind of approach ignores the very patterns of social and economic relations which in effect constitute particular theologies and ethical worldviews. Theological reflection arrives too late on the scene in restricting its focus to the consequences of the dominant economic theologies. Douglas Meeks argues that this theological gap is, in particular, endemic to theologies in the North:

There is a deficit of theological work with regard to political economy. God concepts have been criticized in relation to racism, sexism, the technological mastery of the environment, and ordinary people's loss of democratic control of their lives. But not enough attention has been given to how God concepts in North Atlantic church and society relate to the deepest assumptions of the market society.[8]

Meeks' critique of theological reflection on political economy in the North challenges our theologies to reflect our concrete participation and collaboration, not only with other disciplines concerned with development, but also with the social movements (both in the North, but more importantly in the South) which attempt to articulate and live out alternatives to the prevailing economic order premised on the values of SAPs. The lack of attention in theology to the theological character of development and economic discourse gives rise to the isolation and co-optation of environmental, feminist, native, labour or poverty concerns by the dominant interests which succeed in defusing and mollifying these challenges to the extent that they remain disparate. The African churches responding to SAPs are involved in the task of renaming development in the context of the oppression and domination of those who have been marginalized by this process, intensified by SAPs. Ela reminds us of the rich tradition of resistance rooted in the consciousness of Africans. For Ela, the African church reflects both the perpetuation of colonialism and resistance to it. It is the poor in Africa who are at the forefront in building communities of resistance:

> Working through historical dynamics, the poor are called by the gospel to ask hard questions and to become participants with the power to change their own living conditions. This is all happening at a moment when the strength of the gospel is being discovered in the midst of the plundering of the Third World, the destruction of its cultures, and its relegation to a simple source of raw materials for the dominant industrial countries. This is a momentous experience of faith... . The most striking development is their will to make common cause in a dynamic directed to create a different society.[9]

So too, in the North, these irruptions of the poor challenge "our images of God, our spiritualities and ethics, and our visions of the mission of the Church in this world".[10]

The perspectives provided by churches and social movements that are responding to the SAP agenda also pose a challenge to the social-scientific framework in which development issues are studied. They challenge the traditional division of disciplines as part of the very process by which an oppressive system is allowed to perpetuate itself. The task, then, is to make clear that development issues are at the same time political, theological, economic, social, cultural, and ecological.

The experience of alternative social movements suggests the interconnectedness of these issues and points to the need to break down the barriers between how issues are named and studied. These barriers often create artificial conflicts which impede both a clearer naming of the problem but also the strategies for change. An ecologically sustainable development ethic challenges traditional ethical frame-works which attempt to view issues as if they stand apart or outside of eco-systems or social systems. By maintaining this arms-length approach to the study of development and ecological issues, moral concerns have been effectively marginalized. The dominance of the current SAP agenda is a testimony to the failure to question the assumptions of the modernization paradigm of development which infect the social sciences and theology. Currently emerging perspectives recognize that the ecological and development crises can only be addressed in a comprehensive manner.

The task of "re-thinking development", currently undertaken by social movements, church-based organizations and NGOs on an international scale, is increasingly sensitive and attuned to the cultural and religious dimensions of development. It is these values, which development theory has tended to overlook, that are being reasserted on an unprecedented scale. Indigenous groups on the brink of extinction demonstrate in a dramatic way that the survival of this planet depends on the continued survival of the diversity of cultural and religious forms that have existed and adapted over the centuries. It is indigenous peoples who are playing a key role in providing alternatives to the wasteful economic models of consumption and rampant destruction of the earth's resources.

Responses to the SAP agenda are becoming more comprehensive. They are refuting the basic claims of SAPs at the level of facts and analysis. It is vital for social scientists to be engaged in the endeavour of countering the "rational" and "hard economic" data presented by institutions like the World Bank to legitimize SAPs. Solidarity groups, as well as political groupings in the North and South, are using this research to great effect in their own struggles and campaigns. NGOs, grassroots groups and church-based organizations are also organizing on an international level and across interest groupings in opposition to SAPs. Currently, there are efforts under way to institute international databases and campaigns on SAPs which draw upon the rapidly growing literature which challenges the SAP agenda.

The insight provided by theological reflection on the SAP agenda lies in the recognition of its comprehensiveness and value-laden character. The strategies adopted to resist this agenda elucidate its implicit values and counter them with alternatives that articulate and respect the diversity of visions committed to social, political, economic and ecological justice:

> God is on the side of the poor, the oppressed, the persecuted. When this faith is proclaimed and lived in a situation of political conflict between the rich and the poor, and when the rich and the powerful reject this faith and condemn it as heresy, we can read the signs and discern something more than a crisis. We are faced with a *kairos*, a moment of truth, a time for decision, a time of grace, a God-given opportunity for conversion and hope.[11]

Endnotes

1. J. de Santa Ana, "Sacralization and Sacrifice in Human Practice," p. 38.
2. H. Daly and J. R. Cobb Jr., *For the Common Good*, p. 234.
3. Jaime Wright, General Secretary of the United Presbyterian Church in Brazil, described the Brazilian economy as based on a "theology of death", to the Canadian Parliament's Standing Committee on External Affairs and International Trade. Cited in Ecumenical Coalition for Economic Justice, *Recolonization or Liberation: The Bonds of Structural Adjustment and Struggles for Emancipation*, (Toronto: Our Times, 1990), p. 87.
4. M. DuBois, "The Governance of the Third World: A Foucauldian Perspective on Power Relations in Development," *Alternatives* 16 (1991), p. 4.
5. H. Bernstein, "Agricultural 'Modernization,'" p. 21.
6. G. Helleiner, "From Adjustment to Development in Sub-Saharan Africa: Conflict, Controversy, Convergence, Consensus? An Overview," (Unpublished), October 1993. The paper provides a concise overview of the experience of SAPs in sub-Saharan Africa and the need for equitable and sustainable alternatives.
7. Jean Marc Ela, "The Granary is Empty," in C.Cadorette *et al* eds, *Liberation Theology: An Introductory Reader*, (New York: Orbis Books, 1992), p. 67.
8. M. Douglas Meeks, *God the Economist: The Doctrine of God and Political Economy*, (Minneapolis: Fortress Press, 1989), p. 1.
9. Ela, "The Granary is Empty," p. 68.
10. L. Cormie, "Revolutions in Reading the Bible," in P. Day *et al* eds, *The Bible and the Politics of Exegesis*, (New York: Pilgrim Press, 1991), p. 175.
11. *The Road to Damascus: Kairos and Conversion*, (London: Catholic Institute for International Relations, 1989), par. 46.

Bibliography

Aboum, A. "Women and Economic Justice: The Invisible Victims." In AACC Women's Desk, *Final Report* 1990.

Abugre, Charles. "A Failed Recipe." *Economic Justice Update* (8 November 1993).

Abugre, Charles. "Understanding the Commodity Problem in the Context of the Changing Order: The Need for a Third World Strategy." (Commodities: Third World Network Briefing Papers for UNCED, Paper No. 16 1992).

Adams, P. *Odious Debts: Loose Lending, Corruption and the Third World's Environmental Legacy*. London: Earthscan, 1991.

Adams, P. and Solomon, L. *In the Name of Progress*. Toronto: Energy Probe, 1985.

Addo, H. *et al. Development as Social Transformation: Reflections on the Global Problematique*. London: Hodder and Stoughton, 1985.

Adedeji, Adebayo. "Foreign Debt and Prospects for Growth in Africa During the 1980s." *Journal of Modern African Studies* 23 (March 1985): 53-74.

Adedeji, Adebayo. "A Preliminary Assessment of the Performance of the African Economy in 1990 and Prospects for 1991." Addis Ababa: UN Economic Commission for Africa, 1991.

Africa Conference Issues Paper. Maastricht, Netherlands, 2-4 July 1990.

Africa Recovery (December 1991).

African Centre for Applied Research and Training in Social Development. *Understanding Africa's Food Problems: Social Policy Perspectives*. London: Hans Zell Publishers, 1990.

"African Crisis, Food Security and Structural Adjustment." (Special Issue) *International Labour Review* 127/6 (1988): 655-812.

African Development Bank, United Nations Development Programme and the World Bank. *The Social Dimensions of Adjustment in Africa: A Policy Agenda*. Washington: The World Bank, 1990.

African Network of the Churches Participation and Development. "Luanda Declaration: Our Christian Response to the 'War Against the Dispossessed.'" Luanda May 1989.

Ahiadeke, Clement. "Cooperation or Isolation? A Review of Structural Adjustment Programmes in Sub-Saharan Africa, with Particular Reference to Ghana." (Paper delivered to The Council for the Development of Economic and Social Research in Africa Conference: Politics of Adjustment) Dakar, September 1991.

"Aide-Memoire on Discussions of the Second Meeting of the Non-Aligned Movement Advisory Group of Experts on Debt." (February 1993).

Akiyama, T. and Duncan, R. C. "Coffee and Cocoa Trends." *Finance and Development* (March 1983): 31-3.

All Africa Conference of Churches. "Consultation of the Churches' Role in the Moblization for Child Survival and Development." Addis Ababa: All Africa Conference of Churches, October 1991.

All Africa Conference of Churches. "Maseru Declaration on the Debt Crisis as it Affects Human Rights." Maseru, Lesotho: All Africa Conference of Churches, September 1990.

All Africa Conference of Churches General Secretariat. "The Right Time for Change: What Hope for a Crisis-Stricken Africa?" Nairobi: All Africa Conference of Churches, 1990.

All Africa Conference of Churches Women's Desk. *Church Women's Consultation on Economic Justice*. Nairobi: All Africa Conference of Churches – Women's Desk, 1990.

All Africa Conference of Churches Women's Desk. *Final Report: Consultation on Women and Economic Justice*. Nairobi: All Africa Conference of Churches – Women's Desk, 1990.

Amara, Hamid Ait and Founou-Tchuigoua, Bernard. eds. *African Agriculture: The Critical Choices*. London: Zed Books, 1990.

Amin, S. "Apropos the Green Movement." In Addo, H. *et. al.*, *Development as Social Transformation: Reflections on the Global Problematique* 271-81.

Amin, S. *Maldevelopment: Anatomy of a Global Failure*. London: Zed Books, 1990.

Amin, S. Arrighi, G., Frank, A.G., Wallerstein, I. *Transforming the Revolution: Social Movements and the World System*. New York: Monthly Review Press, 1990.

Anani, Kofi, V. "Transnational Elite Interests as Manifested in the Socio-Economic Recovery Programmes in Sub-Saharan Africa." (Paper prepared for Ten Days for World Development) May 1992.

Asante, S.K.B. *African Development: Adebayo Adedeji's Alternative Strategies*. London: Hans Zell, 1991.

Assmann, Hugo. "Theologial Reflection on Foreign Debt: Some Guidelines". In World Council of Churches' Commission on the Churches Participation in Development, *Debt Resource Materials* 1 (1988): 13-26.

Association of Christian Lay Centres in Africa. *Annual Report*. Nairobi: ACLCA, 1990.

Attwood, D.W., Bruneau, T. C. and Galaty, J. G. *Power and Poverty: Development and Development Projects in the Third World*. Boulder: Westview Press, 1988.

Ayari, C. "What Strategy for Africa's Development?" *Africa Report* 28 (September/October 1983): 8-11.

Ayres, R. *Banking on the Poor*. Cambridge: MIT Press, 1983.

Bahro, R. *From Red to Green: Interviews with New Left Review*. London: Verso, 1984.

Bahro, R. "Capitalism's Global Crisis." *New Statesman* 17 (December 1982): 26-9.

Bahro, R. *Socialism and Survival*. London: Heretic Books, 1982.

Balassa, B. "External Shocks and Policy Response in Sub-Saharan Africa, 1973-78." *Finance and Development* 21 (March 1984): 10-12.

Balassa, B. *New Directions in the World Economy*. London: MacMillan Press, 1989.

"The Bankers Dig In." *South* (April 1987): 19-25.

Barker, Jonathan. *The Politics of Agriculture in Tropical Africa*. Beverley Hills: Sage Publications, 1984.

Barker, Jonathan. *Rural Communities Under Stress. Peasant Farmers and the State in Africa*. Cambridge: Cambridge University Press, 1989.

Barnet, R. J. "But What About Africa? On the Global Economy's Lost Continent." *Harper's* 280 (May 1990): 43-51.

Barrett, Leonard. "Tradition versus Modernization: Methodological Issues Exemplified from African Religions." In C. W. Fu and G. E. Spiegler eds, *Movements and Issues in World Religions*. New York: Greenwood Press, 1987.

Bates, Robert, H. *Markets and States in Tropical Africa: The Political Bias of Agricultural Policies*. Berkeley: University of California Press, 1981.

Bates, Robert, H. "The Political Basis for Agricultural Policy Reform." In Commins, Stephen K. ed., *Africa's Development Challenges and the World Bank*: 115-32.

Bauer, P. T. *Reality and Rhetoric: Studies in the Economics of Development*. Cambridge: Harvard University Press, 1984.

Baum, G. "The Grand Vision: It Needs Social Action." In Lonergan A. and Richards, C. eds, *Thomas Berry and the New Cosmology*: 51-6.

Beckman, Bjorn. "Empowerment or Repression? The World Bank and the Politics of African Adjustment." (Paper to a Symposium on the Social and Political Context of Structural Adjustment in Sub-Saharan Africa) Dakar, Senegal, 17-19 October 1990.

Bennett, J. *The Hunger Machine*. Toronto: CBC Enterprises, 1987.

Berger, Peter, L. *Pyramids of Sacrifice: Political Ethics and Social Change*. New York: Basic Books Inc., 1974.

Berlan, J. P. "The Commodification of Life." *Monthly Review* 41 (1989): 24-30.

Bernstein, Henry. "Agricultural 'Modernization' and the Era of Structural Adjustment: Observations on Sub-Saharan Africa." *Journal of Peasant Studies* 18/1 (1990): 3-35.

Bernstein, Henry *et al.* eds. *The Food Question: Profits vs. People*. London: Earthscan, 1990.

Berry, Thomas. *The Dream of the Earth*. San Francisco: Sierra Club Books, 1988.

Berry, Thomas. "Economics: Its Effect on the Life Systems of the World." In Lonergan A. and Richards, C. eds, *Thomas Berry and the New Cosmology*, 5-26.

"Beyond UNPAAERD: From Talk to Action." (NGO Position Paper for the Final Review of UNPAAERD) September 1991.

Bienefeld, Manfred. "Old Recipes, New Rhetoric: Structural Adjustment in 1990." *Southern Africa Report* 6 (November 1990): 9-13.

Bienefeld, Manfred. *Structural Adjustment and Rural Labour Markets in Tanzania*. Geneva: International Labour Organization, 1991.

Bienen, Henry. "The Politics of Trade Liberalization in Africa." *Economic Development and Cultural Change* (1990): 713-32.

Biggs, M. *Adjust or Protect*. Ottawa: North-South Institute, 1980.

Blaikie, P. *The Political Economy of Soil Erosion in Developing Countries*. London: Longman, 1985.

Blaikie, P. and Brookfield, H. *Land Degradation and Society*. London: Methuen, 1987.

Blomstrom, M. and Hettne, B. *Development Theory in Transition: The Dependency Debate and Beyond*. London: Zed Books, 1984.

"Blood and Treasure." *Barrons* (June 18, 1980).

Boer, Jan, H. *Christians and Moblilization*. Jos: Christian Council of Nigeria, 1989.

Boesen, J. *et al. Tanzania: Crisis and Struggle for Survival*. Uppsala: Scandinavian Institute of African Studies, 1986.

Bonino, Jose Miguez. *Toward a Christian Political Ethic*. New York: Orbis Books, 1983.

Bookchin, M. *The Modern Crisis*. Montreal: Black Rose Books, 1987.

Boone, Kathleen. *The Bible Tells Them So: The Discourse of Protestant Fundamentalism*. Albany: SUNY Press, 1989.

Boulding, Elise. "Cultural Perspectives on Development: The Relevance of Sociology and Anthropology." *Alternatives* XIV (1989): 109-22.

Bradby, B. "The Destruction of the Natural Economy." *Economy and Society* 4 (1975): 127-61.

Bright, C. and Geyer, M. "For a Unified History of the World in the Twentieth Century." *History Review* 39 (1987).

Broad, Robin. *Unequal Alliance: The World Bank and the Philippines*. Berkeley: University of California Press, 1988.

Brodhead, Tim. *Bridges of Hope? Canadian Voluntary Agencies and the Third World*. Ottawa: North-South Institute, 1988.

Brown, Lester *et al. State of the World 1988*. New York: Norton and Co., 1988.

Brown, Lester *et al. State of the World 1989*. New York: Norton and Co., 1989.

Brown, Lester *et al. State of the World 1990*. New York: Norton and Co., 1990.

Brown, Michael, B, and Tiffen, Pauline. *Shortchanged: Africa and World Trade*. Amsterdam: Transnational Institute, 1992.

Brown, R. "The IMF and Paris Club Rescheduling: A Conflicting Role." (Working paper – Sub-series on Money, Finance and Development – No. 30, May 1990).

Brush, Stephen B. "Diversity and Change in Andean Agriculture." In Little, Peter *et al.*, *Lands at Risk in the Third World: Local Level Perspectives*: 271-89.

Bryant, Coralie, ed. *Poverty, Policy, and Food Security in Southern Africa*. Boulder: Lynne Reinmer, 1988.

Buchanan, James *et al. Toward a Theory of the Rent Seeking Society*. College Station: Texas A & M Press, 1990.

Burgess, R. "The Concept of Nature in Geography and Marxism." *Antipode* 10 (1978): 1-11.

Burton, D. J. "The Political Economy of Environmentalism." *Kapitalistate* 9 (1981): 147-57.

Buttel, F and Kenney, M. "Biotechnology: Prospects and Dilemmas for Third World Development." *Development and Change* 16 (January 1985): 61-91.

Buttel, F., Kenney, M. and Kloppenburg, J. "From Green Revolution to Bio-Revolution: Some Observations on the Changing Technological Bases of Economic Transformation in the Third World. "*Economic Development and Cultural Change* 34 (1985): 31-55.

Campbell, Bonnie K. "Canadian Development Assistance to Africa in the Context of Structural Adjustment." (Paper presented to the 1993 Annual Meeting, African Studies Association) December 4-7, 1993.

Campbell, Bonnie K. ed. *Political Dimensions of the International Debt Crisis.* London: MacMillan, 1989.

Campbell, Bonnie, K. and Loxley, John, eds. *Structural Adjustment in Africa.* London: Macmillan Press Ltd., 1989.

Campbell, Bruce. "The Environmental Implications of Free Trade Agreements." Toronto: Canadian Environmental Law Association, 1993.

Canadian Council for International Co-operation. "International Trade and Agriculture: The GATT Agenda." (Conference Proceedings) Montreal, December 1988.

Cardoso, F. H. "Development and the Environment: The Brazilian Case." *CEPAL Review* 12 (1980): 111-27.

Carleton, D. "The New International Division of Labor, Export-Oriented Growth and State Repression in Latin America." In Lopez, G.A. and Stohl, M. eds *Dependance, Development and State Repression*: 211-36.

Carty, R. "Giving for Gain: Foreign Aid and CIDA." In Swift, R. and Clarke, R. eds, *Ties that Bind.* Toronto: Between the Lines, 1982: 149-211.

Catholic Bishops of Zambia. "Economics, Politics and Justice." (1990 Pastoral Statement) September 1990.

Caulfield, C. *In the Rainforest.* London: Picador, 1986.

Cavanagh, J. "Peruvian Promise Lures Investors." *Euromoney* (Sept. 1989).

Cheru, Fantu. *The Silent Revolution in Africa: Debt, Development and Democracy.* London: Zed Books, 1989. ·

Chossudovsky Michel. "The Global Creation of Third World Poverty."*Third World Resurgence* 17 (1992): 13-20.

Churches' Drought Action in Africa Studies Subcommittee. *Report on the Root Causes of Hunger and Food Insufficiency in Africa.* Nairobi: All Africa Conference of Churches, 1986.

Clairmonte, F. F. and Cavanagh, J. "Third World Debt: The Approaching Holocaust." *Economic and Political Weekly* xxi (1986): 1361-4.

Clark, A. *Mosaic or Patchwork? Canadian Policy Toward Sub-Saharan Africa in the 1980s.* Ottawa: North-South Institute, 1991.

Clark, G. and Manuh, T. "Women Traders in Ghana and the Structural Adjustment Program." In Gladwin, C., *Structural Adjustment and African Women Farmers*.

Classens, Stijn, *et al*. *Market-Based Debt Reduction for Developing Countries: Principles and Prospects*. Washington: The World Bank, 1990.

Cleary, S. *Renewing the Earth: Development for a Sustainable Future*. London: Catholic Fund for Overseas Development, 1989.

Cleaver, K. "The Population, Agriculture and Environment Nexus in Sub-Saharan Africa." *World Bank Draft Discussion Paper* (May 1990).

Collins, Jane L. "Labor Scarcity and Ecological Change." In Little, Peter *et al*., *Lands at Risk in the Third World: Local Level Perspectives*, 19-37.

Commander, Simon, ed. *Structural Adjustment and Agriculture: Theory and Practice in Africa and Latin America*. London: Overseas Development Institute, 1989.

Commins, Stephen, K. *Africa's Development Challenges and the World Bank: Hard Questions, Costly Choices*. London: Lynne Rienner Publishers, 1988.

Commonwealth Expert Group on Women and Structural Adjustment. *Engendering Adjustment in the 1990s*. London: Commonwealth Secretariat, 1990.

Conway, Gordon R. and Barbier, Edward B. *After the Green Revolution: Sustainable Agriculture for Development*. London: Earthscan, 1990.

Cormie, L. "Christian Responsibility for the World of the Free Market? Catholicism and the Construction of the Post-World War II Global Order." (Unpublished) 1991.

Cormie, L. "Revolution in Reading the Bible." In Peggy Day and David Jobling eds, *The Bible and the Politics of Exegesis*. New York: Pilgrim Press, 1991: 173-93.

Cormie, L. "The Sociology of National Development and Salvation History". In Baum G. ed., *Sociology and Human Destiny*. New York: Paulist Press, 1980: 56-79.

Cornia, A. C., Jolly, R. and Stewart, F. eds, *Adjustment with a Human Face*. Vols. 1 and 2. Oxford: UNICEF/Oxford: Oxford University Press, 1987.

Crook, Clive. "The IMF and World Bank." *The Economist* (October 12, 1991).

Culpepper, R. and Hardy, M. *Private Foreign Investment and Development: A Partnership for the 1990s?* Ottawa: The North-South Institute, 1990.

D'Aquino, T. *et al*., *Party Democracy in Canada: Issues for Reform*. Methuen: Toronto, 1983.

Daly, Herman, E. and Cobb, John, B. Jr. *For the Common Good: Redirecting the Economy Toward Community, the Environment and a Sustainable Future*. Boston: Beacon Press, 1989.

de Silva, S. B. D. *The Political Economy of Underdevelopment*. London: Routledge & Kegan Paul, 1982.

De Santa Ana, Julio. "Sacralization and Sacrifice in Human Practice." In World Council of Churches' Commission on the Churches Participation in Development, *Sacrifice and Humane Economic Life*. Geneva: World Council of Churches, 1992.

"Debt-Equity: My Kingdom for a Loan." *South* (February 1987): 95-8.

"Delink with West, Africa Urged." *ACLCA News* 1/2 (1989).

Derenoncourt, L. "Structural Adjustment in West Africa: NGO Observations from Senegal, Burkina Faso and Ghana." Washington, D.C.: Development Group for Alternative Policies, INC., 1991

Development GAP. *The Other Side of the Story: The Real Impact of World Bank and IMF Structural Adjustment Programs.* Washington, D. C., 1993.

"Dicing with Debt." *New Internationalist* (November 1988).

Dinham, B. and Hines, C. *Agribusiness in Africa.* Trenton: Africa World Press, 1984.

Dowd, Douglas. *The Waste of Nations: Dysfunction in the World Economy.* Boulder and London: Westview Press, 1989.

DuBois, Marc. "The Governance of the Third World: A Foucauldian Perspective on Power Relations in Development." *Alternatives* 16 (1991).

Economic Coalition for Economic Justice. "Collapse of Gatt Talks: A Dangerous Opportunity." *Economic Justice Report* 2/1 (March 1991).

Ecumenical Coalition for Economic Justice. "The Debt Has Already Been Paid." *GATT-Fly Report* (February 1989).

Ecumenical Coalition for Economic Justice. "To Pay Is To Die; We Want To Live." *GATT-Fly Report* VIII (October 1987).

Ecumenical Coalition for Economic Justice. *Recolonization or Liberation: The Bonds of Structural Adjustment and Struggles for Emancipation.* Toronto: Our Times, 1990.

Ecumenical Coalition for Economic Justice. "U.S. 'Trade' Strategy: 'Do as We Say; Not as We Do'." *Economic Justice Report* 3/2 (May 1992).

Ecumenical Coalition for Economic Justice. "Which Way for the Americas." Ottawa: Canadian Centre for Policy Alternatives, 1993,

Ehrenreich, B. and Fuentes A. *Women in the Global Factory.* Boston: South End Press, 1983.

Ekins, P. ed. *The Living Economy: A New Economics in the Making.* London: Routledge & Kegan Paul, 1986.

Ela, Jean Marc. "The Granary is Empty." In Cadorette, C. *et al.* eds, *Liberation Theology: An Introductory Reader.* New York: Orbis Books, 1992.

Ela, Jean Marc. *My Faith as an African.* Trans. John P. Brown and Susan Perry. Maryknoll, N.Y.: Orbis Books, 1988.

Elabor-Idemudia, Patience. "Women and Economic Reforms: Development or Burden?" (Unpublished) 1992.

Elabor-Idemudia, P., Mihevc, J. and Shettima, K. "World Bank Takes Control of UNCED's Environment Fund." *Economic Justice Update* (Summer, 1992): 1,4.

Elegant, S. "NGOs Concerned over World Bank Role in 'Green Fund'." *Third World Economics* (16-30 September 1991): 7.

Ellison, M.M. *The Centre Cannot Hold – The Search For a Global Economy of Justice.* Washington D.C.: University Press of America, 1983.

Elson, Diane, ed. *Male Bias in the Development Process.* Manchester: Manchester University Press, 1991.

Endely, Joyce, B. "Strategies and Programmes for Women in Africa's Agricultural Sector." In Suliman, M., ed., *Alternative Development Strategies for Africa*, 132-9.

Esteva, G. "Regenerating People's Space." In Mendlovitz, S.H. and Walker, R.B.J. eds. *Towards a Just World Peace*: 271-98.

"Farmers Adjust to Economic Reforms." *African Farmer* 3 (April 1990).

Fasu, A. K. "Exports and Economic Growth: The African Case." *World Development* 18 (June 1990): 831-5.

Final Review and Appraisal of the Implementation of the United Nations Programme of Action for Africa Economic Recovery and Development 1986-1990 (UNPAAERD): Report of the Secretary General. New York: North South Round Table, 1991

Foster, John, W. "Criteria for New Covenants." *Ecumenical Church Consultation on Third World Debt Task Force on the Churches and Corporate Responsibility.* April 1987.

Fribourg, M. and Hettne, B. "The Greening of the World: Towards a Non-Deterministic Model of Global Processes." In Addo, H. *et al.*, *Development as Social Transformation*, 204-70.

Friends of the Earth (Netherlands). *Debt and Environment in the Third World.* Netherlands: Friends of the Earth, 1991.

Gakou, M. L. *The Crisis in African Agriculture.* London: United Nations University and Zed Books, 1987.

Gaidzanwa, Rudo, B. "Structural Adjustment and Debt." (Paper prepared for The European Debt and Development Network) Munich, July 1992.

Galeano, E. *Open Veins of Latin America: Five Centuries of the Pillage of a Continent.* New York: Monthly Review Press, 1974.

Gallagher, Mark. *Rent-Seeking and Economic Growth.* Boulder: Westview Press, 1991.

Galtung, J. *Development, Environment and Technology: Towards A Technology for Self-Reliance.* New York: United Nations, 1979.

Gathaka, Jephthah, K. "Economic and Social Problems Created by Debt and Economic Crisis: Biblical Exposition on Nehemia 5:1-13." (Paper delivered to the All Africa Council of Churches International Affairs Conference on The Debt Crisis as it Affects Human Rights) Maseru, September 1990.

Gathaka, Jephthah, K. "Sounds from African Churches." (Paper presented at the Institute of Church and Society Conference on Nigeria's External Debt) Jos, November 1990.

GATT-Fly, Ecumenical Coalition for Economic Justice. "The Debt Has Already Been Paid." *GATT-Fly Report* 10/1 (February 1989).

Genetic Resources for Our World (GROW) 2 (1989).

George, Susan. *The Debt Boomerang: How Third World Debt Harms Us All.* London: Pluto Press, 1992.

George, Susan. *A Fate Worse Than Debt.* London: Penguin Books, 1988.

George, Susan. *Ill Fares the Land: Essays on Food, Hunger and Power.*

Washington: Institute for Policy Studies, 1986.

Gibbon, P. "A Political Economy of the World Bank 1970-1990." (Paper delivered to the Council for the Development of Economic and Social Research in Africa) Dakar, Senegal. 9-12 September 1991.

Gifford, Paul. *Christianity: To Save or Enslave?* Harare: Ecumenical Documentation and Information Centre of Eastern and Southern Africa, 1990.

Gifford, Paul. "Christian Fundamentalism and Development." *Review of African Political Economy* 52 (1991).

Gifford, Paul. *The New Religious Right in Southern Africa.* Harare: Baobab Books, 1988.

Gladwin, Christina H., ed. *Structural Adjustment and African Women Farmers.* Gainesville: University of Florida Press, 1991.

Gligo, Nicolo. "The Environmental Dimension in Agricultural Development in Latin America." *CEPAL Review* 12 (1980): 129-43.

Good, Kenneth. "Debt and the One-Party State in Zambia." *Journal of Modern African Studies* 27 (2) 1989: 297-313.

Goodman, D. and Redclift, M. *From Peasant to Proletarian: Capitalist Development and Agrarian Transitions.* Oxford: Basil Blackwell, 1981.

Goodman, D. *et al. From Farming to Biotechnology.* Oxford: Basil Blackwell, 1987.

Gorz, Andre. *Ecology as Politics.* Montreal: Black Rose Books, 1980.

Goulet, Denis. "Beyond Moralism: Ethical Strategies in Global Development." In McFadden T. ed., *Theology Confronts A Changing World.* West Mystic: Twenty-Third Publications, 1977: 12-39.

Goulet, Denis. "Can Values Shape Third World Technological Policy?" In Ghosh, P.K. ed., *Technology Policy and Development – A Third World Perspective.* Westport: Greenwood Press, 1984: 50-74.

Goulet, Denis. "The Challenge of Development Economics." *Communications and Development Review* 2 (1978): 18-23.

Goulet, Denis. *The Cruel Choice: A New Concept in the Theory of Development.* New York: Atheneum, 1972.

Goulet, Denis. "Development as Liberation: Policy Lessons From Case Studies." *World Development* 7 (1979): 555-66.

Goulet, Denis. "Development Experts: The One-Eyed Giants." *World Development* 8 (1980): 481-9.

Goulet, Denis. "Goals in Conflict: Corporate Success and Global Justice?" In Williams, O. F. and Houck, J. W. *The Judaeo-Christian Vision and the Modern Corporation.* South Bend: University of Notre Dame Press, 1982: 218-47.

Goulet, Denis. *Mexico: Development Strategies For The Future.* Notre Dame: University of Notre Dame Press, 1983.

Goulet, Denis. *The Myth of Aid: The Hidden Agenda of the Development Reports.* Maryknoll: Orbis Books, 1971.

Goulet, Denis. *A New Moral Order – Development Ethics and Liberation Theology.* New York: Orbis Books, 1974.

Goulet, Denis. "Obstacles to World Development: An Ethical Reflection." *World Development* 11 (1983): 609-24.

Goulet, Denis. "Three Rationalities in Development Decision-Making." *World Development* 14 (1986): 601-17.

Goulet, Denis. "Secular History and Theology." *World Justice* 8 (1966): 5-18.

Goulet, Denis. "Socialization and Cultural Development." *Interchange* 10 (1979-80): 1-9.

Goulet, Denis. *Survival With Integrity – Sarvodaya at the Crossroads.* Sri Lanka: Marga Institute, 1981.

Goulet, Denis. *The Uncertain Promise: Value Conflicts in Technology Transfer.* New York: IDOC, 1977.

Gran, G. *Development By People: Citizen Construction of a Just World.* New York: Praeger Publishers, 1983.

Granberg-Michaelson, W. *A Worldly Spirituality: The Call to Redeem Life on Earth.* San Francisco: Harper and Row, 1984.

Green, R. H. "The Broken Pot: The Social Fabric, Economic Disaster and Adjustment in Africa." In Odimode, B. ed., *The IMF, the World Bank and the African Debt.* Vol. 2. London: Zed Books, 1989.

Greene, Joshua. "The Debt Problem of Sub-Saharan Africa." *Finance and Development* 26/2 (June 1989): 9-12.

Greenpeace and Friends of the Earth. "Financing Ecological Destruction." 1988, 13-18.

Greenpeace International. "The World Bank's Greenwash: Touting Environmentalism While Trashing the Planet." Greenpeace (April 1992).

Guha, R. "Radical American Environmentalism and Wilderness Preservation: A Third World Critique." *Environmental Ethics* II (Spring 1989): 71-83.

Gulhati, R. "Who Makes Economic Policy in Africa and How?" *World Development* 18 (August 1990): 1147-61.

Gupta, Avijit. *Ecology and Development in the Third World.* London: Routledge, 1988.

Gutierrez, G. *A Theology of Liberation.* New York: Orbis Books (1973), 1988.

Guyer, Jane. "Women's Work and Production Systems: A Review of Two Reports on the Agricultural Crisis." *Review of African Political Economy* 22-3 (1983).

Gylmah-Boadl, E. "Adjustment, State Reconstruction and Democratization: Reflections on the Ghanaian Experience." (Paper delivered to Council for the Development of Economic and Social Research in Africa Conference: The Politics of Adjustment), Dakar, September 1991.

Hagen, E. *On the Theory of Social Change.* MIT: Center for International Studies, 1962.

Hallpike, Christopher. *The Foundations of Primitive Thought.* Oxford: Clarendon Press, 1979.

Hardin, G. "The Tragedy of the Commons." *Science* (December 13, 1968).

Harsch, Ernest. "After Adjustment." *Africa Report* 34/3 (May-June 1989): 46-50.

Harsch, Ernest. "On the Road to Recovery." *Africa Report* 34: 4 (July-August 1989): 21-6.

Hawley, Edward, A. "The African Right to Development: World Policy and the Debt Crisis." *Africa Today* 37 (1990): 5-14.

Hayter, Theresa and Catherine Watson. *Aid: Rhetoric and Reality*. London and Sydney: Pluto Press, 1985.

Helleiner, G. K. "External Resource Flows, Debt Relief and Economic Development in Sub-Saharan Africa." November 1992: 20. (Unpublished.)

Helleiner, G. K. "From Adjustment to Development in Sub-Saharan Africa: Conflict, Controversy, Convergence, Consensus? An Overview." October 1993.

Helleiner, G. K. "The IMF, The World Bank and Africa's Adjustment and External Debt Problems: An Unofficial View." University of Toronto, February 1991. (Unpublished.)

Hellinger, Doug. "Banking on Deception." (Development GAP Inter-Press Service Column #4, July 1991).

Herbst, J. "The Structural Adjustment of Politics in Africa." *World Development* 18, July 1990: 949-58.

Hewitt, Adrian and Singer, Hans. "How to Foster Diversification, Not Dependence." *Africa Recovery* 4/3-4, (October-December 1990): 36-8.

Hickey, T. A. and Hickey A. A., "Development Activities by American Missionaries in Sub-Saharan Africa." *Sociology and Social Research* 72 (October 1987): 17-19.

Hinkelammert, Franz, J. "The Sacrifical Cycle as a Justification for Western Domination: the Western Iphigenia in Latin America." In World Council of Churches' Commission on the Churches Participation in Development, *Sacrifice and Humane Economic Life*. Geneva: World Council of Churches, 1992.

Hirschmann, A. O. *The Strategy of Economic Development*. New York: W. W. and Norton Co., 1978.

Hobbelink, Henk. *Biotechnology and the Future of World Agriculture*. London: Zed Books, 1991.

Hoffman, S. *Duties Beyond Borders*. Syracuse: Syracuse University Press, 1981.

Hoogvelt, A. "The New International Division of Labour." In Bush, R., Johnston G. and Coates, D. eds, *The World Order – Socialist Perspectives*. Cambridge: Polity Press, 1987: 65-86.

Horowitz, Michael M. and Salem-Murdock, Muneera. "The Political Economy of Desertification in White Nile Province, Sudan." In Little, Peter *et al.*, *Lands at Risk in the Third World: Local Level Perspectives*, 95-114.

Hoselitz, B. F. and Moore, W.E., eds. *Industrialization and Society*. Mouton: UNESCO, 1966.

Howard, Ross. "UN Body Criticizes Development Aid: Report Urges Wealthy Countries to Divert Spending to Basic Neeeds." *Globe and Mail*, May 21, 1991.

Hulsberg, W. *The German Greens: A Social and Political Profile*. London: Verso, 1988.

Humphreys, Charles and William Jaeger, "Africa's Adjustment and Growth." *Finance and Development* 26/2 (June 1989): 6-8.

Hutchful, E. "From Revolution to Monetarism: The Economics and Politics of the Adjustment Programme in Ghana. In Campbell, B. and Loxley, J. eds, *Structural Adjustment in Africa*: 92-131.

Hyden, Goran. "Debt: The Development Trap." *Africa Report* 32 (November/December 1987): 24-7.

IDS (Institute for Development Studies) Bulletin 19 (January 1988) (Special issue on Adjustment in Africa).

Ihonvbere, Julius, O. "The Dynamics of Change in Eastern Europe and Their Implication for Africa." University of Toronto: Dept. of Political Science. (Unpublished.)

Ihonvbere, Julius, O. "Africa in the 1990s and Beyond: Alternative Analyses and Prescriptions." University of Toronto: Dept. of Political Science. (Unpublished.)

Ihonvbere, Julius, O. "Making Structural Adjustment Work in Africa: Towards a Policy and Research Agenda." University of Toronto: Dept. of Political Science. (Unpublished.)

Ihonvbere, Julius, O. "Economic Crisis, Structural Adjustment and the Poor in Nigeria." University of Toronto: Dept. of Political Science. (Unpublished.)

Imam, Ayesha, M. "Gender Analysis and African Social Sciences in the 1990s." *Africa Development* 3/4 (1990): 1-17.

Imunde, Lawford. *Salt in the Stew: Theological Basis for Christian Participation in Social Transformation*. Nairobi: All Africa Conferernce of Churches, 1989.

Inter Pares. "The World Economic Disorder." *Bulletin* 12 (1990).

International Monetary Fund. *Annual Report* 1990.

International Development Research Centre. *Economic Adjustment and Long-Term Development in Uganda*. Ottawa: IDRC, 1987.

International Conference on Popular Participation in the Recovery and Development Process in Africa. *African Charter for Popular Participation in Development and Transformation*. Arusha, Tanzania: February 1990.

"Is the World Bank Biting Off More Than it Can Chew?" *Forbes* (May 26, 1980).

Jaffe, Hosea. *A History of Africa*. London: Zed Books, 1988 (1985).

Juma, C. *The Gene Hunters: Biotechnology and the Scramble for Seeds*. Princeton: Princeton University Press, 1989.

Katoneene, J. "Social Tranformation: Conceptual Framework." *ACLCA News* 1/3 (1989).

Kanji, Nazeen. "The Gender Specific Effects of Structural Adjustment Policies: Shifting the Costs of Social Reproduction." (Paper for the Workshop on Economic Policy, Equity and Health) Harare, February 1991.

Kanyinga, Karuti and Gathaka, Jephthah, K. "In Search of Debt Crisis' Solution: Structural Adjustment Programmes (SAPs); Recolonization or Liberation and Alternatives?" (Paper presented for the National Council of Churches of Kenya Workshop: The Debt and Economic Crisis in Africa) Nairobi, March 1991.

Karliner, J. "Central America's Other War." *World Policy Journal* 6 (Fall 1989): 787-809

Kenney, M. *Biotechnology: The University-Industrial Complex*. New Haven: Yale University Press, 1986.

Khan, Haider, Ali. "Economic Modeling of Structural Adjustment Programmes: Impact on Human Conditions." *Africa Today* 37 (1990): 29-38.

Khor Kok Peng, Martin. "UN Restructuring Against South's Interests." *Third World Economics* 42 (1-15 June 1992): 19-20.

Khor Kok Peng, Martin. *The Uruguay Round and Third World Sovereignty*. Penang: Third World Network, 1990.

Klein, J. M. "Debt Relief for African Countries." *Finance and Development* 24 (December 1987): 10-13.

Klitgaard, Robert. *Tropical Gangsters: One Man's Experience with Development and Decadence in Deepest Africa*. Basic Books, 1990.

Kloppenburg, J. R. and Kleinman, D. L. "Plant Genetic Resources: The Common Bond." In Kloppenburg, J. R. ed., *Seeds and Sovereignty: The Use and Control of Plant Genetic Resources*. Durham, North Carolina: Duke University Press, 1988.

Kloppenburg, J. R. "The Social Impacts of Biogenetic Technology in Agriculture: Past and Future." In Bernard G.M. and Geisler C.C. eds, *Social Consequences and Challenges of New Agricultural Technologies*. Boulder: Westview Press, 1984: 291-321.

Kloppenburg, J. R. *First the Seed: The Political Economy of Plant Biotechnology, 1492-2000*. Cambridge: Cambridge University Press, 1988.

Kneen, B. Editorial, *Rams Horn* 79 (December 1990).

Kneen, B. "Farm Subsidy Wars – Trade Distorting Measures." *The Ram's Horn* 51 (May/June 1988).

Kneen, B. *From Land to Mouth*. Toronto: New Canada Publications, 1989.

Kneen, B. "Grain Prices: Who's to Blame?" *The Ram's Horn* 88 (October 1991): 1-5.

Krueger, A. O. "The Political Economy of the Rent-Seeking Society." *American Economic Review* 64 (1974): 291-301.

Krueger, A. O. *et al*. "Agricultural Incentives in Developing Countries: Measuring the Effect of Sectoral and Economywide Policies." *World Bank Economic Review* 2/3 (September 1988).

Krueger, A. O. "Import Substitution Versus Export Promotion." *Finance and Development* 22 (June 1985): 20-1.

Krugman, Paul R. *Rethinking International Trade*. Cambridge: MIT Press, 1990.

Lal, Deepak. "The Misconceptions of Development Economics, *Finance and Review* (June 1985): 10-13.

Lal, Deepak. *The Poverty of Development Economics*. Cambridge: Harvard University Press, 1985.

Lancaster, Carol. "Economic Restructuring in Sub-Saharan Africa." *Current History* 88/538 (May 1989): 213-16.

Lancaster, Carol. "The Search for a Growth Strategy for Africa." *Africa Report* 29, (March/April 1984): 50-53.

Lancaster, Carol and Williamson, John. *African Debt and Financing*. Washington: Institute for International Economics, 1986.

Landell-Mills, Pierre, Ramgopal Agarwala and Stanley Please, "From Crisis to Sustainable Growth in Sub-Saharan Africa." *Finance and Development* 26/4 December 1989: 26-9.

Lawrence, Peter, ed. *World Recession and the Food Crisis in Africa.* London: James Currey Ltd., 1986.

Lerner, David. *The Passing of Traditional Society.* Glencoe, Ill.: The Free Press, 1958.

"Leaked World Bank Memo Sparks Debate." *BankCheck* (Winter 1992): 1,6.

Levitt, Kari Polanyi. "Debt, Adjustment and Development: Looking to the 1990s." (Paper delivered to the Association of Caribbean Economists), Port of Spain, May 1990.

Lipton, Michael. *Why Poor People Stay Poor: Urban Bias in World Development.* Cambridge Mass.: Harvard University Press, 1977.

Little, P. D. and Horowitz, M.M. "Social Science Perspectives on Land, Ecology, and Development." In Little, Peter *et al.*, *Lands at Risk in the Third World: Local Level Perspectives.*

Little, P. D., Horowitz, M.M., Nyerges, A.E. *Lands at Risk in the Third World: Local Level Perspectives.* Boulder and London: Westview Press, 1987.

Lombardi, Richard W. *Debt Trap: Rethinking the Logic of Development.* New York: Praeger, 1985.

Lonergan, A. and Richards, C. eds. *Thomas Berry and the New Cosmology.* Mystic, Connecticut: Twenty-Third Publications, 1987.

Looney, R. E. "Military Expenditures and Socio-economic Development in Africa: A Summary of Recent Empirical Research." *Journal of Modern African Studies* 26 (June 1988): 319-25.

Looney, Robert E. "The Influence of Arms Imports on Third World Debt." *Journal of Developing Areas* 23 (January 1989): 221-32.

Lopez, G.A. and Stohl, M. eds. *Dependance, Development and State Repression.* New York: Greenwood Press, 1989.

Lowe Morna, Colleen. "Damas Mbogoro: The Business of Development." *Africa Report* 34 (March/April 1989): 43-4.

Lowe Morna, Colleen. "A New Development Compact?" *Africa Report* 35/1 (March-April 1990): 50-53.

Lowe Morna, Colleen. "Surviving Structural Adjustment." *Africa Report* 34/5 (September-October 1989): 45-8.

Loxley, John. "Crisis in Africa – Berg's Diagnosis and Prescription." In Barker, J. *The Politics of Agriculture in Rural Africa.*

Loxley, John. *Debt and Disorder.* Boulder: Westview Press, 1986.

Loxley, John. *Ghana: The Long Road to Recovery 1983-90.* Ottawa: The North-South Institute, 1991.

M'Passou, D. *Towards a Theology of Development.* Chilema, Malawi: Christian Communication Programme, 1987.

Mackenzie, Fiona. "Exploring the Connections: Structural Adjustment, Gender and the Environment." (Unpublished Draft) 1991.

Mahjoub, Azzam, ed. *Adjustment or Delinking? The African Experience.* London: Zed Books, 1990.

March, K. S. and Taqqu, R. L. *Women's Informal Association in Developing Countries: Catalysts for Change?* Boulder and London: Westview Press, 1986.

Marke, Erika. "The Nineties: The Decade of Women's Development." In *Church Women's Consultation on Economic Justice.* Nairobi: AACC Women's Desk, 1990.

Masilo, B. *ACLA News* 3/1 (1991).

Mathias, Erich. "It Was the Best of Times, It Was the Worst of Times: A Discussion on Economics From a Justice and Faith Perspective." New York: United Churches of Christ Board for World Missions (Africa Office), 1992.

Mazur, Robert E. *Breaking the Links: Development Theory and Practice in Southern Africa.* Africa World Press, 1990.

McClelland, D. "The Achievement Motive in Economic Growth." In Bert F. Hoselitz and Wilbert E. Moore, eds, *Industrialization and Society.* Mouton: UNESCO, 1966.

McCullum, Hugh. "Africa's Debt: The Children Pay." *United Church Observer*, (June 1989): 18-25.

McDaniel, J. *Earth, Sky, Gods and Mortals: Developing an Ecological Spirituality.* Mystic: Twenty-Third Publications, 1990.

Meagher, K. "Institutionalizing the Bio-Revolution: Implications for Nigerian Smallholders." (Unpublished), 1990.

Mearns, Robin. *Environmental Implications of Structural Adjustment: Reflections on Scientific Method.* IDS Discussion Paper No. 284, University of Sussex, 1991.

Meeks, M. Douglas. *God the Economist: The Doctrine of God and Political Economy.* Minneapolis: Fortress Press, 1989.

Mehretu, Assefu. *Regional Disparity in Sub-Saharan Africa: Structural Readjustment of Uneven Development.* Boulder: Westview Press, 1989.

Mello, John W. *et al*, eds. *Accelerating Food Production in Sub-Saharan Africa.* Baltimore: John Hopkins Univ. Press, 1987.

Mendlovitz, S. II. and Walker, R, B. J., eds. *Towards a Just World Peace: Perspectives from Social Movements.* London: Butterworths, 1987.

Messerschmidt, Donald A. "Conservation and Society in Nepal: Traditional Forest Management and Innovative Development." In Little, Peter *et al.*, *Lands at Risk in the Third World: Local Level Perspectives*: 373-98.

Mies, Maria. *Patriarchy and Accumulation on a World Scale.* London: Zed Books, 1986.

Mills, Cadman Atta. *Structural Adjustment in Sub-Saharan Africa.* Washington: The World Bank, 1989.

Mills, Patricia J. *Woman, Nature and Psyche.* New Haven: Yale University Press, 1987.

Minutes of Proceedings and Evidence of the Standing Committee on External Affairs and International Trade." Issue Nos. 1-6, 15, 18, 31 (October-December 1989).

Mireku, Ebenezer, "Assessing Structural Adjustment Programmes: The Case of Ghana." (Publication information not given.)

Mistry, Percy, S. *African Debt Revisited: Procrastination or Progress?* The Hague: Forum on Debt and Development, 1991.

Mistry, Percy, S. *African Debt: The Case for Relief for Sub-Saharan Africa.* Oxford International Associates, 1988.

Mistry, Percy, S. "The Multilateral Debt Problems of Indebted Developing Countries." The Hague: FONDAD, October 1993.

Mistry, Percy, S. "The Problem of 'Official' Debt Owed by Developing Countries." (Prepared for Forum on Debt and Development Conference) Brussels, August 1989.

Mkangi, Katama. *Debt Crisis:The African Perspective.* Nairobi: Association of Christian Lay Centres in Africa, May 1990.

Mohammed, A. "Grassroots Perspectives on Africa's Crisis." (Unpublished), 1991.

Mooney, P. R. *Genetic Resources for Our World* 2 (1989).

Mooney, P. R. "Law of the Seed." *Development Dialogue* 1-2 (1983).

Mugambi, J. N. K. "Problems and Promises of the Church in Africa." (Paper prepared for the All Africa Conference of Churches), Kanamai, November 1991.

Mukasa, Paul. "Churches Call For Review of World Bank and IMF." All Africa Press Service, February 25, 1991.

Mullei, A. K. "Determinants of the Effects of Economic Integration among African Countries." *Eastern Africa Economic Review* 3/1 (1987): 21-5.

Munoz, H. ed. *From Dependancy to Development: Strategies to Overcome Underdevelopment and Inequality.* Boulder: Westview Press, 1981.

Musau, E. "The National Council of Churches of Kenya is in the Forefront in Promoting Women's Activities." In AACC Women's Desk. *Church Women's Consultation.*

Mwereria, Godfrey, K. "The Debt Crisis in Africa." Nairobi: All Africa Conference of Churches (no year given).

Mwereria, Godfrey, K. *The Root Causes of Debt Crisis in Africa: An Agenda for Continental Collective Self-Reliance.* Nairobi: Southern Network for Development, 1990.

Myers, N. and Myers, D. "Increasing Awareness of the Supranational Nature of Emerging Environmental Issues." *Ambio* 11 (1982): 195-201.

National Farmers Union. "NFU Statement on GATT Negotiations to the National Conference on International Trade and Agriculture." Montreal, December 1988.

Ndumbu, Abel, ed. *Africa in the Debt Yoke: The Mission of the Church.* Nairobi: National Council of Churches of Kenya, 1991.

Nelson, Joyce. "The Multinational Free Lunch." *Canadian Forum* 68 (October 1989): 10-15.

Nelson, Joyce. "The New Global Sweatshop. " *Canadian Forum* 68 (September 1989): 10-14.

New Internationalist (June 1990).

New Internationalist (February 1990).

Njoroge, N. J. "Theological Reflection on the Effects of the Economic Crisis on Women in Africa." In All Africa Conference of Churches, *Church Women's Consultation on Economic Justice*. Nairobi: AACC Women's Desk, 1990.

Njoya, T. *ACLCA News* 3/2-3 (1991).

Norgaard, Richard B. "Environmental Economics: An Evolutionary Critique and a Plea for Pluralism." *Journal of Environmental Economics and Management* 12 (1985): 382-94.

North-South Institute. "Structural Adjustment in Africa: External Financing for Development." Ottawa: North-South Institute, February 1988.

Novicki, Margaret, A. "Edward V.K. Jaycox: A New Scenario for Africa." *Africa Report* (November-December 1989): 17-22.

Nsouli, Saleh M. "Structural Adjustment in Sub-Saharan Africa." *Finance and Development* 26/3 (September 1989): 30-33.

Odudoye, M. "To Deal Justly." In AACC Women's Desk, *Final Report*.

O'Neill, Norman and Mustafa, Kemal. *Capitalism, Socialism and the Development Crisis in Tanzania*. Aldershot: Avebury, 1990.

O'Neill, Maureen. "Women and Children First: An Assessment of Structural Adjustment." CDAS Discussion Paper No. 59. Montreal: Centre for Developing-Area Studies (McGill University), November 1989.

Obadina, Elizabeth. "SAPping Nigeria's Poor." *New Internationalist* 208 (June 1990).

Onimode, Bade. *The IMF, The World Bank and The African Debt*. London and New Jersey: The Institute for African Alternatives and Zed Books, 1989 (2 vols.).

Otchere, Isaac, K. "Exploring the Connection Between Export Promotion and Economic Growth: Evidence from Ghana." (Paper delivered to the Canadian Association of African Studies Conference) Montreal, May 1992.

Otim, J. J. *The Taproot of Environmental and Development Crisis in Africa*. ACLCA Publication No. 2, Nairobi: 1992.

Owusu, Francis. "Spatial Implications of Ghana's Structural Adjustment Programme." (Paper delivered to Canadian Association of Africa Studies Conference) Montreal, May 1992.

Oxfam (UK). "The Common Agricultural Policy: Implications of Reform for Developing Countries." Oxford: OXFAM, 1992.

Painter, Michael. "Unequal Exchange: The Dynamics of Settler Impoverishment and Environmental Destruction in Lowland Bolivia." In Little, Peter *et al*. *Lands at Risk in the Third World: Local Level Perspectives*: 164-92.

Parfitt, Trevor W. and Riley, Stephen P. *The African Debt Crisis*. London: Routledge, 1989.

Payer, Cheryl. *Lent and Lost: Foreign Credit and Third World Development*. London: Zed Books, 1991.

Payer, Cheryl. *The World Bank: A Critical Analysis*. New York: Monthly Review Press, 1982.

Pearce, D., Markandya, A. and Barbier, E.B. *Blueprint for a Green Economy.* London: Earthscan Publications, 1989.

Pearson, C.S. ed. *Multi-National Corporations, Environment and the Third World: Business Matters.* Durham: Duke University Press, 1987.

Peet, R. ed. *International Capitalism and Industrial Restructuring.* London: Allen and Unwin, 1987.

Perrings, C. "An Optimal Path to Extinction? Poverty and Resource Degradation in the Open Agrarian Economy." *Journal of Development Economics* 30 (1989): 1-24.

Petersmann, Hans, G. *Financial Assistance to Developing Countries: The Changing Role of the World Bank and International Monetary Fund.* Bonn: Europa Union Verlag GmbH, 1988.

"Pinstripes and Poverty: Inside the World Bank." *The New Internationalist* 214 (December 1990).

Potter, George Ann and George, Susan. "A Debate on the Third World Debt Crisis." *Food Monitor* (Winter 1989).

Poulis, A. and Schwab, P. eds. *Human Rights: Cultural and Ideological Perspectives.* New York: Praeger, 1979.

Pratt, R. C. "The Global Impact of the World Bank." In Torrie, J. ed., *Banking on Poverty.* Toronto: Between the Lines, 1983.

Pratt, R. C. and Hutchinson, R. eds. *Christian Faith and Economic Justice: Toward a Canadian Perspective.* Burlington: Trinity Press, 1988.

Prebisch, Raul. "Biosphere and Development." *CEPAL Review* 12 (1980): 69-84.

Puta-Chekwe, Chisanga. "The Social Cost of Structural Adjustment: Some Evidence From Africa." September 1990. (Unpublished).

Raffer, Kunibert. "Applying Chapter 9 Insolvency to International Debts: An Economically Efficient Solution with a Human Face." *World Development* 18/2 (February 1992): 301-11.

Raghavan, Chakravarthi. "Gains from the Uruguay Round: Facts, Myths and Faith." (Third World Network Features, November 13, 1993).

Raghavan, Chakravarthi. *Recolonization: GATT, the Uruguay Round and the Third World.* Penang: Third World Network, 1990.

Raghavan, Chakravarthi. "Uruguay Round Balance Sheet After Ten Years." (Third World Network Features, December 17, 1993).

Raikes, Philip. *Modernising Hunger: Famine, Food Surplus and Farm Policy in the EEC and Africa.* London: Catholic Institute for International Relations, 1988.

Ramphal, Shridath, S. "Sovereign Default: A Backward Glance." *Third World Quarterly* 11/2 (April 1989): 63-75.

Rau, Bill. *From Feast to Famine: Official Cures and Grassroots Remedies to Africa's Food Crisis.* London: Zed Books, 1991.

Ravenhill, J. "Adjustment with Growth: A Fragile Consensus." *Journal of Modern African Studies* 26 (June 1988): 179-210.

Redclift, Michael. *Development and the Environmental Crisis: Red or Green*

Alternatives. London: Methuen, 1984.

Redclift, Michael. "The Environmental Consequences of Latin America's Agricultural Development: Some Thoughts on the Brundtland Commission Report." *World Development* 17 (1989): 365-77.

Redclift, Michael. "Redefining the Environmental Crisis in the South." In Weston, J. ed., *Red and Green*: 80-100.

Redclift, Michael. "Sustainability and the Market: Survival Strategies on the Bolivian Frontier. *Journal of Development Studies* 23/1 (1986): 93-105.

Redclift, Michael. *Sustainable Development: Exploring the Contradictions*, London: Methuen, 1987.

Reddock, Rhoda. "Towards a Framework for the Study of Women, Gender and Social Movements in Africa." (Draft Working Paper prepared for the Council for the Development of Economic and Social Research in Africa Workshop on Gender Analysis and African Social Science) Dakar, September 1991.

Rempel, H. "Exodus II: An End to the Debt Crisis." (Background paper prepared by the Internatioanl Debt Crisis Committee for the Mennonite Central Committee's Annual Meeting) 1991.

Rempel, Ruth. "Crossing the Desert: A Look at the "Human Face" Approach to Structural Adjustment as it Affects the Low-Income Countries in Sub-Saharan Africa." (Unpublished) 1992.

Rempel, Ruth. "The External Debt of African Nations: Perspectives on Its Causes, Consequences and Cures." (Unpublished) 1991.

Rempel, Ruth. "The "Human Face" of Structural Adjustment in Africa: A Description and Evaluation of "Human Face" Measures Adopted by Low Income Countries in Sub-Saharan Africa." (Unpublished) 1992.

Repetto, R. "Economic Incentives for Sustainable Production". In Schramm, G. and Warford, J. J. eds, *Environmental Management and Economic Development*. Washington D.C.: World Bank, 1989: 69-86.

Review of African Political Economy. (Editorial) 27-8 (1983).

Rich, B. "The Greening of Development Banks: Rhetoric or Reality." *The Ecologist* 15/2 (1989): 44 52.

Rich, B. "Multilateral Development Banks: Their Role in Destroying the Global Environment." *Ecologist* 11/1-2 (1985): 56-68.

Rimmer, Douglas. "Review Article: External Debt and Structural Adjustment in Tropical Africa." *African Affairs* 89 (April 1990): 283-91.

The Road to Damascus: Kairos and Conversion. London: Catholic Institute for International Relations, 1989.

Robertson, Roland and Garrett, William R, eds. *Religion and Global Order*. New York: Paragon Publishers, 1991.

Rodda, Annabel. *Women and the Environment*. London: Zed Books, 1991.

Roddick, J. *The Dance of the Millions: Latin America and the Debt Crisis*. London: Latin America Bureau, 1988.

Sachs, Jeffrey D. ed. *Developing Country Debt and the World Economy*. Chicago: University of Chicago Press, 1989.

Salau, Ademola, T. "Environment and Gender: Ecological Crisis, Women and the Quest for Sustainable Development in Africa." (Paper prepared for the Council for the Development of Economic and Social Research in Africa Workshop on Gender Analysis and African Social Science), Dakar, September 1991.

Samoff, J. "The Intellectual/Financial Complex of Foreign Aid." *Review of African Political Economy* 53 (1992): 60-87.

Sampson, Anthony. *The Money Lenders: Bankers in a Dangerous World.* London: Hodder and Stoughton, 1981.

Sandbrook, R. *The Politics of Africa's Economic Stagnation.* Cambridge: Cambridge University Press, 1985.

Sandbrook, R. *The Politics of Basic Needs.* Toronto: University of Toronto Press, 1982.

Sandbrook, R. "The State and Economic Stagnation in Tropical Africa." *World Development* 14 (March 1986): 319-32.

Santmire, H. Paul. *The Travail of Nature: The Ambiguous Promise of Christian Theology.* Philadelphia: Fortress Press, 1985.

Schatan, Jacobo. *World Debt: Who Is To Pay?* London: Zed Books, 1987.

Schmink, M. and Wood, C.H. "The 'Political Ecology' of Amazonia." In Little, Peter *et al. Lands at Risk in the Third World: Local Level Perspectives*: 38-57.

Scott, James C. *Weapons of the Weak: Everyday Forms of Peasant Resistance.* New Haven: Yale University Press, 1985.

Sells, J. "An Eco-Feminist Critique of Deep Ecology." *Canadian Dimension* 23 (September 1989): 13-15.

Sender, John and Smith, Shelia. "What's Right with the Berg Report and What's Left of its Criticisms." In Lawrence, Peter, ed., *World Recession and the Food Crisis in Africa*: 114-28.

Sevigny, David. *The Paris Club: An Inside View.* Ottawa: The North-South Institute, 1990.

Sheth, D. L. "Alternative Development as Political Practice." In Mendlovitz, S.H. and Walker, R.B.J., eds. *Towards a Just World Peace: Perspectives from Social Movements*: 235-52.

Shipman, A. "Theology and Economy." In AACC Women's Desk. *Church Women's Consultation on Economic Justice.*

Shiva, V. "People's Ecology: The Chipko Movement." In Mendlovitz, S.H. and Walker, R.B.J., eds, *Towards a Just World Peace: Perspectives from Social Movements*: 253-70.

Shiva, V. *Staying Alive: Women, Ecology and Development.* London: Zed Books, 1988.

Shiva, V. *The Violence of the Green Revolution: Third World Agriculture, Ecology and Politics.* London: Zed Books, 1991.

Shiva, V. "Why the World Bank Should Not Be the Guardian of the World's Environment." *Third World Economics* (October 1-15, 1991): 18-19.

Shiva, Vandana. "The World Bank, Agricultural Research and Intellectual

Property Rights." *Third World Economics* (May 1992).

Shivute, Vaino, P. "Agricultural Production: From the Green Revolution to the Bio-Revolution." In Suliman, M. ed., *Alternative Development Strategies for Africa*: 61-71.

Sidel, R. *Women and Children Last*. Harmondsworth: Penguin Books, 1987.

Singer, Hans. "Beyond the Debt Crisis." *Development Journal of SID* 1 (1992): 35-8.

Singer, Hans. "The World Development Report 1987." *World Development* (1988).

Singh, Ajit. "The IMF - World Bank Policy Programme in Africa: A Commentary." In Lawrence, Peter, ed., *World Recession and the Food Crisis in Africa*: 104-13.

Sivanandan, A. "Imperialism and Disorganic Development in the Silicon Age." In R. Peet ed. *International Capitalism and Industrial Restructuring*, 185-200.

Smith, Stephen C. *Industrial Policy in Developing Countries: Reconsidering the Real Sources of Export-Led Growth*. Washington: Economic Policy Institute, 1991.

Sonoko, Karama. "Debt in the Eye of a Storm: The African Crisis in a Global Context." *Africa Today* 37 (1990): 15-28.

Spooner, Brian. "Insiders and Outsiders in Baluchistan: Western and Indigenous Perspectives on Ecology and Development." In Little, Peter *et al.*, *Lands at Risk in the Third World: Local Level Perspectives*: 58-68.

Standing Committee on External Affairs and International Trade. *Securing Our Global Future: Canada's Stake in the Unfinished Business of Third World Debt*. Ottawa: Supply and Services, 1990.

Standing Committee on External Affairs and International Trade. "Unanswered Questions/Uncertain Hopes: A Reply by the Sub-Committee on International Debt to the Government Response to the Report *Securing our Global Future: Canada's Stake in the Unfinished Business of Third World Debt*." Ottawa: House of Commons, March 1991.

Stephen, Gunter. *Pollution Control, Economic Adjustment and Long-Run Equilibrium*. Berlin: Springer-Verlag, 1989.

Stewart, Frances. "The Many Faces of Adjustment." *World Development* 19 (1991): 1847-64.

Stewart, Frances. "The Many Faces of Adjustment II." (Unpublished) 1991.

Stretton, H. *Capitalism, Socialism and the Environment*. Cambridge: Cambridge University Press, 1976.

Suliman, M., ed. *Alternative Development Strategies for Africa*. Vol. 2. London: Institute for African Alternatives, 1991.

Sunkel, O. "Development Styles and the Environment: An Interpretation of the Latin America Case." In Munoz, H. ed., *From Dependancy to Development: Strategies to Overcome Underdevelopment and Inequality*: 93-114.

Sunkel, O. "Economics and Environment in a Development Perspective." *International Social Science Journal* 38 (1986): 411-27.

Sunkel, O. "Environment and Lifestyles: The Latin America Trap." *Mazingira* 10 (1979): 39-49.

Sunkel, O. "The Interaction between Styles of Development and the Environment in Latin America." *CEPAL Review* 12 (1980): 15-49.

Survey of Economic and Social Conditions in Africa, 1987-1988. New York: United Nations, 1990.

Swantz, Marja Liisa. *Women in Development: A Creative Role Denied? The Tanzanian Experience.* London: C. Hurst, 1980.

"Talking Trade." *Left Business Observer* 49 (November 1991).

Taskforce for Churches and Corporate Responsibility et al. *The International Debt Crisis: A Discussion Paper Prepared for the Canadian Churches,* 1989.

Ten Days for World Development. *Action Guide on the International Debt Crisis,* 1989-90.

Ten Days for World Development. *Hungry for Justice,* 1987.

The Addis Ababa Trade Union Declaration on Debt and Debt Servicing in Africa. *Addis Abba: Africa Trade Union Conference on "The External Debt and Debt Servicing."* December 1987.

The Bank Information Centre. *Funding Ecological and Social Destruction: The World Bank and International Monetary Fund.* Washington: The Bank Information Center, 1989.

The Khartoum Declaration: Towards a Human-Focused Approach to Socio-Economic Recovery and Development in Africa. Khartoum: Economic Commission for Africa, March 1988.

"The Lagos Plan of Action." *UN Chronicle* 21 (March 1984): xii-xix.

The Uganda Economic Study Team. *Economic Adjustment and Long-Term Development in Uganda.* Ottawa: International Development Research Centre, November 1987.

Thomson, R. "Canadian Trade and Aid Relations with Nicaragua." Canada-Caribbean-Central American Policy Alternatives, 1984.

Tisdell, C. "Sustainable Development: Differing Perspectives of Ecologists and Economists, and Their Relevance to LDCs." *World Development* 16 (1988): 373-84.

Todaro, M. *Economic Development in the Third World.* London: Longman, 1985.

Tolba, Mostafa, K. "Present Development Styles and Environmental Problems." *CEPAL Review* 12 (1980): 9-14.

Tolen, Aaron. "Africa Through New Eyes." Geneva: World Council of Churches Central Committee, September 1991.

Tomassini, L. "Environmental Factors, Crisis in the Centres and Change in International Relations of the Peripheral Countries." *CEPAL Review* 12 (1980): 145-74.

Torrie, Jill, ed. *Banking on Poverty: The Global Impact of the IMF and World Bank.* Toronto: Between the Lines, 1983.

Toward Sustained Development: A Joint Program of Action for Sub-Saharan Africa." *Finance and Development* 21 (December 1984): 29-30.

Toye, J. *et. al. Aid and Power: The World Bank and Policy Based Lending.* Vols.

1 and 2. London: Routledge, 1991.

"Trade Specialist Calls Current Rules Outdated." *IMF Survey* (July 15, 1991).

Trainer, T. *Developed to Death: Rethinking Third World Development.* London: Merlin Press, 1989.

"Trillion Dollar Debt." *African Concord* 5/34 (December 24, 1990): 18-19.

Turok, Ben. *Africa: What Can be Done?* London: Zed Books, 1987.

"Twins that won't tango." *The Economist* (March 11, 1989): 17-18.

UK Debt Crisis Network. *Media Briefings: IMF/World Bank Annual Meetings.* Berlin: September 1988.

Ul Haq, Mahbub. "Enlarging People's Choices: Focusing on Human Development." Ottawa: The North South Institute, 1990. (Unpublished.)

United Nations Development Programme and World Bank. *African Development Indicators.* Washington: World Bank, 1992.

United Nations Economic Commission for Africa. *African Alternative Framework to Structural Adjustment Programmes for Socio-Economic Recovery and Transformation.* Addis Ababa: UNECA, 1989.

United Nations Economic Commission for Africa. *African Charter for Popular Participation in Development.* Addis Ababa: UNECA, 1990.

United Nations Economic Commission for Africa. *Critical Economic Situation in Africa.* Addis Ababa: UNECA, 1991.

United Nations Economic Commission for Africa. "ECA Preliminary Observations on the World Bank Report: *Africa's Adjustment and Growth in the 1980s*". Addis Ababa, April 1989.

United Nations Economic Commission for Africa. *Economic Report on Africa 1990.* Addis Ababa, 1990.

United Nations Secretary General. *Tackling Africa's Economic Crisis.* New York: United Nations, 1991.

United Nations Secretary General's Expert Group on Africa's Commodity Problems. *Africa's Commodity Problems: Towards a Solution.* Geneva: United Nations, 1990.

US Treasury Department. *United States Participation in Multilateral Development Banks in the 1980s.* Washington, 1982.

Vallely, Paul. *Bad Samaritans: First World Ethics and Third World Debt.* London: Hodder and Stoughton, 1990.

Van Ufford, Philip Q. and Schoffeleers, Matthew. *Religion and Development: Towards an Integrated Approach.* Amsterdam: Free University Press, 1988.

Vickers, Jeanne. *Women and the World Economic Crisis.* London: Zed Books, 1991.

Wallerstein, I. *The Capitalist World Economy.* London: Cambridge University Press, 1979.

Wallerstein, I. "Dependency in an Interdependant World: The Limited Possibilities of Transformation Within the Capitalist World Economy." In Munoz, H. ed., *From Dependency to Development: Strategies to Overcome Underdevelopment and Inequality*: 267-94.

Watkins, Kevin. "Agriculture and Food Security in the GATT Uruguay Round." *Review of African Political Economy* 50 (1991): 38-50.

Watkins, Kevin. *Fixing the Rules: North-South Issues in International Trade and the GATT Uruguay Round*. London: Catholic Institute for International Relations, 1992.

Weiner, Myron, ed. *Modernization: The Dynamics of Growth*. New York: Basic Books, 1966.

Weir D. and Schapiro, M. *Circle of Poison*. San Francisco: Institute for Food and Development Policy, 1981.

Weissman, S. R. "Structural Adjustment in Africa: Insights from the Experience of Ghana and Senegal." *World Development* 18 (December 1990): 1621-34.

Weston, A. "North-South Institute Briefing." Ottawa: North-South Institute, June 1992.

Weston, J. "The Greens, 'Nature' and the Social Environment." In Weston J. ed., *Red and Green: The New Politics of the Environment*: 11-29.

Weston J. ed. *Red and Green: The New Politics of the Environment*. London: Pluto Press, 1986.

White, L. "The Historical Roots of our Ecological Crisis." In Barbour, I.G. ed., *Western Man and Environmental Ethics*. Reading: Addison Wellesley, 1973: 18-30.

Wilber, C. K. and Grimes, L. M. "Analyzing the Moral Defense of Free Market Capitalism – Part 1." *New Oxford Review* (March 1992): 7-10.

Wilson, Michael. "The International Debt Problem." April 1987. (Unpublished).

Winter, Gibson. *Liberating Creation*. New York: Crossroad, 1981.

Wisner, Ben. *Power and Need in Africa*. Trenton: Africa World Press, 1989.

Wittwer, S. H. "The New Agriculture: A View of the Twenty-First Century." In Rosenblum, J. W. ed. *Agriculture in the Twenty-First Century*. New York: Wiley and Sons, 1983: 337-67.

Wolf, E. *Europe and the People Without History*. Los Angeles: University of California Press, 1982.

Wolf, E.C. *Beyond the Green Revolution*. Washington D.C.: Worldwatch Institute, 1986.

Wolfe, Marshall. "The Environment in the Political Arena." *CEPAL Review* 12 (1980): 85-101.

World Bank. *Accelerated Development in Sub-Saharan Africa: An Agenda for Action*. Washington, D.C.: The World Bank, 1981.

World Bank. *Adjustment Lending: An Evaluation of Ten Years of Experience*. Washington: The World Bank, 1988.

World Bank. *Adjustment Lending Policies and Sustainable Growth*. Washington: The World Bank, 1990.

World Bank. *Africa's Adjustment and Growth in the 1980s*. Washington: The World Bank and UNDP, 1989.

World Bank. *Annual Report* 1991. Washington: World Bank, 1991.

World Bank. *Assistance Strategies to Reduce Poverty*. Washington: World Bank, 1991.

World Bank. *Financing Adjustment with Growth in Sub-Saharan Africa, 1986-90*. Washington: The World Bank, 1986.

World Bank. *Making Adjustment Work for the Poor in Africa*. Washington: World Bank, 1990.

World Bank. *Possible Effects of Trade Liberalization on Trade in Primary Commodities*. Staff Working Paper No. 193, 1975.

World Bank. *Price Prospects for Major Primary Commodities, 1988-2000*. Vol. II. Washington D.C., 1989.

World Bank. *The Social Dimensions of Adjustment in Africa: A Political Agenda*. Washington: The World Bank, 1990.

World Bank. *Sub-Saharan Africa: From Crisis to Sustainable Growth: A Long-Term Perspective Study*. Washington, D.C., 1989.

World Bank. *Toward Sustained Development in Sub-Saharan Africa*. Washington: The World Bank, 1984.

World Bank. *Women and Development*. Washington: World Bank, 1990.

World Bank. *World Debt Tables 1990-91, 1991-2, 1992-3, 1993-4: External Debt of Developing Countries*. Vols. 1-2, Washington: World Bank, 1990, 1991, 1992, 1993.

World Bank. *World Development Report*. Washington: Oxford University Press, 1978, 1981, 1988-1993.

World Commission on Environment and Development. *Our Common Future*. Oxford: Oxford University Press, 1987.

World Council of Churches. "Testimony of Mr. Cosmas M. Musumali and Mr. A. J. Annorbah-Sarpei – Ecumenical Hearing on the International Monetary System and the Churches' Responsibility." In World Council of Churches' Commission on the Churches Participation in Development. *Debt Resource Materials* 2 (1988): 13-18.

Worsley, P. *The Three Worlds: Culture and World Development*. London: Weidenfeld and Nicolson, 1984.

Wright, Nancy E. "Disastrous Decade: Africa's Experience with Structural Adjustment." *Multinational Monitor* (April 1990): 21-3.

Yoxen, E. *The Gene Business: Who Should Control Biotechnology?* London: Pan Books, 1983.

"Zambia: Churches Confront Government." *Africa Information* (August 17, 1993).

Zuckerman, E. "Adjustment Programs and Social Welfare." *World Bank Discussion Paper* 44 (1989).

Zulu, J. B. and S. M. Nsouli. "Adjustment Programmes in Africa." *Finance and Development* 21 (March 1984): 5-7.

Index